HOLT McDOUGAL

Southwest and Central Asia

Christopher L. Salter

HISTORY

HOLT McDOUGAL

 HOUGHTON MIFFLIN HARCOURT

Author

Dr. Christopher L. Salter

Dr. Christopher L. "Kit" Salter is Professor Emeritus of geography and former Chair of the Department of Geography at the University of Missouri. He did his undergraduate work at Oberlin College and received both his M.A. and Ph.D. degrees in geography from the University of California at Berkeley.

Dr. Salter is one of the country's leading figures in geography education. In the 1980s he helped found the national Geographic Alliance network to promote geography education in all 50 states. In the 1990s Dr. Salter was Co-Chair of the National Geography Standards Project, a group of distinguished geographers who created *Geography for Life* in 1994, the document outlining national standards in geography. In 1990 Dr. Salter received the National Geographic Society's first-ever Distinguished Geography Educator Award. In 1992 he received the George Miller Award for distinguished service in geography education from the National Council for Geographic Education. In 2006 Dr. Salter was awarded Lifetime Achievement Honors by the Association of American Geographers for his transformation of geography education.

Over the years, Dr. Salter has written or edited more than 150 articles and books on cultural geography, China, field work, and geography education. His primary interests lie in the study of the human and physical forces that create the cultural landscape, both nationally and globally.

ISBN-13 978-0-547-48487-7

1 2 3 4 5 6 7 8 9 10 0914 19 18 17 16 15 14 13 12 11 10

4500263433   ^ B C D E F G

Reviewers

Academic Reviewers

Elizabeth Chako, Ph.D.
Department of Geography
The George Washington
    University

Altha J. Cravey, Ph.D.
Department of Geography
University of North Carolina

Eugene Cruz-Uribe, Ph.D.
Department of History
Northern Arizona University

Toyin Falola, Ph.D.
Department of History
University of Texas

Sandy Freitag, Ph.D.
Director, Monterey Bay History
    and Cultures Project
Division of Social Sciences
University of California,
    Santa Cruz

Oliver Froehling, Ph.D.
Department of Geography
University of Kentucky

Reuel Hanks, Ph.D.
Department of Geography
Oklahoma State University

Phil Klein, Ph.D.
Department of Geography
University of Northern Colorado

B. Ikubolajeh Logan, Ph.D.
Department of Geography
Pennsylvania State University

Marc Van De Mieroop, Ph.D.
Department of History
Columbia University
New York, New York

Christopher Merrett, Ph.D.
Department of History
Western Illinois University

Thomas R. Paradise, Ph.D.
Department of Geosciences
University of Arkansas

Jesse P. H. Poon, Ph.D.
Department of Geography
University at Buffalo–SUNY

Robert Schoch, Ph.D.
CGS Division of Natural Science
Boston University

Derek Shanahan, Ph.D.
Department of Geography
Millersville University
Millersville, Pennsylvania

David Shoenbrun, Ph.D.
Department of History
Northwestern University
Evanston, Illinois

Sean Terry, Ph.D.
Department of Interdisciplinary
    Studies, Geography and
    Environmental Studies
Drury University
Springfield, Missouri

Educational Reviewers

Dennis Neel Durbin
Dyersburg High School
Dyersburg, Tennessee

Carla Freel
Hoover Middle School
Merced, California

Tina Nelson
Deer Park Middle School
Randallstown, Maryland

Don Polston
Lebanon Middle School
Lebanon, Indiana

Robert Valdez
Pioneer Middle School
Tustin, California

Teacher Review Panel

Heather Green
LaVergne Middle School
LaVergne, Tennessee

John Griffin
Wilbur Middle School
Wichita, Kansas

Rosemary Hall
Derby Middle School
Birmingham, Michigan

Rose King
Yeatman-Liddell School
St. Louis, Missouri

Mary Liebl
Wichita Public Schools USD 259
Wichita, Kansas

Jennifer Smith
Lake Wood Middle School
Overland Park, Kansas

Melinda Stephani
Wake County Schools
Raleigh, North Carolina

Contents

Southwest and Central Asia 1

CHAPTER 1 History of the Fertile Crescent, 7000–500 BC 10

CHAPTER 4 **The Eastern Mediterranean** 90

VIDEO
Jesus' Jerusalem

References

Available @
↗ **hmhsocialstudies.com**

• Facts About the World
• Regions of the World Handbook
• Standardized Test-Taking Strategies
• Economics Handbook

HISTORY™ is the leading destination for revealing, award-winning, original non-fiction series and event-driven specials that connect history with viewers in an informative, immersive and entertaining manner across multiple platforms. HISTORY is part of A&E Television Networks (AETN), a joint venture of Hearst Corporation, Disney/ABC Television Group and NBC Universal, an award-winning, international media company that also includes, among others, A&E Network™, BIO™, and History International™.

HISTORY programming greatly appeals to educators and young people who are drawn into the visual stories our documentaries tell. Our Education Department has a long-standing record in providing teachers and students with curriculum resources that bring the past to life in the classroom. Our content covers a diverse variety of subjects, including American and world history, government, economics, the natural and applied sciences, arts, literature and the humanities, health and guidance, and even pop culture.

The HISTORY website, located at **www.history.com**, is the definitive historical online source that delivers entertaining and informative content featuring broadband video, interactive timelines, maps, games, podcasts and more.

"We strive to engage, inspire and encourage the love of learning..."

Since its founding in 1995, HISTORY has demonstrated a commitment to providing the highest quality resources for educators. We develop multimedia resources for K–12 schools, two- and four-year colleges, government agencies, and other organizations by drawing on the award-winning documentary programming of A&E Television Networks. We strive to engage, inspire and encourage the love of learning by connecting with students in an informative and compelling manner. To help achieve this goal, we have formed a partnership with Houghton Mifflin Harcourt.

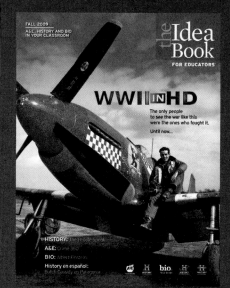

The Idea Book for Educators

Classroom resources that bring the past to life

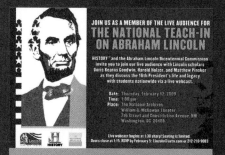

Live webcasts

HISTORY Take a Veteran to School Day

In addition to premium video-based resources, **HISTORY** has extensive offerings for teachers, parents, and students to use in the classroom and in their in-home educational activities, including:

▶ *The Idea Book for Educators* is a biannual teacher's magazine, featuring guides and info on the latest happenings in history education to help keep teachers on the cutting edge.

▶ **HISTORY Classroom (www.history.com/classroom)** is an interactive website that serves as a portal for history educators nationwide. Streaming videos on topics ranging from the Roman aqueducts to the civil rights movement connect with classroom curricula.

▶ **HISTORY email newsletters** feature updates and supplements to our award-winning programming relevant to the classroom with links to teaching guides and video clips on a variety of topics, special offers, and more.

▶ **Live webcasts** are featured each year as schools tune in via streaming video.

▶ **HISTORY Take a Veteran to School Day** connects veterans with young people in our schools and communities nationwide.

In addition to **HOUGHTON MIFFLIN HARCOURT**, our partners include the *Library of Congress*, the *Smithsonian Institution*, *National History Day*, *The Gilder Lehrman Institute of American History*, the *Organization of American Historians*, and many more. HISTORY video is also featured in museums throughout America and in over 70 other historic sites worldwide.

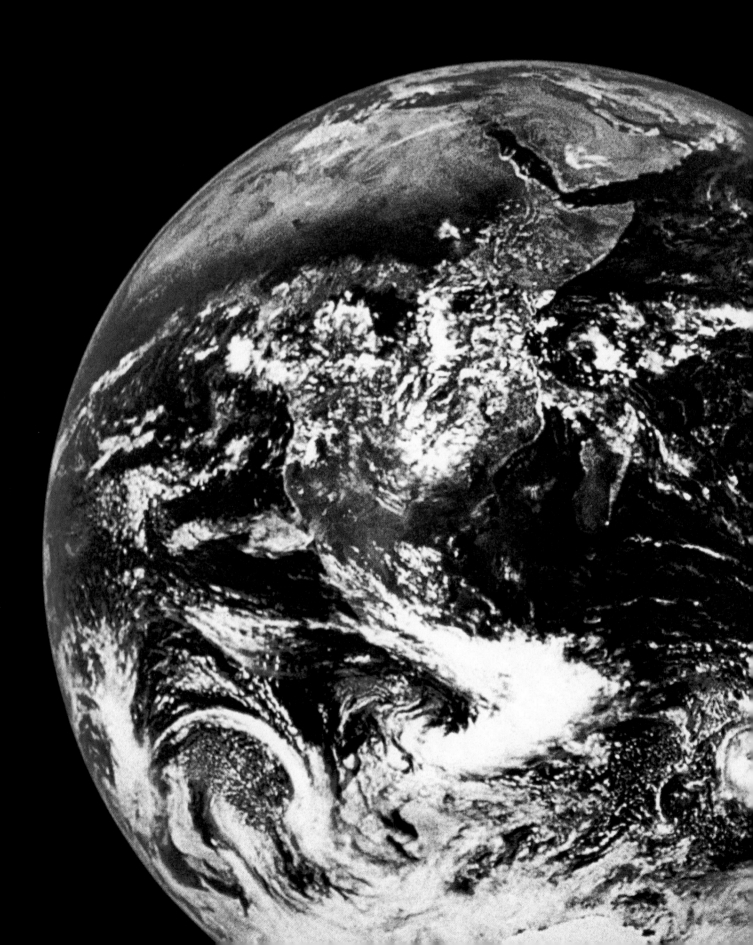

Geography and Map Skills Handbook

Contents

Throughout this textbook, you will be studying the world's people, places, and landscapes. One of the main tools you will use is the map—the primary tool of geographers. To help you begin your studies, this Geography and Map Skills Handbook explains some of the basic features of maps. For example, it explains how maps are made, how to read them, and how they can show the round surface of Earth on a flat piece of paper. This handbook will also introduce you to some of the types of maps you will study later in this book. In addition, you will learn about the different kinds of features on Earth and about how geographers use themes and elements to study the world.

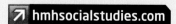 hmhsocialstudies.com **INTERACTIVE MAPS**

Geography Skills With map zone geography skills, you can go online to find interactive versions of the key maps in this book. Explore these interactive maps to learn and practice important map skills and bring geography to life.

You can access all of the interactive maps in this book through the Interactive Student Edition at

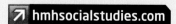 hmhsocialstudies.com

Mapping the Earth
Using Latitude and Longitude

A **globe** is a scale model of the Earth. It is useful for showing the entire Earth or studying large areas of Earth's surface.

To study the world, geographers use a pattern of imaginary lines that circles the globe in east-west and north-south directions. It is called a **grid**. The intersection of these imaginary lines helps us find places on Earth.

The east-west lines in the grid are lines of **latitude**, which you can see on the diagram. Lines of latitude are called **parallels** because they are always parallel to each other. These imaginary lines measure distance north and south of the **equator**. The equator is an imaginary line that circles the globe halfway between the North and South Poles. Parallels measure distance from the equator in **degrees**. The symbol for degrees is °. Degrees are further divided into **minutes**. The symbol for minutes is ´. There are 60 minutes in a degree. Parallels north of the equator are labeled with an N. Those south of the equator are labeled with an S.

The north-south imaginary lines are lines of **longitude**. Lines of longitude are called **meridians**. These imaginary lines pass through the poles. They measure distance east and west of the **prime meridian**. The prime meridian is an imaginary line that runs through Greenwich, England. It represents 0° longitude.

Lines of latitude range from 0°, for locations on the equator, to 90°N or 90°S, for locations at the poles. Lines of longitude range from 0° on the prime meridian to 180° on a meridian in the mid-Pacific Ocean. Meridians west of the prime meridian to 180° are labeled with a W. Those east of the prime meridian to 180° are labeled with an E. Using latitude and longitude, geographers can identify the exact location of any place on Earth.

Lines of Latitude

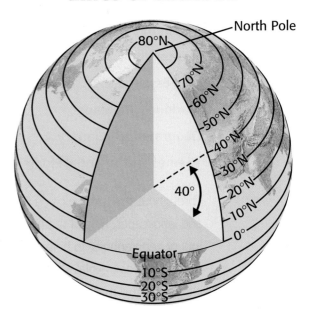

Lines of Longitude

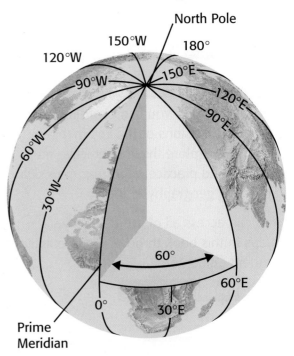

The equator divides the globe into two halves, called **hemispheres**. The half north of the equator is the Northern Hemisphere. The southern half is the Southern Hemisphere. The prime meridian and the 180° meridian divide the world into the Eastern Hemisphere and the Western Hemisphere. Look at the diagrams on this page. They show each of these four hemispheres.

Earth's land surface is divided into seven large landmasses, called **continents**. These continents are also shown on the diagrams on this page. Landmasses smaller than continents and completely surrounded by water are called **islands**.

Geographers organize Earth's water surface into major regions too. The largest is the world ocean. Geographers divide the world ocean into the Pacific Ocean, the Atlantic Ocean, the Indian Ocean, and the Arctic Ocean. Lakes and seas are smaller bodies of water.

Northern Hemisphere

Southern Hemisphere

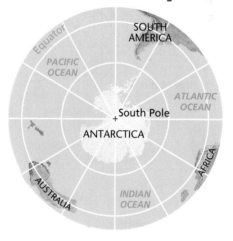

Western Hemisphere

Eastern Hemisphere

Mapmaking
Understanding Map Projections

A **map** is a flat diagram of all or part of Earth's surface. Mapmakers have created different ways of showing our round planet on flat maps. These different ways are called **map projections**. Because Earth is round, there is no way to show it accurately on a flat map. All flat maps are distorted in some way. Mapmakers must choose the type of map projection that is best for their purposes. Many map projections are one of three kinds: cylindrical, conic, or flat-plane.

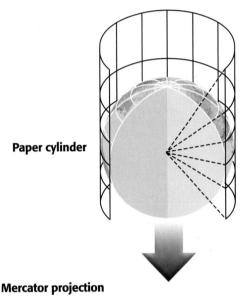

Paper cylinder

Cylindrical Projections

Cylindrical projections are based on a cylinder wrapped around the globe. The cylinder touches the globe only at the equator. The meridians are pulled apart and are parallel to each other instead of meeting at the poles. This causes landmasses near the poles to appear larger than they really are. The map below is a Mercator projection, one type of cylindrical projection. The Mercator projection is useful for navigators because it shows true direction and shape. However, it distorts the size of land areas near the poles.

Mercator projection

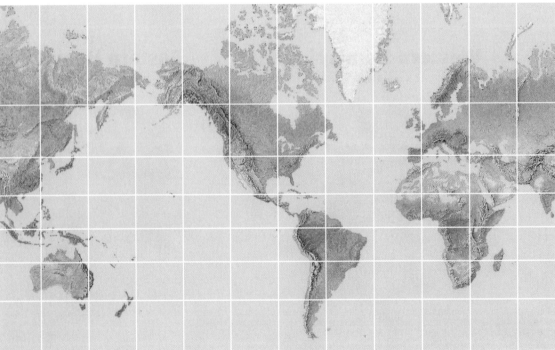

Conic Projections

Conic projections are based on a cone placed over the globe. A conic projection is most accurate along the lines of latitude where it touches the globe. It retains almost true shape and size. Conic projections are most useful for showing areas that have long east-west dimensions, such as the United States.

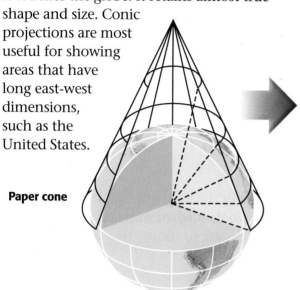

Paper cone

Conic projection

Flat-plane Projections

Flat-plane projections are based on a plane touching the globe at one point, such as at the North Pole or South Pole. A flat-plane projection is useful for showing true direction for airplane pilots and ship navigators. It also shows true area. However, it distorts the true shapes of landmasses.

Flat plane

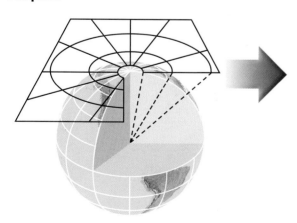

Flat-plane projection

Map Essentials
How to Read a Map

Maps are like messages sent out in code. To help us translate the code, mapmakers provide certain features. These features help us understand the message they are presenting about a particular part of the world. Of these features, almost all maps have a title, a compass rose, a scale, and a legend. The map below has these four features, plus a fifth—a locator map.

❶ Title

A map's **title** shows what the subject of the map is. The map title is usually the first thing you should look at when studying a map, because it tells you what the map is trying to show.

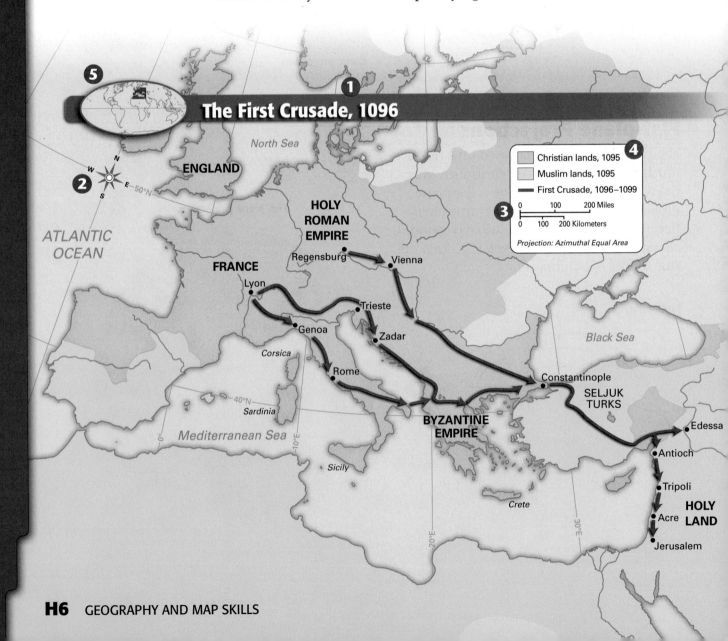

The First Crusade, 1096

North Sea

ENGLAND

HOLY ROMAN EMPIRE

Regensburg

Vienna

FRANCE

Lyon

ATLANTIC OCEAN

Genoa

Trieste

Zadar

Corsica

Rome

Sardinia

Mediterranean Sea

Sicily

BYZANTINE EMPIRE

Crete

Black Sea

Constantinople

SELJUK TURKS

Edessa

Antioch

Tripoli

HOLY LAND

Acre

Jerusalem

Legend
- Christian lands, 1095
- Muslim lands, 1095
- First Crusade, 1096–1099

0   100   200 Miles
0   100   200 Kilometers

Projection: Azimuthal Equal Area

❷ Compass Rose

A directional indicator shows which way north, south, east, and west lie on the map. Some mapmakers use a "north arrow," which points toward the North Pole. Remember, "north" is not always at the top of a map. The way a map is drawn and the location of directions on that map depend on the perspective of the mapmaker. Most maps in this textbook indicate direction by using a compass rose. A **compass rose** has arrows that point to all four principal directions.

❸ Scale

Mapmakers use scales to represent the distances between points on a map. Scales may appear on maps in several different forms. The maps in this textbook provide a **bar scale**. Scales give distances in miles and kilometers.

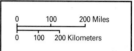

To find the distance between two points on the map, place a piece of paper so that the edge connects the two points. Mark the location of each point on the paper with a line or dot. Then, compare the distance between the two dots with the map's bar scale. The number on the top of the scale gives the distance in miles. The number on the bottom gives the distance in kilometers. Because the distances are given in large intervals, you may have to approximate the actual distance on the scale.

❹ Legend

The **legend**, or key, explains what the symbols on the map represent. Point symbols are used to specify the location of things, such as cities, that do not take up much space on the map. Some legends show colors that represent certain features like empires or other regions. Other maps might have legends with symbols or colors that represent features such as roads. Legends can also show economic resources, land use, population density, and climate.

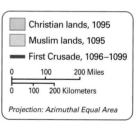

❺ Locator Map

A **locator map** shows where in the world the area on the map is located. The area shown on the main map is shown in red on the locator map. The locator map also shows surrounding areas so the map reader can see how the information on the map relates to neighboring lands.

Working with Maps
Using Different Kinds of Maps

As you study the world's regions and countries, you will use a variety of maps. Political maps and physical maps are two of the most common types of maps you will study. In addition, you will use special-purpose maps. These maps might show climate, population, resources, ancient empires, or other topics.

Political Maps

Political maps show the major political features of a region. These features include country borders, capital cities, and other places. Political maps use different colors to represent countries, and capital cities are often shown with a special star symbol.

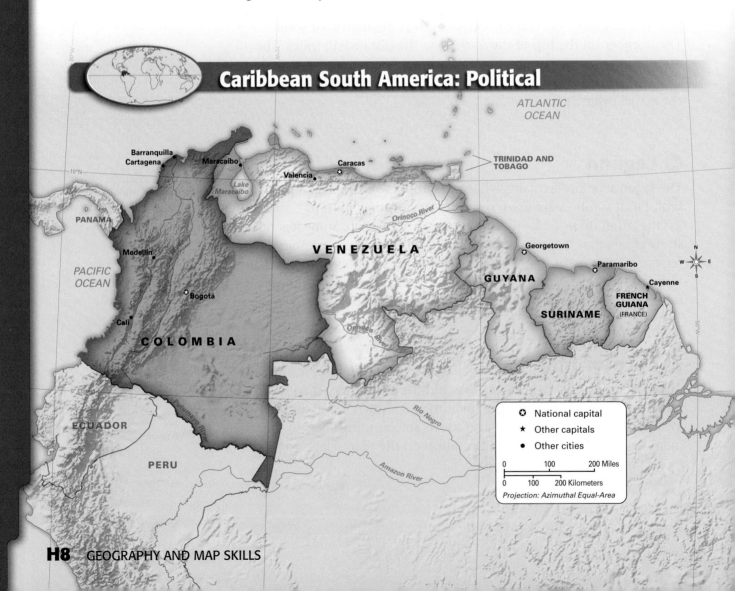

Caribbean South America: Political

ATLANTIC OCEAN

TRINIDAD AND TOBAGO

Barranquilla
Cartagena
Maracaibo
Caracas
Valencia
Lake Maracaibo

PANAMA

Orinoco River

VENEZUELA

Georgetown

PACIFIC OCEAN

Medellín

GUYANA

Paramaribo

Cayenne

Bogotá

Orinoco River

SURINAME

FRENCH GUIANA (FRANCE)

Cali

COLOMBIA

ECUADOR

Rio Negro

PERU

Amazon River

✪ National capital
★ Other capitals
● Other cities

0   100   200 Miles
0   100   200 Kilometers
Projection: Azimuthal Equal-Area

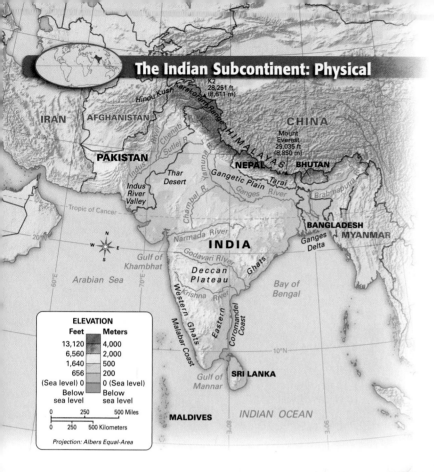

The Indian Subcontinent: Physical

Physical Maps

Physical maps show the major physical features of a region. These features may include mountain ranges, rivers, oceans, islands, deserts, and plains. Often, these maps use different colors to represent different elevations of land. As a result, the map reader can easily see which areas are high elevations, like mountains, and which areas are lower.

Special-Purpose Maps

Special-purpose maps focus on one special topic, such as climate, resources, or population. These maps present information on the topic that is particularly important in the region. Depending on the type of special-purpose map, the information may be shown with different colors, arrows, dots, or other symbols.

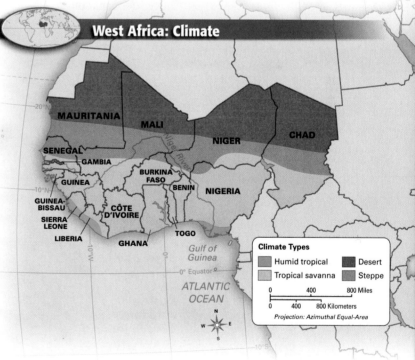

West Africa: Climate

Using Maps in Geography The different kinds of maps in this textbook will help you study and understand geography. By working with these maps, you will see what the physical geography of places is like, where people live, and how the world has changed over time.

Geographic Dictionary

OCEAN
a large body of water

CORAL REEF
an ocean ridge made up of
skeletal remains of tiny sea animals

GULF
a large part of
the ocean that
extends into land

PENINSULA
an area of land that sticks
out into a lake or ocean

ISTHMUS
a narrow piece of land
connecting two larger
land areas

BAY
part of a large
body of water
that is smaller
than a gulf

ISLAND
an area of land
surrounded entirely
by water

DELTA
an area where a
river deposits soil
into the ocean

STRAIT
a narrow body of
water connecting two
larger bodies of water

SINKHOLE
a circular depression
formed when the roof
of a cave collapses

WETLAND
an area of land
covered by
shallow water

RIVER
a natural flow of
water that runs
through the land

LAKE
an inland body
of water

FOREST
an area of densely
wooded land

COAST
an area of land
near the ocean

MOUNTAIN
an area of rugged
land that generally
rises higher than
2,000 feet

VALLEY
an area of low
land between
hills or mountains

GLACIER
a large area of
slow-moving ice

VOLCANO
an opening in Earth's crust
where lava, ash, and gases erupt

CANYON
a deep, narrow valley
with steep walls

HILL
a rounded, elevated
area of land smaller
than a mountain

PLAIN
a nearly
flat area

DUNE
a hill of sand
shaped by wind

OASIS
an area in the
desert with a
water source

DESERT
an extremely dry area with
little water and few plants

PLATEAU
a large, flat,
elevated
area of land

Themes and Essential Elements of Geography

by Dr. Christopher L. Salter

To study the world, geographers have identified 5 key themes, 6 essential elements, and 18 geography standards.

"How should we teach and learn about geography?" Professional geographers have worked hard over the years to answer this important question.

In 1984 a group of geographers identified the 5 Themes of Geography. These themes did a wonderful job of laying the groundwork for good classroom geography. Teachers used the 5 Themes in class, and geographers taught workshops on how to apply them in the world.

By the early 1990s, however, some geographers felt the 5 Themes were too broad. They created the 18 Geography Standards and the 6 Essential Elements. The 18 Geography Standards include more detailed information about what geography is, and the 6 Essential Elements are like a bridge between the 5 Themes and 18 Standards.

Look at the chart to the right. It shows how each of the 5 Themes connects to the Essential Elements and Standards. For example, the theme of Location is related to The World in Spatial Terms and the first three Standards. Study the chart carefully to see how the other themes, elements, and Standards are related.

The last Essential Element and the last two Standards cover The Uses of Geography. These key parts of geography were not covered by the 5 Themes. They will help you see how geography has influenced the past, present, and future.

5 Themes of Geography

Location The theme of location describes where something is.

Place Place describes the features that make a site unique.

Regions Regions are areas that share common characteristics.

Movement This theme looks at how and why people and things move.

Human-Environment Interaction People interact with their environment in many ways.

6 Essential Elements

18 Geography Standards

1. How to use maps and other tools
2. How to use mental maps to organize information
3. How to analyze the spatial organization of people, places, and environments

I. The World in Spatial Terms

4. The physical and human characteristics of places
5. How people create regions to interpret Earth
6. How culture and experience influence people's perceptions of places and regions

II. Places and Regions

7. The physical processes that shape Earth's surface
8. The distribution of ecosystems on Earth

9. The characteristics, distribution, and migration of human populations
10. The complexity of Earth's cultural mosaics

III. Physical Systems

11. The patterns and networks of economic interdependence on Earth
12. The patterns of human settlement
13. The forces of cooperation and conflict

IV. Human Systems

14. How human actions modify the physical environment
15. How physical systems affect human systems
16. The distribution and meaning of resources

V. Environment and Society

17. How to apply geography to interpret the past
18. How to apply geography to interpret the present and plan for the future

VI. The Uses of Geography

Become an Active Reader

Did you ever think you would begin reading your social studies book by reading about *reading*? Actually, it makes better sense than you might think. You would probably make sure you knew some soccer skills and strategies before playing in a game. Similarly, you need to know something about reading skills and strategies before reading your social studies book. In other words, you need to make sure you know whatever you need to know in order to read this book successfully.

Tip #1
Read Everything on the Page!

You can't follow the directions on the cake-mix box if you don't know where the directions are! Cake-mix boxes always have directions on them telling you how many eggs to add or how long to bake the cake. But, if you can't find that information, it doesn't matter that it is there.

Likewise, this book is filled with information that will help you understand what you are reading. If you don't study that information, however, it might as well not be there. Let's take a look at some of the places where you'll find important information in this book.

The Chapter Opener
The chapter opener gives you a brief overview of what you will learn in the chapter. You can use this information to prepare to read the chapter.

The Section Openers
Before you begin to read each section, preview the information under What You Will Learn. There you'll find the main ideas of the section and key terms that are important in it. Knowing what you are looking for before you start reading can improve your understanding.

Boldfaced Words
Those words are important and are defined somewhere on the page where they appear—either right there in the sentence or over in the side margin.

Maps, Charts, and Artwork
These things are not there just to take up space or look good! Study them and read the information beside them. It will help you understand the information in the chapter.

Questions at the End of Sections
At the end of each section, you will find questions that will help you decide whether you need to go back and re-read any parts before moving on. If you can't answer a question, that is your cue to go back and re-read.

Questions at the End of the Chapter
Answer the questions at the end of each chapter, even if your teacher doesn't ask you to. These questions are there to help you figure out what you need to review.

Tip #2

Use the Reading Skills and Strategies in Your Textbook

Good readers use a number of skills and strategies to make sure they understand what they are reading. In this textbook you will find help with important reading skills and strategies such as "Using Context Clues," and "Re-Reading."

We teach the reading skills and strategies in several ways. Use these activities and lessons and you will become a better reader.

- First, on the opening page of every chapter we identify and explain the reading skill or strategy you will focus on as you work through the chapter. In fact, these activities are called "Focus on Reading."

- Second, as you can see in the example at right, we tell you where to go for more help. The back of the book has a reading handbook with a full-page practice lesson to match the reading skill or strategy in every chapter.

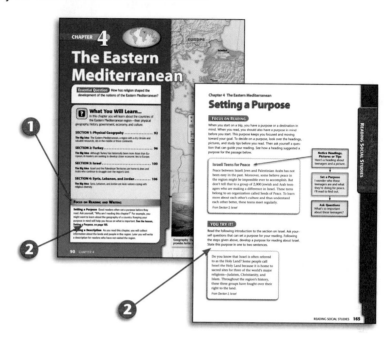

- Third, we give you short practice activities and examples as you read the chapter. These activities and examples show up in the margin of your book. Again, look for the words, "Focus on Reading."

- Finally, we provide another practice activity in the Chapter Review at the end of every chapter. That activity gives you one more chance to make sure you know how to use the reading skill or strategy.

Tip #3

Pay Attention to Vocabulary

It is no fun to read something when you don't know what the words mean, but you can't learn new words if you only use or read the words you already know. In this book, we know we have probably used some words you don't know. But, we have followed a pattern as we have used more difficult words.

- First, at the beginning of each section you will find a list of key terms that you will need to know. Be on the lookout for those words as you read through the section. You will find that we have defined those words right there in the paragraph where they are used. Look for a word that is in boldface with its definition highlighted in yellow.

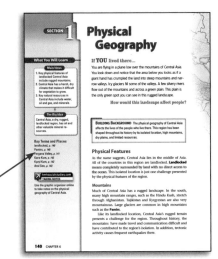

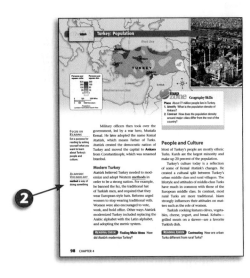

- Second, when we use a word that is important in all classes, not just social studies, we define it in the margin under the heading Academic Vocabulary. You will run into these academic words in other textbooks, so you should learn what they mean while reading this book.

Tip #4

Read Like a Skilled Reader

You won't be able to climb to the top of Mount Everest if you do not train! If you want to make it to the top of Mount Everest then you must start training to climb that huge mountain.

Training is also necessary to become a good reader. You will never get better at reading your social studies book—or any book for that matter—unless you spend some time thinking about how to be a better reader.

Skilled readers do the following:

1. They preview what they are supposed to read before they actually begin reading. When previewing, they look for vocabulary words, titles of sections, information in the margin, or maps or charts they should study.

2. They get ready to take some notes while reading by dividing their notebook paper into two parts. They title one side "Notes from the Chapter" and the other side "Questions or Comments I Have."

3. As they read, they complete their notes.

4. They read like **active readers**. The Active Reading list below shows you what that means.

5. Finally, they use clues in the text to help them figure out where the text is going. The best clues are called signal words. These are words that help you identify chronological order, causes and effects, or comparisons and contrasts.

Chronological Order Signal Words: *first, second, third, before, after, later, next, following that, earlier, subsequently, finally*

Cause and Effect Signal Words: *because of, due to, as a result of, the reason for, therefore, consequently, so, basis for*

Comparison/Contrast Signal Words: *likewise, also, as well as, similarly, on the other hand*

Active Reading

There are three ways to read a book: You can be a turn-the-pages-no-matter-what type of reader. These readers just keep on turning pages whether or not they understand what they are reading. Or, you can be a stop-watch-and-listen kind of reader. These readers know that if they wait long enough, someone will tell them what they need to know. Or, you can be an active reader. These readers know that it is up to them to figure out what the text means. Active readers do the following as they read:

Predict what will happen next based on what has already happened. When your predictions don't match what happens in the text, re-read the confusing parts.

Question what is happening as you read. Constantly ask yourself why things have happened, what things mean, and what caused certain events. Jot down notes about the questions you can't answer.

Summarize what you are reading frequently. Do not try to summarize the entire chapter! Read a bit and then summarize it. Then read on.

Connect what is happening in the section you're reading to what you have already read.

Clarify your understanding. Be sure that you understand what you are reading by stopping occasionally to ask yourself whether you are confused by anything. Sometimes you might need to re-read to clarify. Other times you might need to read further and collect more information before you can understand. Still other times you might need to ask the teacher to help you with what is confusing you.

Visualize what is happening in the text. In other words, try to see the events or places in your mind. It might help you to draw maps, make charts, or jot down notes about what you are reading as you try to visualize the action in the text.

Social Studies Words

As you read this textbook, you will be more successful if you learn the meanings of the words on this page. You will come across these words many times in your social studies classes, like geography and history. Read through these words now to become familiar with them before you begin your studies.

Social Studies Words

WORDS ABOUT TIME

AD	refers to dates after the birth of Jesus
BC	refers to dates before Jesus's birth
BCE	refers to dates before Jesus's birth, stands for "before the common era"
CE	refers to dates after Jesus's birth, stands for "common era"
century	a period of 100 years
decade	a period of 10 years
era	a period of time
millennium	a period of 1,000 years

WORDS ABOUT THE WORLD

climate	the weather conditions in a certain area over a long period of time
geography	the study of the world's people, places, and landscapes
physical features	features on Earth's surface, such as mountains and rivers
region	an area with one or more features that make it different from surrounding areas
resources	materials found on Earth that people need and value

WORDS ABOUT PEOPLE

anthropology	the study of people and cultures
archaeology	the study of the past based on what people left behind
citizen	a person who lives under the control of a government
civilization	the way of life of people in a particular place or time
culture	the knowledge, beliefs, customs, and values of a group of people
custom	a repeated practice or tradition
economics	the study of the production and use of goods and services
economy	any system in which people make and exchange goods and services
government	the body of officials and groups that run an area
history	the study of the past
politics	the process of running a government
religion	a system of beliefs in one or more gods or spirits
society	a group of people who share common traditions
trade	the exchange of goods or services

Academic Words

What are academic words? They are important words used in all of your classes, not just social studies. You will see these words in other textbooks, so you should learn what they mean while reading this book. Review this list now. You will use these words again in the chapters of this book.

Academic Words

classical	referring to the cultures of ancient Greece or Rome	**implicit**	understood though not clearly put into words
complex	difficult, not simple	**method**	a way of doing something
establish	to set up or create	**principle**	basic belief, rule, or law
explicit	fully revealed without vagueness	**procedure**	a series of steps taken to accomplish a task
ideals	ideas or goals that people try to live up to	**role**	a part or function
impact	effect, result		

> Academic Words features provide definitions for important terms that will help you understand social studies content.

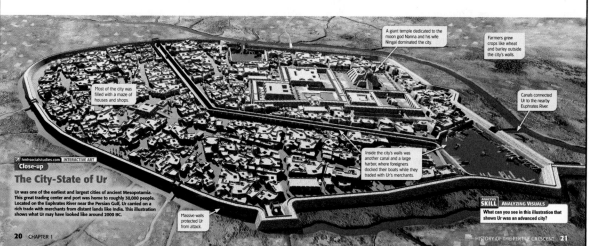

ACADEMIC VOCABULARY
role a part or function

Sargon was emperor, or ruler of his empire, for more than 50 years. However, the empire lasted only a century after his death. Later rulers could not keep the empire safe from invaders. Hostile tribes from the east raided and captured Akkad. A century of chaos followed.

Eventually, however, the Sumerian city-state of Ur rebuilt its strength and conquered the rest of Mesopotamia. Political stability was restored. The Sumerians once again became the most powerful civilization in the region.

READING CHECK Summarizing How did Sargon build an empire?

Religion Shapes Society

Religion was very important in Sumerian society. In fact, it played a **role** in nearly every aspect of life. In many ways, religion was the basis for all of Sumerian society.

Sumerian Religion

The Sumerians practiced **polytheism**, the worship of many gods. Among the gods they worshipped were Enlil, lord of the air; Enki, god of wisdom; and Inanna, goddess of love and war. The sun and moon were represented by the gods Utu and Nanna. Each city-state considered one god to be its special protector.

The Sumerians believed that their gods had enormous powers. Gods could bring good harvests or disastrous floods. They could bring illness, or they could bring good health and wealth. The Sumerians believed that success in life depended on pleasing the gods. Every Sumerian had to serve and worship the gods.

Priests, people who performed or led religious ceremonies, had great status in Sumer. People relied on them to help gain the gods' favor. Priests interpreted the wishes of the gods and made offerings to them. These offerings were made in temples, special buildings where priests performed their religious ceremonies.

Sumerian Social Order

Because of their status, priests occupied a high level in Sumer's **social hierarchy**, the division of society by rank or class. In fact, priests were just below kings. The kings of Sumer claimed that they had been chosen by the gods to rule.

Below the priests were Sumer's skilled craftspeople, merchants, and traders. Trade had a great **impact** on Sumerian society. Traders traveled to faraway places and exchanged grain for gold, silver, copper, lumber, and precious stones.

Below traders, farmers and laborers made up the large working class. Slaves were at the bottom of the social order.

ACADEMIC VOCABULARY
impact effect, result

A giant temple dedicated to the moon god Nanna and his wife Ningal dominated the city.

Farmers grew crops like wheat and barley outside the city's walls.

Most of the city was filled with a maze of houses and shops.

Canals connected Ur to the nearby Euphrates River.

Inside the city's walls was another canal and a large harbor, where foreigners docked their boats while they traded with Ur's merchants.

hmhsocialstudies.com INTERACTIVE ART
Close-up

The City-State of Ur

Ur was one of the earliest and largest cities of ancient Mesopotamia. This great trading center and port was home to roughly 30,000 people. Located on the Euphrates River near the Persian Gulf, Ur carried on a rich trade with merchants from distant lands like India. This illustration shows what Ur may have looked like around 2000 BC.

Massive walls protected Ur from attack.

ANALYSIS SKILL ANALYZING VISUALS
What can you see in this illustration that shows Ur was an advanced city?

20 CHAPTER 1

HISTORY OF THE FERTILE CRESCENT 21

Making This Book Work for You

Studying geography will be easy for you with this textbook. Take a few minutes now to become familiar with the easy-to-use structure and special features of your book. See how it will make geography come alive for you!

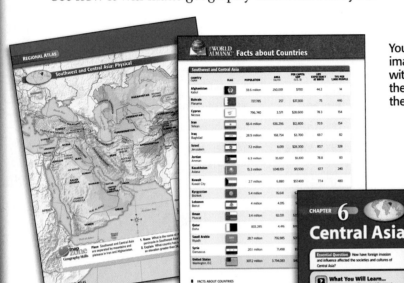

Your book begins with a satellite image, a regional atlas, and a table with facts about each country. Use these pages to get an overview of the region you will study.

Chapter

Each chapter includes an introduction, a Social Studies Skills activity, Chapter Review pages, and a Standardized Test Practice page.

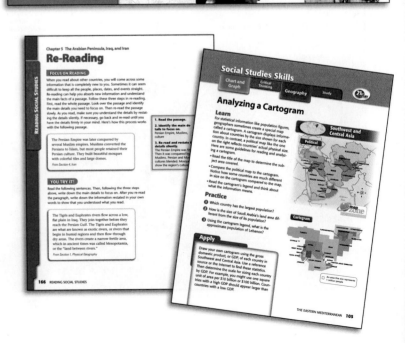

Reading Social Studies Chapter reading lessons give you skills and practice to help you read the textbook. More help with each lesson can be found in the back of the book. Margin notes and questions in the chapter make sure you understand the reading skill.

Social Studies Skills The Social Studies Skills lessons give you an opportunity to learn, practice, and apply an important skill. Chapter Review questions then follow up on what you learned.

Section

The section opener pages include Main Ideas, an overarching Big Idea, and Key Terms and Places. In addition, each section includes these special features.

If YOU Lived There . . . Each section begins with a situation for you to respond to, placing you in a place that relates to the content you will be studying in the section.

Building Background Building Background connects what will be covered in each section with what you already know.

Short Sections of Content The information in each section is organized into small chunks of text that you can easily understand.

Taking Notes Suggested graphic organizers help you read and take notes on the important ideas in the section.

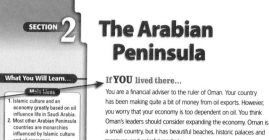

SECTION 2

The Arabian Peninsula

What You Will Learn...

Main Ideas

1. Islamic culture and an economy greatly based on oil influence life in Saudi Arabia.
2. Most other Arabian Peninsula countries are monarchies influenced by Islamic culture and oil resources.

The Big Idea

Most countries of the Arabian Peninsula share three main characteristics: Islamic religion and culture, monarchy as a form of government, and valuable oil resources.

Key Terms

Shia, p. 120
Sunni, p. 120
OPEC, p. 121

hmhsocialstudies.com
TAKING NOTES

Use the graphic organizer online to take notes on the countries of the Arabian Peninsula.

If YOU lived there...

You are a financial adviser to the ruler of Oman. Your country has been making quite a bit of money from oil exports. However, you worry that your economy is too dependent on oil. You think Oman's leaders should consider expanding the economy. Oman is a small country, but it has beautiful beaches, historic palaces and mosques, and colorful markets.

How would you suggest expanding the economy?

BUILDING BACKGROUND Oman and all the countries of the Arabian Peninsula have valuable oil resources. In addition to oil, these countries share two basic characteristics: Islamic religion and monarchy as a form of government. The largest country, and the one with the most influence in the region, is Saudi Arabia.

Saudi Arabia

Saudi Arabia is by far the largest of the countries of the Arabian Peninsula. It is also a major religious and cultural center and has one of the region's strongest economies.

People and Customs

Nearly all Saudis are Arabs and speak Arabic. Their culture is strongly influenced by Islam, a religion founded in Saudi Arabia by Muhammad. Islam is based on submitting to God and on messages Muslims believe God gave to Muhammad. These messages are written in the Qur'an, the holy book of Islam.

Nearly all Saudis follow one of two main branches of Islam. **Shia** Muslims believe that true interpretation of Islamic teaching can only come from certain religious and political leaders called imams. **Sunni** Muslims believe in the ability of the majority of the community to interpret Islamic teachings. About 85 percent of Saudi Muslims are Sunni.

120 CHAPTER 5

With about 10 million people, Istanbul, shown here, is Turkey's largest city.

electronics. About 30 perce[...] labor force works in agric[...] cotton, sugar beets, and [...] major crops.

Turkey is rich in natural resources, which include oil, coal, and iron ore. Water is also a valuable resource in the region. Turkey has spent billions of dollars building dams to increase its water supply. On one hand, these dams provide hydroelectricity. On the other hand, some of these dams have restricted the flow of river water into neighboring countries.

READING CHECK Finding Main Ideas What kind of government does Turkey have?

SUMMARY AND PREVIEW In this section you learned about Turkey's history, people, government, and economy. Next, you will learn about Israel.

Turkey Today

Turkey's government meets in the capital of Ankara, but **Istanbul** is Turkey's largest city. Istanbul's location will serve as an economic bridge to Europe as Turkey plans to join the European Union.

Government

Turkey's legislature is called the National Assembly. A president and a prime minister share executive power.

Although most of its people are Muslim, Turkey is a secular state. **Secular** means that religion is kept separate from government. For example, the religion of Islam allows a man to have up to four wives. However, by Turkish law a man is permitted to have just one wife. In recent years Islamic political parties have attempted to increase Islam's role in Turkish society.

Economy and Resources

As a member of the European Union, Turkey's economy and people would benefit by increased trade with Europe. Turkey's economy includes modern factories as well as village farming and craft making.

Among the most important industries are textiles and clothing, cement, and

---

Section 2 Assessment

hmhsocialstudies.com
ONLINE QUIZ

Reviewing Ideas, Terms, and Places

1. a. **Recall** What city did both the Romans and Ottoman Turks capture?
   b. **Explain** In what ways did Atatürk try to modernize Turkey?
2. a. **Recall** What ethnic group makes up 20 percent of Turkey's population?
   b. **Draw Conclusions** What makes Turkey **secular**?
   c. **Elaborate** Why do you think Turkey wants to be a member of the European Union?

Critical Thinking

3. **Summarizing** Using the information in your notes, summarize Turkey's history and Turkey today.

Turkey's History	Turkey Today

FOCUS ON WRITING

4. **Describing Turkey** A description of Turkey might include details about its people, culture, government, and economy. Take notes on the details you think are important and interesting.

THE EASTERN MEDITERRANEAN **99**

Reading Check Questions end each section of content so you can check to make sure you understand what you just studied.

Summary and Preview The Summary and Preview connects what you studied in the section to what you will study in the next section.

Section Assessment Finally, the section assessment boxes make sure that you understand the main ideas of the section. We also provide assessment practice online!

Scavenger Hunt

Are you ready to explore the world of geography? *Holt McDougal: Southwest and Central Asia* is your ticket to this exciting world. Before you begin your journey, complete this scavenger hunt to get to know your book and discover what's inside.

On a separate sheet of paper, fill in the blanks to complete each sentence below. In each answer, one letter will be in a yellow box. When you have answered every question, copy these letters in order to reveal the answer to the question at the bottom of the page.

1 According to the Table of Contents, the title of Chapter 2 is ☐☐☐☐☐☐ and Christianity. What is Section 3 of that chapter called?

2 Page 198 is the beginning of the ☐☐☐☐☐. What would you use this section of the book for?

3 The second word of the Main Ideas on page 144 is ☐☐☐☐☐☐.

4 The Case Study feature on pages 124–125 is called Oil in ☐☐☐☐☐ ☐☐☐☐☐☐.

5 The third word of the English and Spanish Glossary is ☐☐☐☐☐☐☐☐☐☐☐. What is its definition?

6 Look up Kabul in the Gazetteer. According to the entry, it is located in the country of ☐☐☐☐☐☐☐☐☐☐☐.

7 Page 180 of the Atlas is a map of ☐☐☐☐☐☐.

Fact!

The oldest known permanent settlement in the world is in Southwest Asia. What is it called?

☐☐☐☐☐☐☐

Southwest and Central Asia

The Caspian Sea

The vast Caspian Sea, which is the world's largest inland body of water, contains valuable resources like oil.

Great Mountains

In Central Asia, high mountain ranges such as the Tian Shan separate the region from other parts of Asia.

Huge Deserts

Southwest Asia is home to huge deserts such as the Rub' al-Khali, or "Empty Quarter," which is virtually uninhabited.

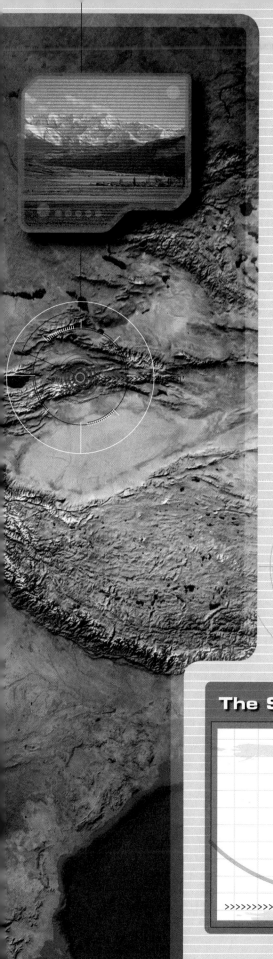

Southwest and Central Asia

Explore the Satellite Image
Vast deserts, high mountains, and large rivers stand out clearly on this satellite image of Southwest and Central Asia. How do you think these features influence life in the region?

The Satellite's Path

>44'56.08<

>>>>>>>>665.00'87<

567.476.348

+355

+766
+808

+966

456.094.

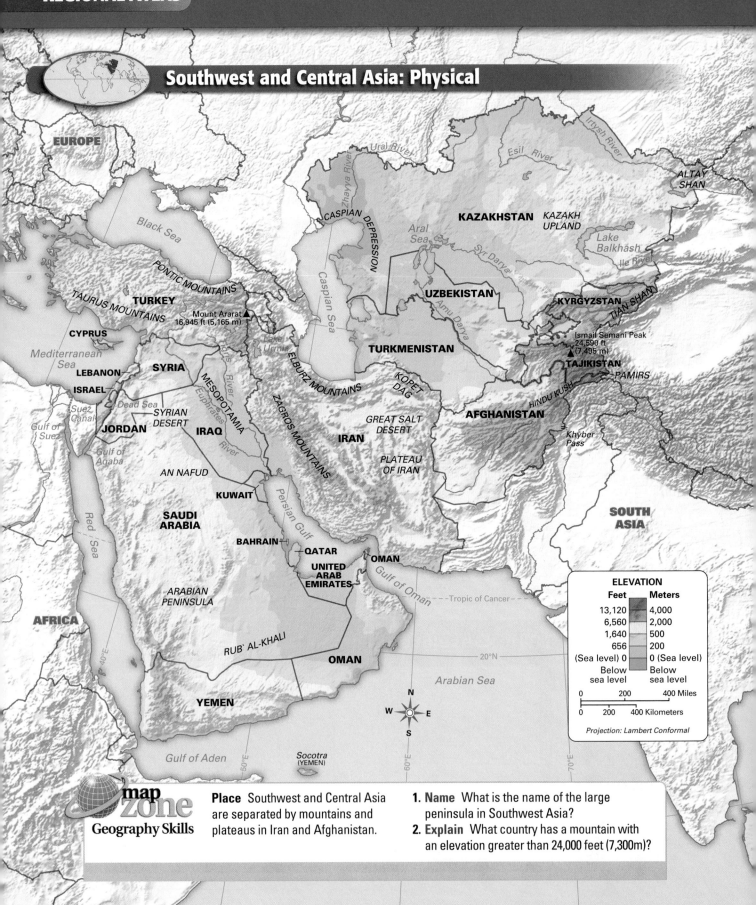

Southwest and Central Asia: Physical

EUROPE

Black Sea

Ural River

Esil River

Irtysh River

ALTAY SHAN

CASPIAN DEPRESSION

Aral Sea

KAZAKHSTAN

KAZAKH UPLAND

Lake Balkhash

Ile River

PONTIC MOUNTAINS

Zhayyk River

Caspian Sea

Syr Darya

TAURUS MOUNTAINS

TURKEY

Mount Ararat ▲
16,945 ft (5,165 m)

UZBEKISTAN

KYRGYZSTAN

TIAN SHAN

CYPRUS

Lake Urmia

ELBURZ MOUNTAINS

TURKMENISTAN

Amu Darya

Ismail Semani Peak
24,590 ft
(7,495 m) ▲

Mediterranean Sea

LEBANON

SYRIA

Tigris River

MESOPOTAMIA

KOPET DAG

TAJIKISTAN

PAMIRS

ISRAEL

Dead Sea

Euphrates River

ZAGROS MOUNTAINS

GREAT SALT DESERT

HINDU KUSH

Suez Canal

SYRIAN DESERT

AFGHANISTAN

Gulf of Suez

JORDAN

IRAQ

IRAN

PLATEAU OF IRAN

Khyber Pass

Gulf of Aqaba

AN NAFUD

KUWAIT

SOUTH ASIA

Red Sea

SAUDI ARABIA

Persian Gulf

BAHRAIN

QATAR

UNITED ARAB EMIRATES

OMAN

Gulf of Oman

ARABIAN PENINSULA

Tropic of Cancer

AFRICA

RUB' AL-KHALI

OMAN

20°N

Arabian Sea

YEMEN

N
W   E
S

Gulf of Aden

Socotra
(YEMEN)

ELEVATION

Feet		Meters
13,120		4,000
6,560		2,000
1,640		500
656		200
(Sea level) 0		0 (Sea level)
Below sea level		Below sea level

0   200   400 Miles

0   200   400 Kilometers

Projection: Lambert Conformal

map zone
Geography Skills

Place Southwest and Central Asia are separated by mountains and plateaus in Iran and Afghanistan.

1. **Name** What is the name of the large peninsula in Southwest Asia?

2. **Explain** What country has a mountain with an elevation greater than 24,000 feet (7,300m)?

Southwest and Central Asia

THE WORLD ALMANAC®
Facts about the World
Geographical Extremes: Southwest and Central Asia

Longest River	Euphrates River, Turkey/Syria/Iraq: 1,700 miles (2,735 km)
Highest Point	Qullai Ismoili Somoni, Tajikistan: 24,590 feet (7,495 m)
Lowest Point	Dead Sea, Israel/Jordan: 1,348 feet (411 m) below sea level
Highest Recorded Temperature	Tirat Tsvi, Israel: 129°F (53.9°C)
Driest Place	Aden, Yemen: 1.8 inches (4.6 cm) average precipitation per year
Largest Country	Kazakhstan: 1,049,155 square miles (2,717,311 square km)
Smallest Country	Bahrain: 257 square miles (666 square km)
Saltiest Lake	Dead Sea, Israel/Jordan: 33 percent salt content
Most Powerful Earthquake	Erzincan, Turkey, 1939: 8.0 magnitude

A high salt content keeps people afloat in the Dead Sea.

⬈ hmhsocialstudies.com

Size Comparison: The United States and Southwest and Central Asia

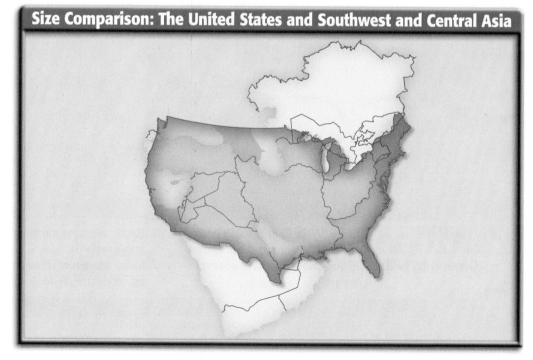

Southwest and Central Asia: Political

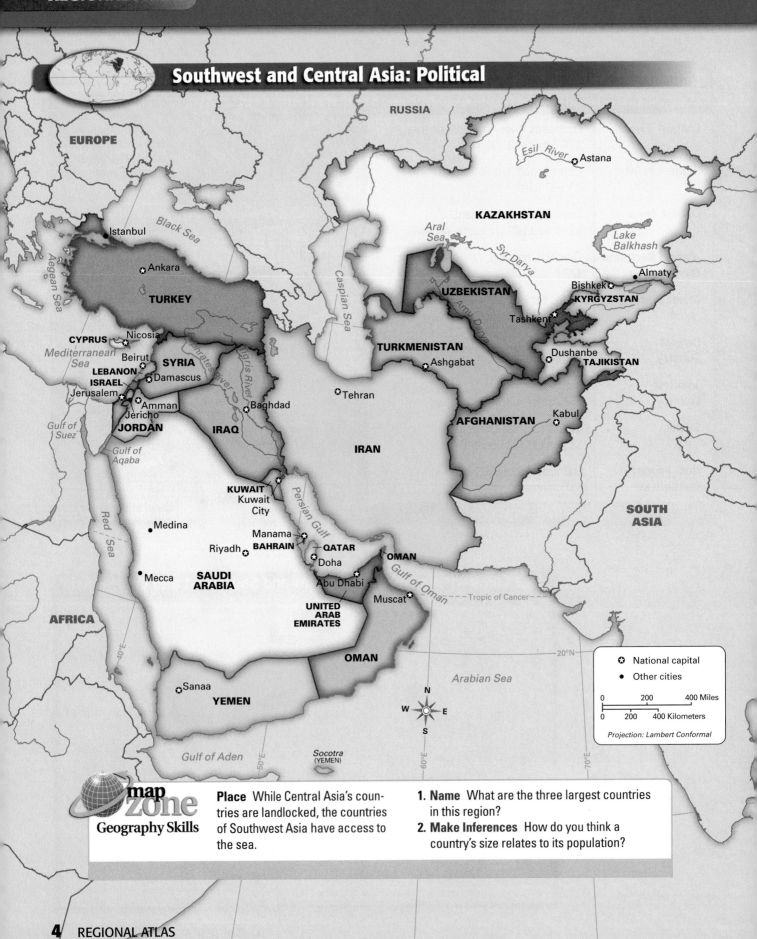

EUROPE

RUSSIA

KAZAKHSTAN

Esil River ✪ Astana

Black Sea

Aral Sea

Lake Balkhash

Syr Darya

Istanbul

✪ Ankara

TURKEY

Aegean Sea

Caspian Sea

UZBEKISTAN

✪ Almaty

Bishkek ✪

KYRGYZSTAN

Tashkent ★

CYPRUS   Nicosia ✪

Mediterranean Sea

Beirut ✪

SYRIA

TURKMENISTAN

Amu Darya

Dushanbe ✪

TAJIKISTAN

LEBANON
ISRAEL

✪ Damascus

Euphrates River

Tigris River

✪ Ashgabat

Jerusalem ✪

Amman ✪

Jericho

JORDAN

✪ Tehran

IRAQ

✪ Baghdad

AFGHANISTAN

Kabul ✪

Gulf of Suez

Gulf of Aqaba

IRAN

SOUTH ASIA

Red Sea

• Medina

KUWAIT

Kuwait City ✪

Persian Gulf

Manama ✪

Riyadh ✪

BAHRAIN

QATAR

✪ Doha

OMAN

SAUDI ARABIA

Abu Dhabi ✪

Gulf of Oman

- - - Tropic of Cancer - - -

Muscat ✪

• Mecca

UNITED ARAB EMIRATES

AFRICA

20°N

OMAN

Arabian Sea

✪ Sanaa

YEMEN

N
W   E
S

Gulf of Aden

Socotra
(YEMEN)

50°E   60°E   70°E

40°E

30°E

Legend
- ✪ National capital
- • Other cities

0	200	400 Miles
0	200	400 Kilometers

Projection: Lambert Conformal

map zone

Geography Skills

Place While Central Asia's countries are landlocked, the countries of Southwest Asia have access to the sea.

1. **Name** What are the three largest countries in this region?
2. **Make Inferences** How do you think a country's size relates to its population?

Southwest and Central Asia

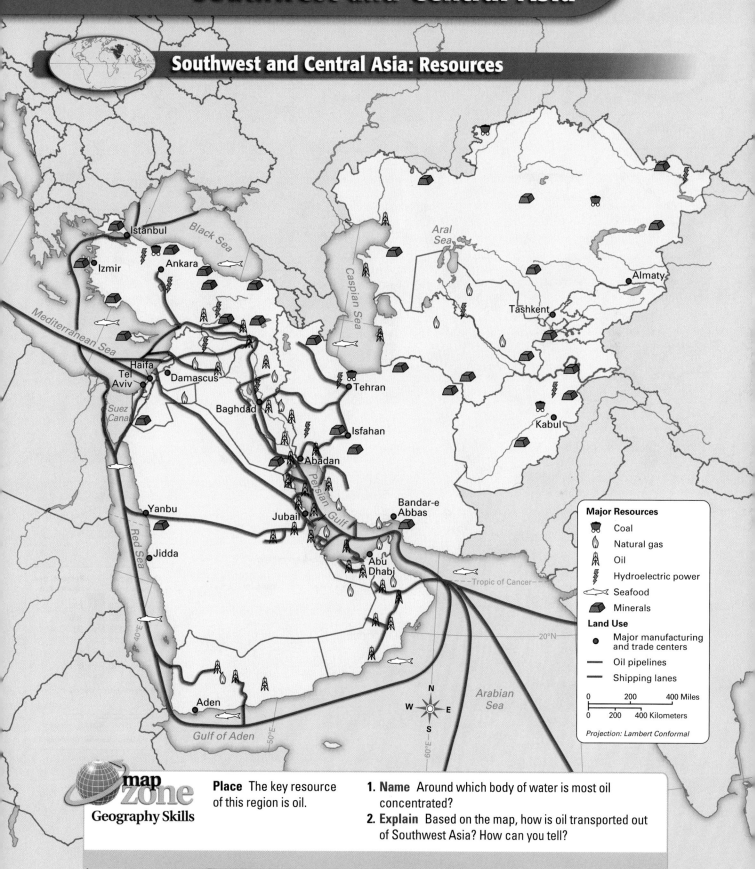

Major Resources

- 🪨 Coal
- 💧 Natural gas
- ⛽ Oil
- ⚡ Hydroelectric power
- 🐟 Seafood
- 💎 Minerals

Land Use

- ● Major manufacturing and trade centers
- — Oil pipelines
- — Shipping lanes

0   200   400 Miles
0   200   400 Kilometers

Projection: Lambert Conformal

map zone
Geography Skills

Place The key resource of this region is oil.

1. **Name** Around which body of water is most oil concentrated?
2. **Explain** Based on the map, how is oil transported out of Southwest Asia? How can you tell?

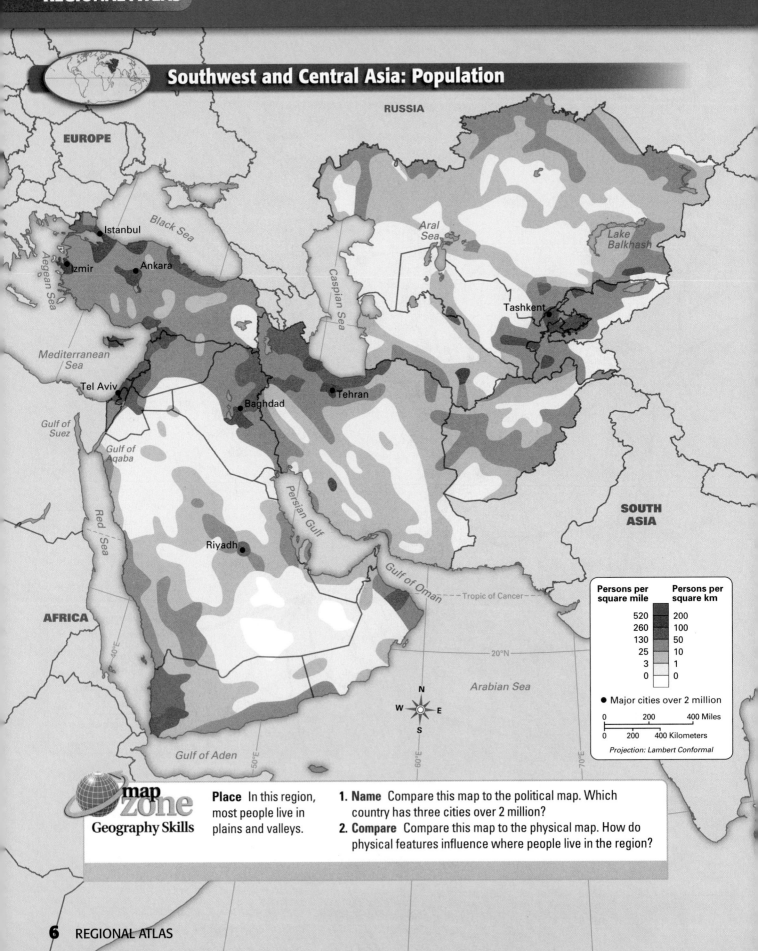

Southwest and Central Asia: Population

RUSSIA

EUROPE

Black Sea

Istanbul

Aegean Sea

Izmir

Ankara

Mediterranean Sea

Tel Aviv

Gulf of Suez

Gulf of Aqaba

Red Sea

AFRICA

Riyadh

Gulf of Aden

Caspian Sea

Aral Sea

Lake Balkhash

Tashkent

Tehran

Baghdad

Persian Gulf

Gulf of Oman

Tropic of Cancer

20°N

Arabian Sea

SOUTH ASIA

Persons per square mile | **Persons per square km**

Persons per square mile	Persons per square km
520	200
260	100
130	50
25	10
3	1
0	0

● Major cities over 2 million

0   200   400 Miles

0   200   400 Kilometers

Projection: Lambert Conformal

map Zone Geography Skills

Place In this region, most people live in plains and valleys.

1. **Name** Compare this map to the political map. Which country has three cities over 2 million?

2. **Compare** Compare this map to the physical map. How do physical features influence where people live in the region?

Southwest and Central Asia

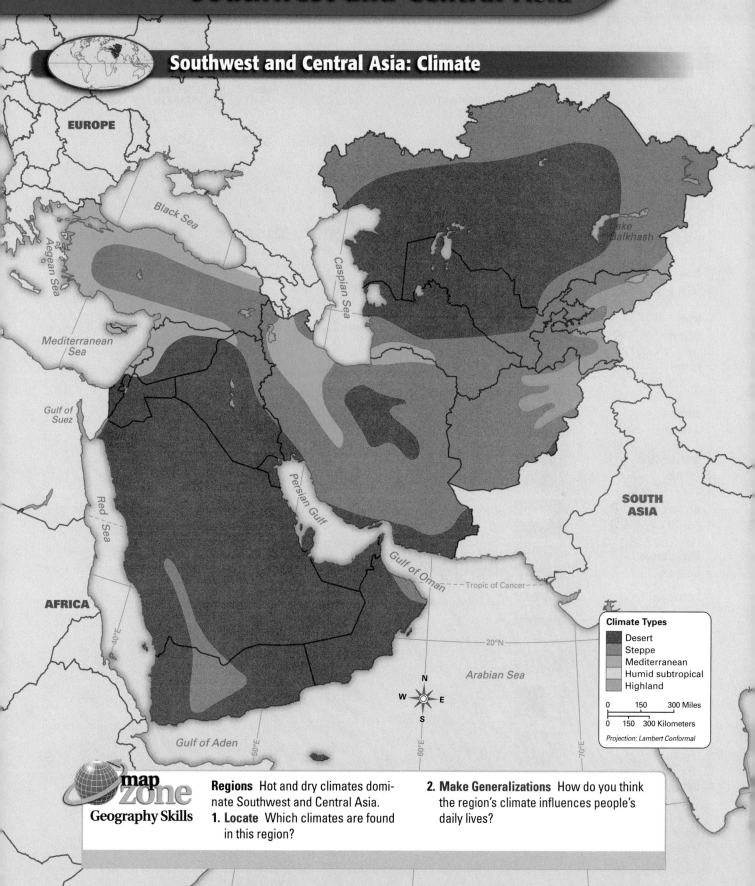

EUROPE

Black Sea

Lake Balkhash

Aegean Sea

Caspian Sea

Mediterranean Sea

SOUTH ASIA

Gulf of Suez

Gulf of Aqaba

Red Sea

Persian Gulf

Gulf of Oman

Tropic of Cancer

AFRICA

40°E

30°E

20°N

60°E

70°E

Arabian Sea

Gulf of Aden

N W E S

Climate Types
- Desert
- Steppe
- Mediterranean
- Humid subtropical
- Highland

0   150   300 Miles

0   150   300 Kilometers

Projection: Lambert Conformal

map zone
Geography Skills

Regions Hot and dry climates dominate Southwest and Central Asia.

1. Locate Which climates are found in this region?

2. Make Generalizations How do you think the region's climate influences people's daily lives?

Southwest and Central Asia

country Capital	FLAG	POPULATION	AREA (sq mi)	PER CAPITA GDP (U.S. $)	LIFE EXPECTANCY AT BIRTH	TVS PER 1,000 PEOPLE
Afghanistan Kabul		33.6 million	250,001	$700	44.2	14
Bahrain Manama		727,785	257	$37,300	75	446
Cyprus Nicosia		796,740	3,571	$28,600	78.3	154
Iran Tehran		66.4 million	636,296	$12,800	70.9	154
Iraq Baghdad		28.9 million	168,754	$3,700	69.7	82
Israel Jerusalem		7.2 million	8,019	$28,300	80.7	328
Jordan Amman		6.3 million	35,637	$5,100	78.8	83
Kazakhstan Astana		15.3 million	1,049,155	$11,500	67.7	240
Kuwait Kuwait City		2.7 million	6,880	$57,400	77.4	480
Kyrgyzstan Bishkek		5.4 million	76,641	$2,200	69.2	49
Lebanon Beirut		4 million	4,015	$11,100	73.5	355
Oman Muscat		3.4 million	82,031	$20,200	74	575
Qatar Doha		833,285	4,416	$110,700	75.3	866
Saudi Arabia Riyadh		28.7 million	756,985	$20,500	76.1	263
Syria Damascus		20.1 million	71,498	$5,000	70.9	68
United States Washington, D.C.		307.2 million	3,794,083	$46,900	78.2	844

country Capital	FLAG	POPULATION	AREA (sq mi)	PER CAPITA GDP (U.S. $)	LIFE EXPECTANCY AT BIRTH	TVS PER 1,000 PEOPLE
Tajikistan Dushanbe		7.3 million	55,251	$1,800	65.1	328
Turkey Ankara		76.8 million	301,384	$11,900	73.2	328
Turkmenistan Ashgabat		4.9 million	188,456	$6,200	68.7	198
United Arab Emirates Abu Dhabi		4.8 million	32,000	$39,900	76	309
Uzbekistan Tashkent		27.8 million	172,742	$2,600	71.8	280
Yemen Sanaa		23.8 million	203,850	$2,400	63	286
United States Washington, D.C.		307.2 million	3,794,083	$46,900	78.2	844

ANALYSIS SKILL ▸ **ANALYZING TABLES**

1. How does the per capita GDP of countries in this region compare to the per capita GDP of the United States?
2. Based on the table, which countries seem to have the highest standard of living?

Oil Giants

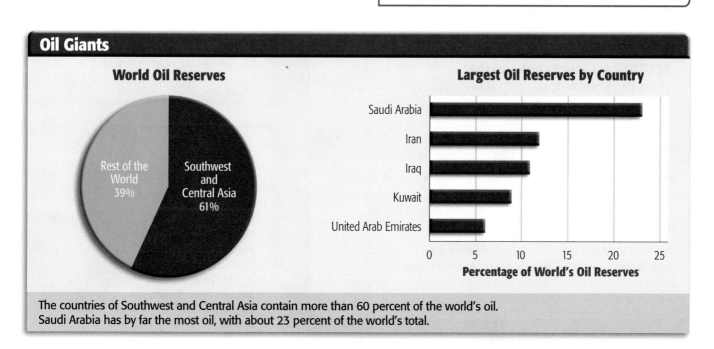

World Oil Reserves

Rest of the World 39%

Southwest and Central Asia 61%

Largest Oil Reserves by Country

Saudi Arabia
Iran
Iraq
Kuwait
United Arab Emirates

0   5   10   15   20   25
Percentage of World's Oil Reserves

The countries of Southwest and Central Asia contain more than 60 percent of the world's oil.
Saudi Arabia has by far the most oil, with about 23 percent of the world's total.

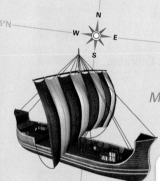

History of the Fertile Crescent

7000–500 BC

Essential Question How did the geography of the Fertile Crescent lead to the development of advanced civilizations?

What You Will Learn...

The world's oldest civilizations developed in the region of Mesopotamia, part of a larger area known as the Fertile Crescent.

FOCUS ON READING AND WRITING

Paraphrasing One way to be sure you understand a passage of text is to paraphrase it, or restate it in your own words. Practice paraphrasing sentences and whole paragraphs as you read this chapter. **See the lesson, Paraphrasing, on page 162.**

Create a Poster Most elementary students have not read or heard much about ancient Mesopotamia. As you read this chapter, you can gather information about the land. Then you can create a colorful poster to share some of what you have learned with a young child.

Mediterranean Sea

Phoenician trading ship

map zone Geography Skills

Regions The Fertile Crescent is a name given by historians to a large area of fertile land in Southwest Asia.

1. **Name** What two rivers are at the heart of the Fertile Crescent?
2. **Interpret** Why do you think this area is called the Fertile Crescent?

Empires The world's first empires were formed in the Fertile Crescent. Soldiers from these empires wore bronze helmets like this one.

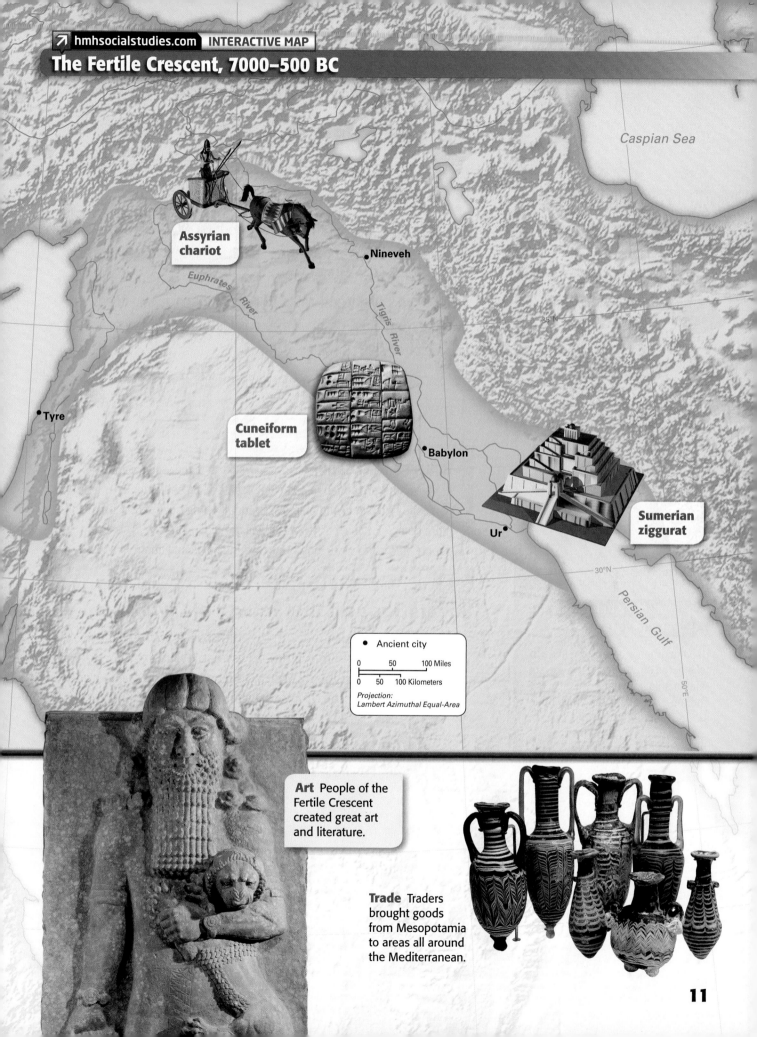

The Fertile Crescent, 7000–500 BC

Assyrian chariot

Nineveh

Caspian Sea

Euphrates River

Tigris River

35°N

Cuneiform tablet

Babylon

Sumerian ziggurat

Tyre

Ur

30°N

Persian Gulf

60°E

• Ancient city

0   50   100 Miles

0   50   100 Kilometers

Projection:
Lambert Azimuthal Equal-Area

Art People of the
Fertile Crescent
created great art
and literature.

Trade Traders
brought goods
from Mesopotamia
to areas all around
the Mediterranean.

11

Geography of the Fertile Crescent

If **YOU** lived there...

You are a farmer in Southwest Asia about 6,000 years ago. You live near a slow-moving river that has many shallow lakes and marshes. The river makes the land in the valley rich and fertile, so you can grow wheat and dates. But in the spring, raging floods spill over the riverbanks, destroying your fields. In the hot summers, you are often short of water.

How can you control the waters of the river?

BUILDING BACKGROUND In several parts of the world, bands of hunter-gatherers began to settle down in farming settlements. They domesticated plants and animals. Gradually, their cultures became more complex. Most early civilizations grew up along rivers, where people learned to work together to irrigate fields and control floods.

Rivers Support the Growth of Civilization

Early peoples settled where crops would grow. Crops usually grew well near rivers, where water was available and regular floods made the soil rich. One region in Southwest Asia was especially well suited for farming. It lay between two rivers.

The Land between the Rivers

The Tigris and Euphrates rivers are the most important physical features of the region sometimes known as Mesopotamia (mes-uh-puh-TAY-mee-uh). Mesopotamia means "between the rivers" in Greek.

As you can see on the map, the region called Mesopotamia lies between Asia Minor and the Persian Gulf. The region is part of the **Fertile Crescent**, a large arc of rich, or fertile, farmland. As you can see on the map, the Fertile Crescent extends from the Persian Gulf to the Mediterranean Sea.

In ancient times, Mesopotamia was made of two parts. Northern Mesopotamia was a plateau bordered on the north and the east by mountains. The southern part of Mesopotamia was a flat plain. The Tigris and Euphrates rivers flowed down from the hills into this low-lying plain.

The Rise of Civilization

Hunter-gatherer groups first settled in Mesopotamia more than 12,000 years ago. Over time, these people learned how to plant crops to grow their own food. Every year, floods on the Tigris and Euphrates rivers brought **silt**, a mixture of rich soil and tiny rocks, to the land. The fertile silt made the land ideal for farming.

The first farm settlements were formed in Mesopotamia as early as 7000 BC. There, farmers grew wheat, barley, and other types of grain. Livestock, birds, and fish were also good sources of food. Plentiful food led to population growth, and villages formed. Eventually, these early villages developed into the world's first civilization.

READING CHECK **Summarizing** What made civilization possible in Mesopotamia?

FOCUS ON READING

Make sure you understand this paragraph by restating it in your own words.

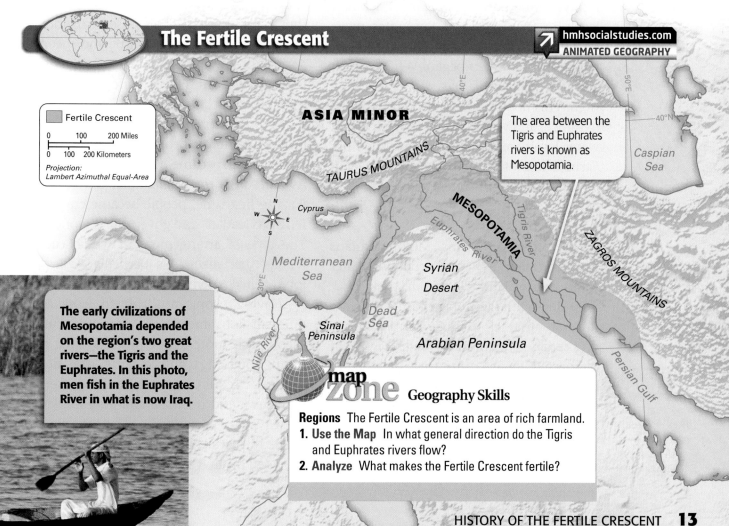

The Fertile Crescent

hmhsocialstudies.com
ANIMATED GEOGRAPHY

Fertile Crescent

0   100   200 Miles
0   100   200 Kilometers
Projection:
Lambert Azimuthal Equal-Area

ASIA MINOR

TAURUS MOUNTAINS

Cyprus

Mediterranean Sea

The area between the Tigris and Euphrates rivers is known as Mesopotamia.

Caspian Sea

MESOPOTAMIA

Euphrates River

Tigris River

ZAGROS MOUNTAINS

Syrian Desert

Dead Sea

Sinai Peninsula

Nile River

Arabian Peninsula

Persian Gulf

The early civilizations of Mesopotamia depended on the region's two great rivers—the Tigris and the Euphrates. In this photo, men fish in the Euphrates River in what is now Iraq.

map zone **Geography Skills**

Regions The Fertile Crescent is an area of rich farmland.
1. **Use the Map** In what general direction do the Tigris and Euphrates rivers flow?
2. **Analyze** What makes the Fertile Crescent fertile?

Early farmers faced the challenge of learning how to control the flow of river water to their fields in both rainy and dry seasons.

1 Early settlements in Mesopotamia were located near rivers. Water was not controlled, and flooding was a continual problem.

2 Later, people built canals to protect houses from flooding and to move water to their fields.

Farming and Cities

Although Mesopotamia had fertile soil, farming wasn't easy there. The region received little rain. This meant that water levels in the Tigris and Euphrates rivers depended on rainfall in eastern Asia Minor where the two rivers began. When a great amount of rain fell, water levels got very high. This flooding destroyed crops, killed livestock, and washed away homes. When water levels were too low, crops dried up. Farmers knew that they needed to develop a way to control the rivers' flow.

Controlling Water

To solve their problems, Mesopotamians used **irrigation**, a way of supplying water to an area of land. To irrigate their land, they dug out large storage basins to catch rainwater that fell to the north. Then they dug **canals**, human-made waterways, that connected these basins to a network of ditches. These ditches brought water to the fields. To protect their fields from flooding, farmers built up the rivers' banks. These built-up banks held back floodwaters even when river levels were high.

People still build dikes, or earthen walls along rivers or shorelines, to hold back water.

Food Surpluses

Irrigation increased the amount of food farmers were able to grow. In fact, farmers could produce a food **surplus**, or more than they needed. Farmers also used irrigation to water grazing areas for cattle and sheep. As a result, Mesopotamians ate a variety of foods. Fish, meat, wheat, barley, and dates were plentiful.

Because irrigation made farmers more productive, fewer people needed to farm. Some people became free to do other jobs. As a result, new occupations developed. For the first time, people became crafters, religious leaders, and government workers. The type of arrangement in which each worker specializes in a particular task or job is called a **division of labor**.

Having people available to work on different jobs meant that society could accomplish more. Large projects, such as raising buildings and digging irrigation systems, required specialized workers, managers, and organization. To complete these types of projects, the Mesopotamians needed structure and rules. These could be provided by laws and government.

③ With irrigation, the people of Mesopotamia were able to grow more food.

④ Food surpluses allowed some people to stop farming and concentrate on other jobs, like making clay pots or tools.

Appearance of Cities

Over time, Mesopotamian settlements grew both in size and complexity. They gradually developed into cities between 4000 and 3000 BC.

Despite the growth of cities, society in Mesopotamia was still based on agriculture. Most people still worked in farming jobs. However, cities were becoming important places. People traded goods there, and cities provided leaders with power bases.

Cities were the political, religious, cultural, and economic centers of civilization.

READING CHECK **Analyzing** Why did the Mesopotamians create irrigation systems?

SUMMARY AND PREVIEW Mesopotamia's rich, fertile lands supported productive farming, which led to the development of cities. In Section 2 you will learn about some of the first city builders.

Section 1 Assessment

hmhsocialstudies.com
ONLINE QUIZ

Reviewing Ideas, Terms, and Places

1. **a. Identify** Where was Mesopotamia?
   b. Explain How did the **Fertile Crescent** get its name?
   c. Evaluate What was the most important factor in making Mesopotamia's farmland fertile?
2. **a. Describe** Why did farmers need to develop a system to control their water supply?
   b. Explain In what ways did a **division of labor** contribute to the growth of the Mesopotamian civilization?
   c. Elaborate How might managing large projects prepare people for running a government?

Critical Thinking

3. **Identifying Cause and Effect** Farmers who used the rivers for irrigation were part of a cause-effect chain. Use a chart like this one to show that chain.

   | River levels were uneven. | → | | → | | → | People enjoy many foods. |

FOCUS ON WRITING

4. **Understanding Geography** Think of the images you could use on your poster. Would you want to show an image of the canals or rivers? Where could you find pictures to show important features?

River Valley Civilizations

All of the world's earliest civilizations had at least one thing in common—they arose in river valleys that were good locations for farming. Three key factors made river valleys good for farming. First, the fields that bordered the rivers were flat, which made it easier for farmers to plant crops. Second, the soils were nourished by flood deposits and silt, which made them very fertile. Finally, the river provided the water farmers needed for irrigation.

Natural Highways River travel allowed early civilizations to trade goods and ideas. These people are traveling on the Euphrates River, one of the two main rivers of ancient Mesopotamia.

Mediterranean Sea

A F R I C A

Memphis ●

EGYPT

Caspian Sea

MESOPOTAMIA

Tigris River

Euphrates River

Ur ●

Red Sea

Nile River

A R A B I A N
P E N I N S U L A

From Village to City With the development of agriculture, people settled into farming villages. Over time, some of these villages grew into large cities. These ancient ruins are near Memphis, Egypt.

Gifts of the River River water was key to farming in early civilizations. This farmer is using water from the Huang He (Yellow River) in China to water her crops.

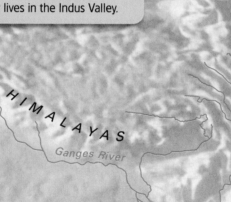

A S I A

New Activities Food surpluses allowed people to pursue other activities, like crafts, art, and writing. This tile designer lives in the Indus Valley.

Harappa

Mohenjo Daro

INDUS VALLEY

H I M A L A Y A S

Indus River

Ganges River

INDIA

CHINA

Chang Jiang (Yangzi River)

Huang He (Yellow River)

Arabian Sea

Bay of Bengal

N W E S

River valley

0   500   1,000 Miles
0 500 1,000 Kilometers

map zone Geography Skills

Human-Environment Interaction Four of the world's earliest civilizations arose on the banks of large rivers.
1. **Locate** Where were the four earliest river valley civilizations located?
2. **Explain** Why did the world's first civilizations all develop in river valleys?

INDIAN OCEAN

The Rise of Sumer

If **YOU** lived there...

You are a crafter living in one of the cities of Sumer. Thick walls surround and protect your city, so you feel safe from the armies of other city-states. But you and your neighbors are fearful of other beings—the many gods and spirits that you have been taught are everywhere. They can bring illness or sandstorms or bad luck.

How might you protect yourself from gods and spirits?

What You Will Learn...

Main Ideas

1. The Sumerians created the world's first advanced society.
2. Religion played a major role in Sumerian society.

The Big Idea

The Sumerians developed the first civilization in Mesopotamia.

Key Terms and Places

Sumer, *p. 18*
city-state, *p. 18*
empire, *p. 19*
polytheism, *p. 20*
priests, *p. 21*
social hierarchy, *p. 21*

hmhsocialstudies.com
TAKING NOTES

Use the graphic organizer online to take notes on the Sumerian civilization.

BUILDING BACKGROUND As civilizations developed along rivers, their societies and governments became more advanced. Religion became a main characteristic of these ancient cultures. Kings claimed to rule with the approval of the gods, and ordinary people wore charms and performed rituals to avoid bad luck.

An Advanced Society

In southern Mesopotamia, a people known as the Sumerians (soo-MER-ee-unz) developed the world's first civilization. No one knows where they came from or when they moved into the region. All we know is that by 3000 BC, several hundred thousand Sumerians had settled in Mesopotamia, in a land they called **Sumer** (soo-muhr). There they built an advanced society.

City-States of Sumer

Most people in Sumer were farmers. They lived mainly in rural, or countryside, areas. The centers of Sumerian society, however, were the urban, or city, areas. The first cities in Sumer had about 10,000 residents. Over time, the cities grew. Historians think that by 2000 BC, some of Sumer's largest cities had more than 100,000 residents.

As a result, the basic political unit of Sumer combined the two parts. This unit was the city-state. A **city-state** consisted of a central city and all the countryside around it. The amount of farmland controlled by a city-state depended on its military strength. Stronger city-states controlled larger areas.

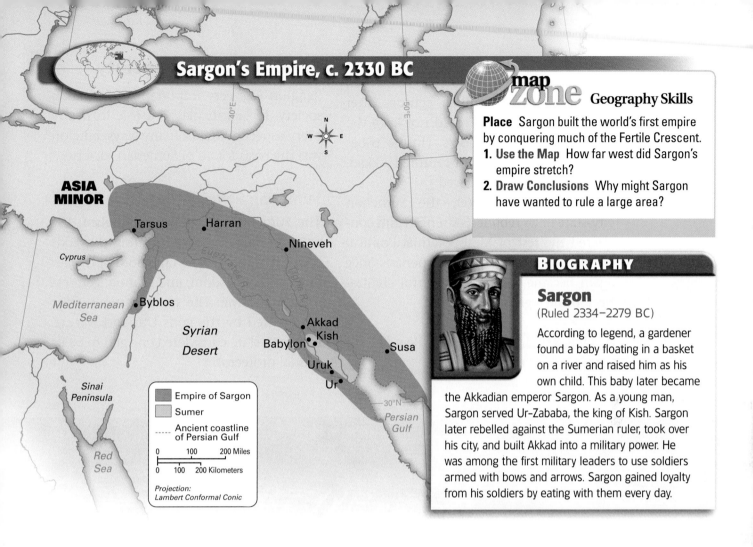

Sargon's Empire, c. 2330 BC

map zone Geography Skills

Place Sargon built the world's first empire by conquering much of the Fertile Crescent.
1. **Use the Map** How far west did Sargon's empire stretch?
2. **Draw Conclusions** Why might Sargon have wanted to rule a large area?

ASIA MINOR

Tarsus

Harran

Nineveh

Cyprus

Mediterranean Sea

Byblos

Syrian Desert

Babylon

Akkad

Kish

Uruk

Ur

Susa

Sinai Peninsula

Red Sea

Persian Gulf

30°N

Empire of Sargon

Sumer

Ancient coastline of Persian Gulf

0   100   200 Miles
0   100   200 Kilometers

Projection:
Lambert Conformal Conic

BIOGRAPHY

Sargon
(Ruled 2334–2279 BC)

According to legend, a gardener found a baby floating in a basket on a river and raised him as his own child. This baby later became the Akkadian emperor Sargon. As a young man, Sargon served Ur–Zababa, the king of Kish. Sargon later rebelled against the Sumerian ruler, took over his city, and built Akkad into a military power. He was among the first military leaders to use soldiers armed with bows and arrows. Sargon gained loyalty from his soldiers by eating with them every day.

City-states in Sumer fought each other to gain more farmland. As a result of these conflicts, the city-states built up strong armies. Sumerians also built strong, thick walls around their cities for protection.

Individual city-states gained and lost power over time. By 3500 BC, a city-state known as Kish had become quite powerful. Over the next 1,000 years, the city-states of Uruk and Ur fought for dominance. One of Uruk's kings, known as Gilgamesh, became a legendary figure in Sumerian literature.

Rise of the Akkadian Empire

In time, another society developed along the Tigris and Euphrates. This society was built by the Akkadians (uh-KAY-dee-uhns). They lived just north of Sumer, but they were not Sumerians. They even spoke a different language than the Sumerians.

In spite of their differences, however, the Akkadians and the Sumerians lived in peace for many years.

That peace was broken in the 2300s BC when Sargon sought to extend Akkadian territory. He built a new capital, Akkad (A-kad), on the Euphrates River, near what is now the city of Baghdad. Sargon was the first ruler to have a permanent army. He used that army to launch a series of wars against neighboring kingdoms.

Sargon's soldiers defeated all the city-states of Sumer. They also conquered northern Mesopotamia, finally bringing the entire region under his rule. With these conquests, Sargon established the world's first **empire**, or land with different territories and peoples under a single rule. Sargon's huge empire stretched from the Persian Gulf to the Mediterranean Sea.

ACADEMIC
VOCABULARY
role a part or
function

Sargon was emperor, or ruler of his empire, for more than 50 years. However, the empire lasted only a century after his death. Later rulers could not keep the empire safe from invaders. Hostile tribes from the east raided and captured Akkad. A century of chaos followed.

Eventually, however, the Sumerian city-state of Ur rebuilt its strength and conquered the rest of Mesopotamia. Political stability was restored. The Sumerians once again became the most powerful civilization in the region.

READING CHECK **Summarizing** How did Sargon build an empire?

Religion Shapes Society

Religion was very important in Sumerian society. In fact, it played a **role** in nearly every aspect of life. In many ways, religion was the basis for all of Sumerian society.

Sumerian Religion

The Sumerians practiced **polytheism**, the worship of many gods. Among the gods they worshipped were Enlil, lord of the air; Enki, god of wisdom; and Inanna, goddess of love and war. The sun and moon were represented by the gods Utu and Nanna. Each city-state considered one god to be its special protector.

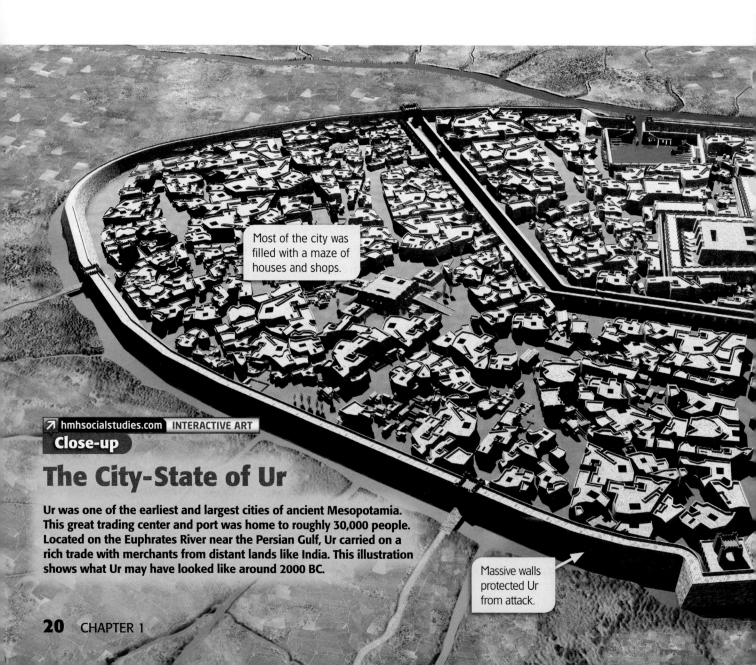

Most of the city was filled with a maze of houses and shops.

↗ hmhsocialstudies.com **INTERACTIVE ART**
Close-up

The City-State of Ur

Ur was one of the earliest and largest cities of ancient Mesopotamia. This great trading center and port was home to roughly 30,000 people. Located on the Euphrates River near the Persian Gulf, Ur carried on a rich trade with merchants from distant lands like India. This illustration shows what Ur may have looked like around 2000 BC.

Massive walls protected Ur from attack.

The Sumerians believed that their gods had enormous powers. Gods could bring good harvests or disastrous floods. They could bring illness, or they could bring good health and wealth. The Sumerians believed that success in life depended on pleasing the gods. Every Sumerian had to serve and worship the gods.

Priests, people who performed or led religious ceremonies, had great status in Sumer. People relied on them to help gain the gods' favor. Priests interpreted the wishes of the gods and made offerings to them. These offerings were made in temples, special buildings where priests performed their religious ceremonies.

Sumerian Social Order

Because of their status, priests occupied a high level in Sumer's **social hierarchy**, the division of society by rank or class. In fact, priests were just below kings. The kings of Sumer claimed that they had been chosen by the gods to rule.

Below the priests were Sumer's skilled craftspeople, merchants, and traders. Trade had a great impact on Sumerian society. Traders traveled to faraway places and exchanged grain for gold, silver, copper, lumber, and precious stones.

Below traders, farmers and laborers made up the large working class. Slaves were at the bottom of the social order.

ACADEMIC VOCABULARY

impact effect, result

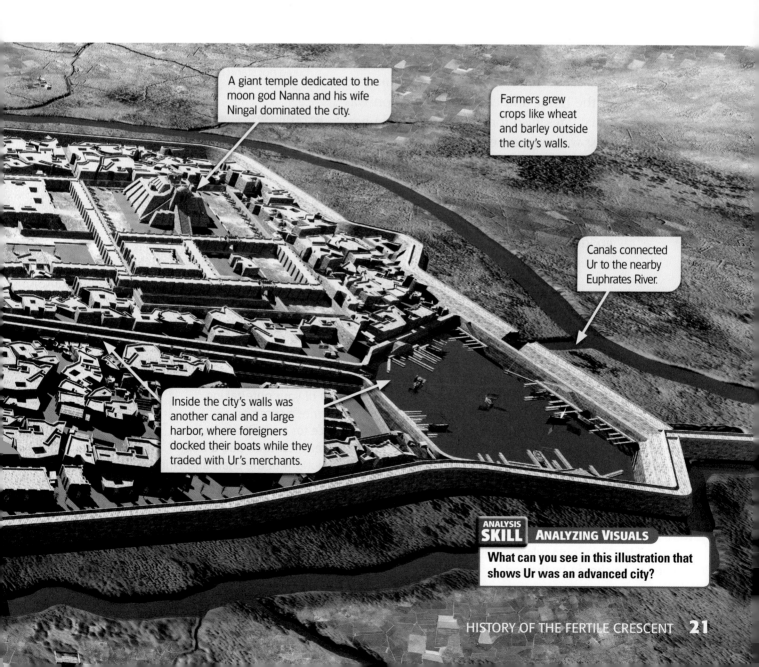

A giant temple dedicated to the moon god Nanna and his wife Ningal dominated the city.

Farmers grew crops like wheat and barley outside the city's walls.

Canals connected Ur to the nearby Euphrates River.

Inside the city's walls was another canal and a large harbor, where foreigners docked their boats while they traded with Ur's merchants.

ANALYSIS SKILL **ANALYZING VISUALS**

What can you see in this illustration that shows Ur was an advanced city?

Sumerian Society

Sumerian society was divided into different groups. This ancient artifact shows Sumerian leaders celebrating a military victory while a musician plays an instrument.

Men and Women in Sumer

Sumerian men and women had different roles. In general, men held political power and made laws while women took care of the home and children. Education was usually reserved for men, but some upper-class women were educated as well.

Some educated women were priestesses in Sumer's temples. They helped shape Sumerian culture. One, Enheduanna, the daughter of Sargon, wrote hymns to the goddess Inanna. The first known female writer in history, she wrote these verses:

" My Queen,
[all] the Anunna, the great gods,
Fled before you like fluttering bats,
Could not stand before your awesome face, "
–Enheduanna, from *Adoration of Inanna of Ur*

READING CHECK **Analyzing** How did trade affect Sumerian society?

SUMMARY AND PREVIEW In this section you learned about Sumerian city-states, religion, and society. In Section 3, you will read about Sumerian achievements.

Section 2 Assessment

hmhsocialstudies.com
ONLINE QUIZ

Reviewing Ideas, Terms, and Places

1. **a. Recall** What was the basic political unit of Sumer?
   b. Explain What steps did Sumerian **city-states** take to protect themselves from their rivals?
   c. Elaborate How do you think that Sargon's creation of an **empire** changed the later history of Mesopotamia? Defend your answer.
2. **a. Identify** What is **polytheism**?
   b. Draw Conclusions Why do you think **priests** were so influential in ancient Sumerian society?
   c. Elaborate Why would rulers benefit if they claimed to be chosen by the gods?

Critical Thinking

3. **Summarizing** In the right column of your note-taking chart, write a summary sentence for each of the four characteristics. Then add a box at the bottom of the chart and write a sentence summarizing the Sumerian civilization.

Characteristics	Notes
Cities	
Government	
Religion	
Society	

Summary Sentence:

Focus on Writing

4. **Gathering Information About Sumer** You will need some pictures of Sumerian society on your poster. Note two or three things to add.

Sumerian Achievements

If YOU lived there...

You are a student at a school for scribes in Sumer. Learning all the symbols for writing is very hard. Your teacher assigns you lessons to write on your clay tablet, but you can't help making mistakes. Then you have to smooth out the surface and try again. Still, being a scribe can lead to important jobs for the king. You could make your family proud.

Why would you want to be a scribe?

BUILDING BACKGROUND Sumerian society was advanced in terms of religion and government organization. The Sumerians were responsible for many other achievements, which were passed down to later civilizations.

Invention of Writing

The Sumerians made one of the greatest cultural advances in history. They developed **cuneiform** (kyoo-NEE-uh-fohrm), the world's first system of writing. The Sumerians did not have pens, pencils, or paper, though. Instead, they used sharp tools called styluses to make wedge-shaped symbols on clay tablets.

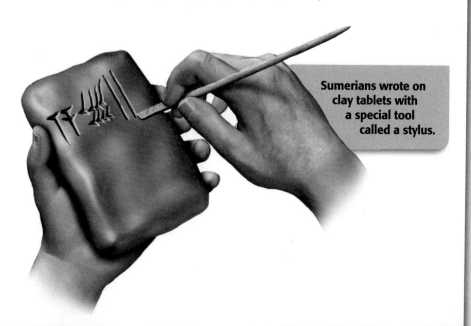

Sumerians wrote on clay tablets with a special tool called a stylus.

What You Will Learn...

Main Ideas

1. The Sumerians invented the world's first writing system.
2. Advances and inventions changed Sumerian lives.
3. Many types of art developed in Sumer.

The Big Idea

The Sumerians made many advances that helped their society develop.

Key Terms

cuneiform, *p. 23*
pictographs, *p. 24*
scribe, *p. 24*
epics, *p. 24*
architecture, *p. 26*
ziggurat, *p. 26*

hmhsocialstudies.com
TAKING NOTES

Use the graphic organizer online to take notes about the achievements and advances made by the Sumerians.

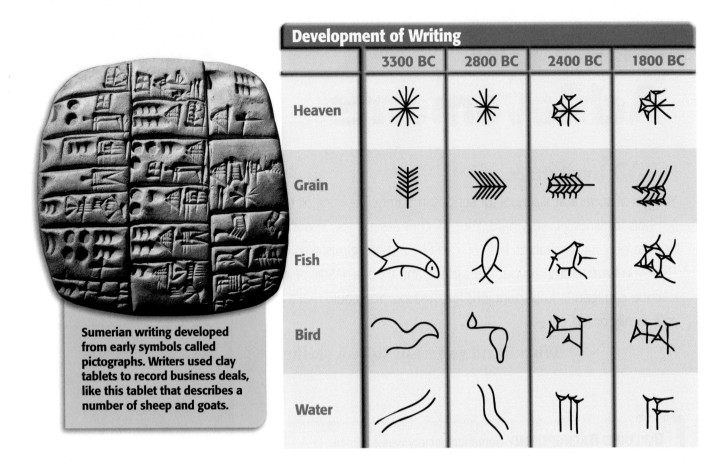

Development of Writing

	3300 BC	2800 BC	2400 BC	1800 BC
Heaven				
Grain				
Fish				
Bird				
Water				

Sumerian writing developed from early symbols called pictographs. Writers used clay tablets to record business deals, like this tablet that describes a number of sheep and goats.

Earlier written communication had used **pictographs**, or picture symbols. Each pictograph represented an object, such as a tree or an animal. In cuneiform, symbols could also represent syllables, or basic parts of words. As a result, Sumerian writers could combine multiple symbols to express more **complex** ideas such as "joy" or "powerful."

Sumerians first used cuneiform to keep business records. A **scribe**, or writer, would be hired to keep track of the items people traded. Government officials and temples also hired scribes to keep their records. Becoming a scribe was a way to move up in social class.

Sumerian students went to school to learn to read and write. Like today, though, some students did not want to study. A Sumerian story tells of a father who urged his son to do his schoolwork:

ACADEMIC VOCABULARY

complex
difficult, not simple

❝ Go to school, stand before your 'school-father,' recite your assignment, open your schoolbag, write your tablet . . . After you have finished your assignment and reported to your monitor [teacher], come to me, and do not wander about in the street. ❞
–Sumerian essay quoted in *History Begins at Sumer*, by Samuel Noah Kramer

In time, Sumerians put their writing skills to new uses. They wrote works on history, law, grammar, and math. They also created works of literature. Sumerians wrote stories, proverbs, and songs. They wrote poems about the gods and about military victories. Some of these were **epics**, long poems that tell the stories of heroes. Later, people used some of these poems to create *The Epic of Gilgamesh*, the story of a legendary Sumerian king.

READING CHECK **Generalizing** How was cuneiform first used in Sumer?

Advances and Inventions

Writing was not the only great Sumerian invention. These early people made many other advances and discoveries.

Technical Advances

One of the Sumerians' most important developments was the wheel. They were the world's first people to build wheeled vehicles, such as carts. Using the wheel, Sumerians invented a device that spins clay as a craftsperson shapes it into bowls. This device is called a potter's wheel.

The plow was another important Sumerian invention. Pulled by oxen, plows broke through the hard clay soil of Sumer to prepare it for planting. This technique greatly increased farm production. The Sumerians also invented a clock that used falling water to measure time.

Sumerian advances improved daily life. Sumerians built sewers under city streets. They used bronze to make strong tools and weapons. They even produced makeup and glass jewelry.

Math and Science

Another area in which Sumerians excelled was math. In fact, they developed a math system based on the number 60. Based on this system, they divided a circle into 360 degrees. Dividing a year into 12 months—a factor of 60—was another Sumerian idea. Sumerians also calculated the areas of rectangles and triangles.

Sumerian scholars studied science, too. They wrote long lists to record their study of the natural world. These tablets included the names of thousands of animals, plants, and minerals.

The Sumerians also made advances in medicine. Using ingredients from animals, plants, and minerals, they produced many healing drugs. Among the items used in these medicines were milk, turtle shells, figs, and salt. The Sumerians catalogued their medical knowledge, listing treatments according to symptoms and body parts.

READING CHECK **Categorizing** What areas of life were improved by Sumerian inventions?

THE IMPACT TODAY

We still use a base-60 system when we talk about 60 seconds in a minute and 60 minutes in an hour.

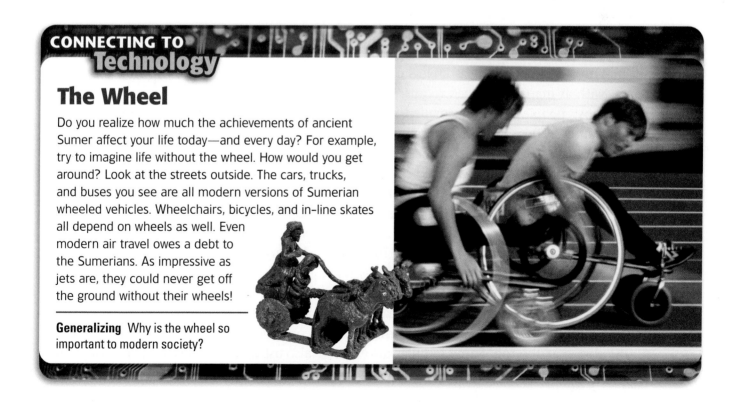

CONNECTING TO Technology

The Wheel

Do you realize how much the achievements of ancient Sumer affect your life today—and every day? For example, try to imagine life without the wheel. How would you get around? Look at the streets outside. The cars, trucks, and buses you see are all modern versions of Sumerian wheeled vehicles. Wheelchairs, bicycles, and in-line skates all depend on wheels as well. Even modern air travel owes a debt to the Sumerians. As impressive as jets are, they could never get off the ground without their wheels!

Generalizing Why is the wheel so important to modern society?

Sumerian Achievements

The Sumerians' artistic achievements included beautiful works of gold, wood, and stone.

Cylinder seals like this one were carved into round stones and then rolled over clay to leave their mark.

This stringed musical instrument is called a lyre. It features a cow's head and is made of silver decorated with shell and stone.

The Arts of Sumer

The Sumerians' skills in the fields of art, metalwork, and **architecture**—the science of building—are well known to us. The ruins of great buildings and fine works of art have provided us with many examples of the Sumerians' creativity.

Architecture

Most Sumerian rulers lived in large palaces. Other rich Sumerians had two-story homes with as many as a dozen rooms. However, most people lived in smaller, one-story houses. These homes had six or seven rooms arranged around a small courtyard. Large and small houses stood side by side along the narrow, unpaved streets of the city. Bricks made of mud were the houses' main building blocks.

City centers were dominated by their temples, the largest and most impressive buildings in Sumer. A **ziggurat**, a pyramid-shaped temple, rose high above each city. Outdoor staircases led to a platform and a shrine at the top. Some temples also had columns to make them more attractive.

FOCUS ON READING

What was a cylinder seal? Describe one in your own words.

The Arts

Sumerian sculptors produced many fine works. Among them are the statues of gods created for temples. Sumerian artists also sculpted small objects out of ivory and rare woods. Sumerian pottery is better known for its quantity than its quality. Potters turned out many items, but few were works of beauty.

Jewelry was a popular item in Sumer. The jewelers of the region made many beautiful works out of imported gold, silver, and gems. Earrings and other items found in the region show that Sumerian jewelers knew rather advanced methods for putting gold pieces together.

Cylinder seals are perhaps Sumer's most famous works of art. These small objects were stone cylinders engraved with designs. When rolled over clay, the designs would leave behind their imprint. Each seal left its own distinct imprint. As a result, a person could show ownership of a container by rolling a cylinder over the container's wet clay surface. People could also use cylinder seals to "sign" documents or to decorate other clay objects.

The Sumerians were the first people in Mesopotamia to build large temples called ziggurats.

This gold dagger was found in a royal tomb. The bull's head is made of gold and silver.

ANALYSIS SKILL **ANALYZING VISUALS**

What animal is shown in two of these works?

Some cylinder seals showed battle scenes. Others displayed worship rituals. Some were highly decorative, covered with hundreds of carefully cut gems.

The Sumerians also enjoyed music. Kings and temples hired musicians to play on special occasions. Sumerian musicians played reed pipes, drums, tambourines, and harplike stringed instruments called lyres. Children learned songs in school. People sang hymns to gods and kings.

Music and dance provided entertainment in marketplaces and homes.

READING CHECK **Drawing Inferences** What might historians learn from cylinder seals?

SUMMARY AND PREVIEW The Sumerians greatly enriched their society. Next, you will learn about the later peoples who lived in Mesopotamia.

Section 3 Assessment

Reviewing Ideas, Terms, and Places

1. **a. Identify** What is **cuneiform**?
   b. Analyze Why do you think writing is one of history's most important cultural advances?
   c. Elaborate What current leader would you choose to write an **epic** about, and why?
2. **a. Recall** What were two early uses of the wheel?
   b. Explain Why do you think the invention of the plow was so important to the Sumerians?
3. **a. Describe** What was the basic Sumerian building material?
   b. Make Inferences Why do you think cylinder seals developed into works of art?

Critical Thinking

4. **Identifying Effects** In a chart like this one, identify the effect of each Sumerian advance you listed in your notes.

Advance/ Achievement	Effect

FOCUS ON WRITING

5. **Evaluating Information** What will you include on your poster to show Sumerian achievements? A ziggurat? A piece of jewelry? A musical instrument? Make a list of the pictures you think would be most interesting to elementary students.

Later Peoples of the Fertile Crescent

What You Will Learn...

Main Ideas

1. The Babylonians conquered Mesopotamia and created a code of law.
2. Invasions of Mesopotamia changed the region's culture.
3. The Phoenicians built a trading society in the eastern Mediterranean region.

The Big Idea

After the Sumerians, many cultures ruled parts of the Fertile Crescent.

Key Terms and Places

Babylon, *p. 28*
Hammurabi's Code, *p. 29*
chariot, *p. 30*
alphabet, *p. 33*

hmhsocialstudies.com
TAKING NOTES

Use the graphic organizer online to take notes on the later empires of the Fertile Crescent.

If **YOU** lived there...

You are a noble in ancient Babylon, an adviser to the great king Hammurabi. One of your duties is to collect all the laws of the kingdom. They will be carved on a tall block of black stone and placed in the temple. The king asks your opinion about the punishments for certain crimes. For example, should common people be punished more harshly than nobles?

How will you advise the king?

BUILDING BACKGROUND Many peoples invaded Mesopotamia. A series of kings conquered the lands between the rivers. Each new culture inherited the earlier achievements of the Sumerians. Some of the later invasions of the region also introduced new skills and ideas that still influence civilization today, such as a written law code.

The Babylonians Conquer Mesopotamia

Although Ur rose to glory after the death of Sargon, repeated foreign attacks drained its strength. By 2000 BC, Ur lay in ruins. With Ur's power gone, several waves of invaders battled to gain control of Mesopotamia.

Rise of Babylon

Babylon was home to one such group. That city was located on the Euphrates near what is now Baghdad, Iraq. Babylon had once been a Sumerian town. By 1800 BC, however, it was home to a powerful government of its own. In 1792 BC, Hammurabi (ham-uh-RAHB-ee) became Babylon's king. He would become the city's greatest ruler.

Hammurabi's Code

Hammurabi was a brilliant war leader. His armies fought many battles to expand his power. Eventually, Hammurabi brought all of Mesopotamia into his empire, called the Babylonian Empire after his capital city.

Hammurabi was not only skilled on the battlefield, though. He was also an able ruler who could govern a huge empire. He used tax money to pay for building and irrigation projects. He also brought wealth through increased trade. Hammurabi is best known, however, for his code of laws.

Hammurabi's Code was a set of 282 laws that dealt with almost every part of daily life. There were laws on everything from trade, loans, and theft to marriage, injury, and murder. It contained some ideas that are still found in laws today.

Under Hammurabi's Code, each crime brought a specific penalty. However, social class did matter. For example, injuring a rich man brought a greater penalty than injuring a poor man.

Hammurabi's Code was important not only for how thorough it was but also because it was written down for all to see. People all over the empire could read exactly what was against the law.

Hammurabi ruled for 42 years. During his reign, Babylon became the major city in Mesopotamia. However, after his death, Babylonian power declined. The kings that followed faced invasions from the people Hammurabi had conquered. Before long, the Babylonian Empire came to an end.

READING CHECK **Analyzing** What was Hammurabi's most important accomplishment?

Primary Source

HISTORIC DOCUMENT
Hammurabi's Code

The Babylonian ruler Hammurabi is credited with putting together the earliest known written collection of laws. The code set down rules for both criminal and civil law and informed citizens about what was expected of them.

196. If a man put out the eye of another man, his eye shall be put out.

197. If he break another man's bone, his bone shall be broken.

198. If he put out the eye of a freed man, or break the bone of a freed man, he shall pay one gold mina.

199. If he put out the eye of a man's slave, or break the bone of a man's slave, he shall pay one-half of its value.

221. If a physican heal the broken bone or diseased soft part of a man, the patient shall pay the physician five shekels in money.

222. If he were a freed man he shall pay three shekels.

223. If he were a slave his owner shall pay the physician two shekels.

–Hammurabi, from *The Code of Hammurabi,* translated by L. W. King

ANALYSIS SKILL **ANALYZING PRIMARY SOURCES**

How do you think Hammurabi's code of laws affected citizens of that time?

Invasions of Mesopotamia

Several other civilizations developed in and around the Fertile Crescent. As their armies battled for land, control of the region passed from one empire to another.

Hittites and Kassites

FOCUS ON READING

Make sure you understand this paragraph by restating it in your own words.

A people known as the Hittites built a strong kingdom in Asia Minor, in what is today Turkey. Their success came, in part, from two key military advantages they had over rivals. First, the Hittites were among the first people to master ironworking. This meant they could make stronger weapons than their foes. Second, the Hittite army skillfully used the **chariot**, a wheeled, horse-drawn cart used in battle. Chariots allowed Hittite soldiers to move quickly around a battlefield. Archers riding in the chariots fired arrows at the enemy.

Using these advantages, Hittite forces captured Babylon around 1595 BC. Hittite rule did not last long, however. Soon after taking Babylon, the Hittite king was killed by an assassin. The kingdom plunged into chaos. The Kassites, a people who lived north of Babylon, captured the city and ruled for almost 400 years.

Assyrians

Later, in the 1200s BC, a group called the Assyrians (uh-SIR-ee-unz) from northern Mesopotamia briefly gained control of Babylon. However, their empire was soon overrun by invaders. After this defeat, the Assyrians took about 300 years to recover their strength. Then, starting about 900 BC, they began to conquer all of the Fertile Crescent. They even took over parts of Asia Minor and Egypt.

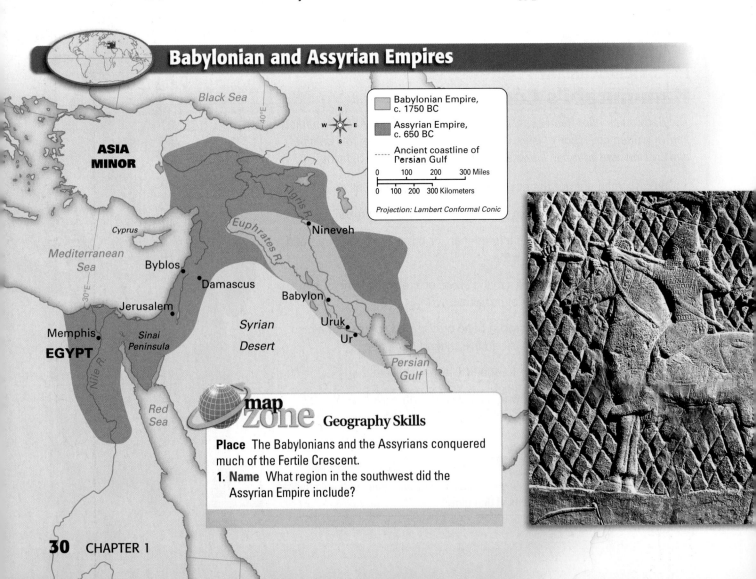

Babylonian and Assyrian Empires

Babylonian Empire, c. 1750 BC

Assyrian Empire, c. 650 BC

Ancient coastline of Persian Gulf

0   100   200   300 Miles
0   100   200   300 Kilometers

Projection: Lambert Conformal Conic

Black Sea

ASIA MINOR

Cyprus

Mediterranean Sea

Byblos

Damascus

Jerusalem

Memphis

EGYPT

Sinai Peninsula

Red Sea

Nile R.

Tigris R.

Euphrates R.

Nineveh

Babylon

Syrian Desert

Uruk

Ur

Persian Gulf

map zone Geography Skills

Place The Babylonians and the Assyrians conquered much of the Fertile Crescent.
1. Name What region in the southwest did the Assyrian Empire include?

The key to the Assyrians' success was their strong army. Like the Hittites, the Assyrians used iron weapons and chariots. The army was very well organized, and every soldier knew his role.

The Assyrians were fierce in battle. Before attacking, they spread terror by looting villages and burning crops. Anyone who still dared to resist them was killed.

After conquering the Fertile Crescent, the Assyrians ruled from their capital city, Nineveh (NI-nuh-vuh). They demanded heavy taxes from across the empire. Areas that resisted the Assyrians' demands were harshly punished.

Assyrian kings ruled their large empire through local leaders. Each governed a small area, collected taxes, enforced laws, and raised troops for the army. Roads were built to link distant parts of the empire. Messengers on horseback were sent to deliver orders to faraway officials.

Chaldeans

In 652 BC a series of wars broke out in the Assyrian Empire over who should rule. These wars greatly weakened the empire.

Sensing this weakness, the Chaldeans (kal-DEE-unz), a group from the Syrian Desert, led other peoples in an attack on the Assyrians. In 612 BC, they destroyed Nineveh and the Assyrian Empire.

In its place, the Chaldeans set up a new empire of their own. Nebuchadnezzar (neb-uh-kuhd-NEZ-uhr), the most famous Chaldean king, rebuilt Babylon into a beautiful city. According to legend, his grand palace featured the famous Hanging Gardens. Trees and flowers grew on its terraces and roofs. From the ground the gardens seemed to hang in the air.

The Chaldeans greatly admired the ideas and culture of the Sumerians. They studied the Sumerian language and built temples to Sumerian gods.

At the same time, Babylon became a center for astronomy. Chaldeans charted the positions of the stars and kept track of economic, political, and weather events. They also created a calendar and solved complex problems of geometry.

READING CHECK **Sequencing** List in order the peoples who ruled Mesopotamia.

The Assyrian Army

The Assyrian army was the most powerful fighting force the world had ever seen. Large and well organized, it featured iron weapons, war chariots, and giant war machines used to knock down city walls.

ANALYZING VISUALS What kinds of weapons can you see in this carving?

The Phoenicians sailed throughout the Mediterranean, seeking trade goods and founding new cities.

The Phoenicians

At the western end of the Fertile Crescent, along the Mediterranean Sea, was a land known as Phoenicia (fi-NI-shuh). It was not home to a great military power and was often ruled by foreign governments. Nevertheless, the Phoenicians created a wealthy trading society.

Geography of Phoenicia

Today the nation of Lebanon occupies most of what was Phoenicia. Mountains border the region to the north and east. To the west lies the Mediterranean.

The Phoenicians were largely an urban people. Among their chief cities were Tyre, Sidon, and Byblos. These three cities, like many Phoenician cities, still exist today.

Phoenicia had few resources. One thing it did have, however, was cedar. Cedar trees were prized for their timber, a valuable trade item. But Phoenicia's overland trade routes were blocked by mountains and hostile neighbors. Phoenicians had to look to the sea for a way to trade.

THE IMPACT TODAY

Because so many cedar trees have been cut down in Lebanon's forests over the years, very few trees remain.

Expansion of Trade

Motivated by a desire for trade, the people of Phoenicia became expert sailors. They built one of the world's finest harbors at the city of Tyre. Fleets of fast Phoenician trading ships sailed to ports all around the Mediterranean Sea. Traders traveled to Egypt, Greece, Italy, Sicily, and Spain. They even passed through the Strait of Gibraltar to reach the Atlantic Ocean.

The Phoenicians founded several new colonies along their trade routes. Carthage (KAHR-thij), located on the northern coast of Africa, was the most famous of these. It later became one of the most powerful cities on the Mediterranean.

Phoenicia grew wealthy from its trade. Besides lumber, the Phoenicians traded silverwork, ivory carvings, and slaves. They also made and sold beautiful glass items. In addition, the Phoenicians made purple dye from a type of shellfish. They then traded cloth that had been dyed with this purple color. Phoenician purple fabric was very popular with rich people all around the Mediterranean.

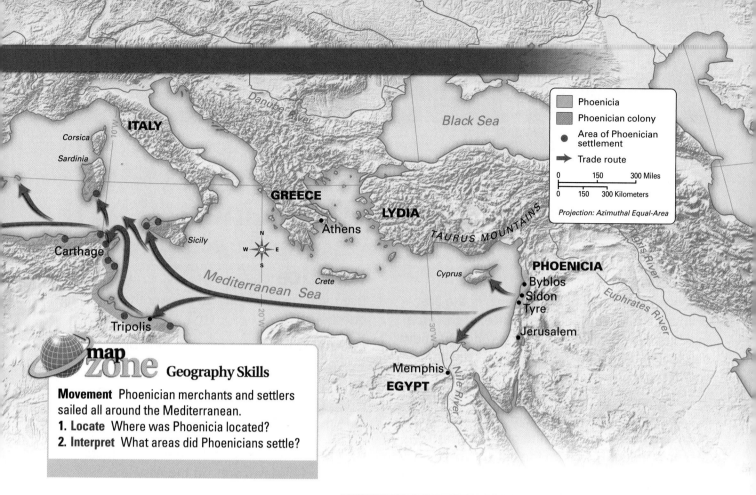

Movement Phoenician merchants and settlers sailed all around the Mediterranean.
1. **Locate** Where was Phoenicia located?
2. **Interpret** What areas did Phoenicians settle?

The Phoenicians' most important achievement, however, wasn't a trade good. To record their activities, Phoenician traders developed one of the world's first alphabets. An **alphabet** is a set of letters that can be combined to form words. This development made writing much easier. It had a major impact on the ancient world and on our own. In fact, the alphabet we use today is based on the Phoenicians'.

READING CHECK Finding Main Ideas What were the Phoenicians' main achievements?

SUMMARY AND PREVIEW Many peoples ruled in the Fertile Crescent after the Sumerians. Some made contributions that are still valued today. Next, you will learn about two religions that developed in the Fertile Crescent and are still alive today—Judaism and Christianity.

Section 4 Assessment

 hmhsocialstudies.com
ONLINE QUIZ

Reviewing Ideas, Terms, and Places
1. **a. Identify** Where was **Babylon** located?
   b. Analyze What does **Hammurabi's Code** reveal about Babylonian society?
2. **a. Describe** What two advantages did Hittite soldiers have over their opponents?
   b. Rank Which empire discussed in this section do you feel contributed the most to modern-day society? Why?
3. **a. Identify** For what trade goods were the Phoenicians known? For what else were they known?
   b. Analyze How did Phoenicia grow wealthy?

Critical Thinking
4. **Categorizing** Use your note-taking diagram with the names of the empires. List at least one advance or achievement made by each empire.

FOCUS ON WRITING

5. **Gathering Information About Later Peoples** Several different peoples contributed to civilization in the Fertile Crescent after the Sumerians. Which ones, if any, will you include on your poster? What will you show?

Sequencing and Using Time Lines

Learn

When you are reading about events in the past, it is important to learn their sequence, or the order in which the events occurred. If you do not know the sequence in which events happen, history will not make any sense.

One way to examine the sequence of events is to construct a time line. A time line is a visual display showing events in the order in which they happened. Events on the left side of the time line occurred first. Events farther to the right occurred later.

Practice

Use the time line below to answer the following questions.

① Around what year did Hammurabi issue his code of laws?

② Which happened earlier, the formation of Sargon's empire or the beginning of Phoenician trade?

③ About how many years after Hammurabi issued his law code did the Assyrians conquer Babylon?

Major Events in the Fertile Crescent

| 2500 BC | 2000 BC | 1500 BC | 1000 BC | 500 BC |

c. 2350 BC
Sargon of Akkad conquers Mesopotamia and forms the world's first empire.

c. 1770 BC
Hammurabi of Babylon issues a written code of laws.

c. 1200 BC
Assyrians take over Babylon.

c. 1000 BC
Phoenicians trade all around the Mediterranean.

Apply

Think about a typical school day. What time do you wake up? What classes do you have? When do you get home? Make a list of events that occur on a typical day. Once you have made your list, rearrange it so that the events are listed in sequence. Then use your list to draw a time line of your day.

Chapter Review

Geography's Impact
video series
Review the video to answer the closing question:
What would life in America be like today without a written code of laws?

Visual Summary

Use the visual summary below to help you review the main ideas of the chapter.

QUICK FACTS

The early Mesopotamians developed irrigation to grow food. As a result, they were able to form cities.

Sumerian advances included ziggurats, the wheel, and the world's first writing system, cuneiform.

Later peoples created the first written laws and the first empires. They also formed great trading networks.

Reviewing Vocabulary, Terms, and Places

Using your own paper, complete the sentences below by providing the correct term for each blank.

1. Mesopotamian farmers built _____ to irrigate their fields.

2. The art and science of building is known as _____.

3. The people of Sumer practiced _____, the worship of many gods.

4. Instead of using pictographs, Sumerians developed a type of writing called _____.

5. Horse-drawn _____ gave the Hittites an advantage during battle.

6. _____ was Hammurabi's capital and one of Mesopotamia's greatest cities.

7. _____ ideas are not simple.

8. Sumerian society was organized in _____, which consisted of a city and the surrounding lands.

Comprehension and Critical Thinking

SECTION 1 *(Pages 12–15)*

9. **a. Describe** Where was Mesopotamia, and what does the name mean?

   b. Analyze How did Mesopotamian irrigation systems allow civilization to develop?

   c. Elaborate Do you think a division of labor is necessary for civilization to develop? Why or why not?

SECTION 2 *(Pages 18–22)*

10. **a. Identify** Who built the world's first empire, and what land did that empire include?

    b. Analyze Politically, how was early Sumerian society organized? How did that organization affect society?

    c. Elaborate Why did the Sumerians consider it everyone's responsibility to keep the gods happy?

SECTION 3 (Pages 23–27)

11. a. Identify What was the Sumerian writing system called, and why is it so significant?

b. Compare and Contrast What were two ways in which Sumerian society was similar to our society today? What were two ways in which it was different?

c. Evaluate Other than writing and the wheel, which Sumerian invention do you think is most important? Why?

SECTION 4 (Pages 28–33)

12. a. Describe What were two developments of the Phoenicians?

b. Draw Conclusions Why do you think several peoples banded together to fight the Assyrians?

c. Evaluate Do you think Hammurabi was more effective as a ruler or as a military leader? Why?

Map Activity

13. The Fertile Crescent On a separate sheet of paper, match the letters on the map with their correct labels.

Babylon   Euphrates River

Phoenicia   Tigris River

Sumer

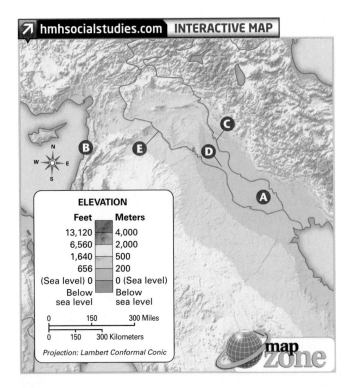

⬈ **hmhsocialstudies.com** **INTERACTIVE MAP**

ELEVATION

Feet	Meters
13,120	4,000
6,560	2,000
1,640	500
656	200
(Sea level) 0	0 (Sea level)
Below sea level	Below sea level

0	150	300 Miles
0	150	300 Kilometers

Projection: Lambert Conformal Conic

map zone

Social Studies Skills

14. Sequencing and Using Time Lines Create a time line that shows the various people who ruled the Fertile Crescent. Remember that the people should appear on your time line in order.

Using the Internet

15. Activity: Looking at Writing The Sumerians made one of the greatest cultural advances in history by developing the world's first system of writing. Through the online book, research the evolution of language and its written forms. Look at one of the newest methods of writing: text messaging. Then write a paragraph explaining why writing is important using abbreviations and symbols used in text messaging.

⬈ **hmhsocialstudies.com**

FOCUS ON READING AND WRITING

Paraphrasing *Read the paragraph below carefully. Then rewrite the paragraph in your own words, taking care to include all the main ideas.*

16

> Mesopotamia was the home of many ancient civilizations. The first of these civilizations was the Sumerians. They lived in Mesopotamia by 3000 BC. There they built cities, created a system of writing, and invented the wheel.

Creating a Poster *Use your notes and the instructions below to help you create a poster.*

17. Using a large poster board, create a poster on the Fertile Crescent. From your list, select 5 or 6 pictures to show. Remember that your audience is young children and think about what would interest them.

Begin by collecting pictures or drawings from magazines or the Internet. Then make a plan for your poster. Decide where you will place each picture and what you will say about each. After you have arranged the pictures, create a title for the poster and center it at the top. Write a one- or two-sentence introduction for your poster. You will have to create a label or short caption for each picture.

Standardized Test Prep

DIRECTIONS: Read questions 1 through 7 and write the letter of the best response. Then read question 8 and write your own well-constructed response.

1 The first people to develop a civilization in Mesopotamia were the

A Akkadians.

B Babylonians.

C Egyptians.

D Sumerians.

2 Which of the following statements about the first writing system is false?

A It was developed by the Babylonians.

B It began with the use of pictures to represent syllables and objects.

C It was recorded on tablets made of clay.

D It was first used to keep business records.

3 In Sumerian society, people's social class or rank depended on their wealth and their

A appearance.

B religion.

C location.

D occupation.

4 Which of the following was the subject of a great Sumerian epic?

A Cuneiform

B Ziggurat

C Gilgamesh

D Babylon

5 What was the most important contribution of the Phoenicians to our civilization?

A purple dye

B their alphabet

C founding of Carthage

D sailing ships

Mesopotamia

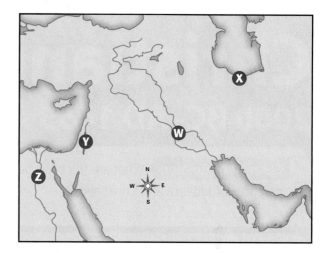

6 The region known as Mesopotamia is indicated on the map above by the letter

A W.

B X.

C Y.

D Z.

7 Hammurabi's Code is important in world history because it was an early

A form of writing that could be used to record important events.

B written list of laws that controlled people's daily life and behavior.

C record-keeping system that enabled the Phoenicians to become great traders.

D set of symbols that allowed the Sumerians to communicate with other peoples.

8 **Extended Response** The early civilizations of Mesopotamia developed in the valleys of two rivers. Look back at the map in the Geography and History feature. All around the world, river valleys were the home of early civilizations. Why was this? Write a short paragraph in which you give at least two reasons why early civilizations were often formed in river valleys.

Judaism and Christianity

2000 BC–AD 1453

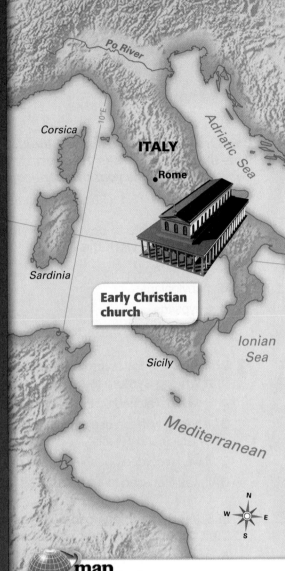

Early Christian church

Essential Question What are the basic beliefs and practices of Judaism and Christianity?

What You Will Learn...

In this chapter you will learn about the origins and spread of two major world religions—Judaism and Christianity.

FOCUS ON READING AND WRITING

Understand Implied Main Ideas Sometimes the main idea of a paragraph or passage is not directly stated; instead it is implied, or suggested. In those cases, you have to examine the details the author provides. Then you decide what point, or main idea, the author is expressing with those details. **See the lesson, Understanding Implied Main Ideas, on page 163.**

Writing a Letter As you read this chapter, think about what it would have been like to witness the events that occurred as Judaism and Christianity developed and spread. Then you will write a letter from the point of view of someone who actually witnessed an event.

map zone Geography Skills

Regions Both Judaism and Christianity began in the region around the Mediterranean Sea.
1. **Locate** Where did Christian missionaries travel?
2. **Make Inferences** Where do you think Judaism and Christianity might have spread to next?

Judaism Jews pray at the Western Wall in Jerusalem. The wall is part of the Second Temple, which was built by ancient Hebrews.

The Jewish and Christian Worlds, 2000 BC–AD 1453

EUROPE

Danube River

Black Sea

Hagia Sophia

Constantinople

40°N

20°E

30°E

GREECE

Aegean Sea

ASIA MINOR

Tigris River

ASIA

SYRIA

Crete

Sea

Christian missionaries

Second Temple

Nazareth

Jerusalem

Moses with the Ten Commandments

30°E

Euphrates River

Nile River

AFRICA

HISTORY   Moses at Mount Sinai

hmhsocialstudies.com   VIDEO

0   100   200 Miles
0   100   200 Kilometers

Projection: Azimuthal Equal-Area

Christianity
Christianity is based on the life and teachings of Jesus, shown here in his mother's arms.

Byzantine Empire
The Byzantine Empire was known for its mosaics.

Origins of Judaism

If YOU were there...

You and your family are herders, looking after large flocks of sheep. Your grandfather is the leader of your tribe. One day your grandfather says that your whole family will be moving to a new country where there is more water and food for your flocks. The trip will be long and difficult.

How do you feel about going to a new land?

BUILDING BACKGROUND Like the family described above, the early Hebrews moved to new lands in ancient times. According to Jewish tradition, their history began when God told an early Hebrew leader to travel west to a new land.

Early History

Sometime between 2000 and 1500 BC a new people appeared in Southwest Asia. They were the Hebrews (HEE-brooz), ancestors of the Israelites and Jews. Much of what is known about their early history comes from the work of archaeologists and from accounts written by Hebrew scribes. These accounts describe their early history and the laws of **Judaism** (JOO-dee-i-zuhm), their religion. In time these accounts became the Hebrew Bible.

Time Line

Early Hebrew History

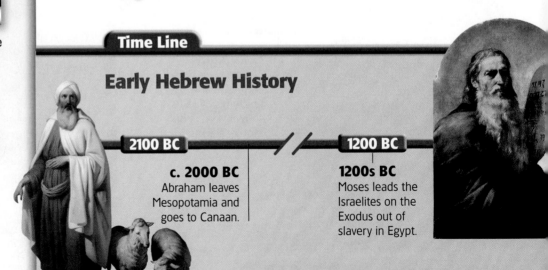

2100 BC

c. 2000 BC
Abraham leaves Mesopotamia and goes to Canaan.

1200 BC

1200s BC
Moses leads the Israelites on the Exodus out of slavery in Egypt.

Beginnings in Canaan and Egypt

The Bible traces the Hebrews back to a man named Abraham. One day, the Bible says, God told Abraham to leave his home in Mesopotamia. He was to take his family on a long journey to the west. God promised to lead Abraham to a new land and make his descendants into a mighty nation.

Abraham left Mesopotamia and settled in **Canaan** (KAY-nuhn) on the Mediterranean Sea. Some of his descendents, the Israelites, lived in Canaan for many years. Later, however, some Hebrews moved to Egypt, perhaps because of famine in Canaan.

The Israelites lived well in Egypt, and their population grew. This growth worried Egypt's ruler, the pharaoh. He feared that the Israelites might soon become too powerful. To stop this from happening, the pharaoh made the Israelites slaves.

The Exodus

According to the Hebrew Bible, a leader named Moses appeared among the Israelites in Egypt. In the 1200s BC, God told Moses to lead the Israelites out of Egypt. Moses went to the pharaoh and demanded that he free the Israelites. The pharaoh refused. Soon afterward a series of terrible plagues, or disasters, struck Egypt.

The plagues frightened the pharaoh so much that he agreed to free the Israelites. Overjoyed with the news of their release, Moses led his people out of Egypt in a journey called the **Exodus**. To the Israelites, the release from slavery proved that God was protecting and watching over them.

For years after their release, the Israelites traveled through the desert, trying to return to Canaan. On their journey, they reached a mountain called Sinai. The Hebrew Bible says that while Moses was on the mountain, God gave him two stone tablets. On the tablets was written a code of moral laws known as the Ten Commandments. These laws shaped Jewish society.

Once the Israelites reached Canaan, they had to fight to gain control of the land. After they conquered Canaan and settled down on the land, the Israelites built their own society.

A Series of Invasions

The Israelites soon faced more threats to their land. Invaders swept through the region in the mid-1000s BC. For a while, strong kings kept Israel together. Israel even grew rich through trade and expanded its territory. With their riches, the Israelites built a great temple to God in Jerusalem.

Some years later when one king died, the Israelites could not agree on who would be the next king. This conflict caused Israel to split into two kingdoms, one called Israel and one called Judah (JOO-duh). The people of Judah became known as Jews.

FOCUS ON READING

Study the details in the first paragraph under A Series of Invasions. What is the main idea?

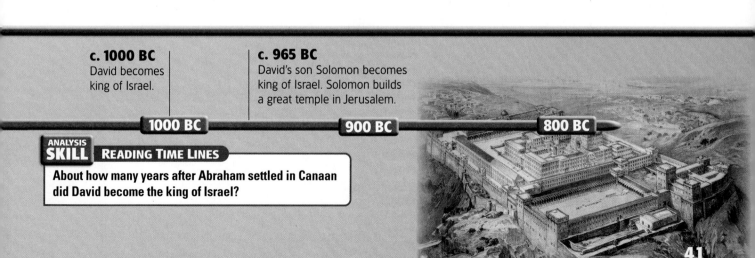

c. 1000 BC
David becomes king of Israel.

c. 965 BC
David's son Solomon becomes king of Israel. Solomon builds a great temple in Jerusalem.

1000 BC   900 BC   800 BC

ANALYSIS SKILL READING TIME LINES

About how many years after Abraham settled in Canaan did David become the king of Israel?

The two new kingdoms lasted for a few centuries. Israel eventually fell to invaders about 722 BC. Judah lasted until 586 BC, when invaders captured Jerusalem and destroyed Solomon's temple. They sent the Jews out of Jerusalem as slaves. When these invaders were themselves conquered, some Jews returned home. Others moved to other places in Southwest Asia. Scholars call the scattering of Jews outside of Israel and Judah the Diaspora (dy-AS-pruh).

The Jews who returned to Jerusalem ruled themselves for about 100 years. They even rebuilt Solomon's temple. Eventually, however, they were conquered by the Romans. The Jews revolted against the Romans, but most gave up after the Romans destroyed their temple. As punishment for the rebellion, the Romans killed or enslaved much of Jerusalem's population. Thousands of Jews fled Jerusalem. Over the next centuries, Jews moved all around the world. Often they were forced to move by other religious groups who discriminated against them.

READING CHECK **Identifying Cause and Effect** How did invasions affect the Jews?

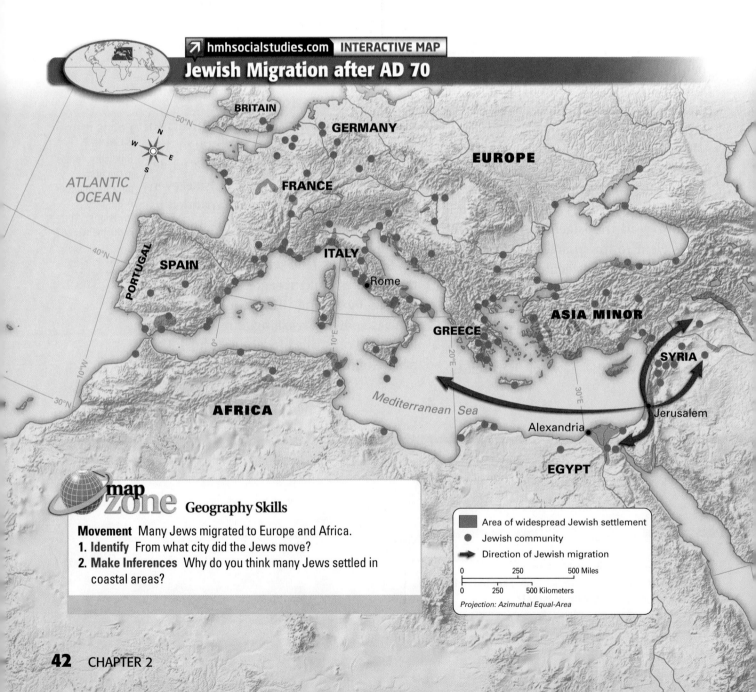

hmhsocialstudies.com **INTERACTIVE MAP**

Jewish Migration after AD 70

Geography Skills

Movement Many Jews migrated to Europe and Africa.
1. **Identify** From what city did the Jews move?
2. **Make Inferences** Why do you think many Jews settled in coastal areas?

■ Area of widespread Jewish settlement
● Jewish community
➜ Direction of Jewish migration

0   250   500 Miles
0   250   500 Kilometers
Projection: Azimuthal Equal-Area

Jewish Beliefs

Wherever Jews live around the world, their religion is the foundation upon which they base their whole society. In fact, much of Jewish culture is based directly on Jewish beliefs. The central concepts of Judaism are belief in one God, justice and righteousness, and observance of religious and moral law.

Belief in One God

Most importantly, Jews believe in one God. The belief in one and only one God is called **monotheism**. Many people believe that Judaism was the world's first monotheistic religion.

Basic Jewish Beliefs

- Belief in and worship of one and only one God
- Commitment to justice, or dealing with people kindly and fairly
- Commitment to righteousness, or doing what is proper
- Observance of religious and moral law

All Jews share the same basic beliefs, but different Jewish communities around the world have their own cultures. These Jews from Eastern Europe carry a Torah, a practice among Jews everywhere.

In the ancient world where most people worshipped many gods, the Jews' worship of only one God set them apart. This worship shaped Jewish society. The Jews believe they have a special responsibility to improve the world. They believe that God guides their history through relationships with Abraham, Moses, and other leaders.

Justice and Righteousness

Also central to the Jews' religion are the ideas of justice and righteousness. To Jews, justice means kindness and fairness in dealing with other people. Everyone deserves justice, even strangers and criminals. Jews are expected to give aid to those who need it, including the poor, the sick, and orphans. Jews are also expected to be fair in business dealings.

Righteousness refers to doing what is proper. Jews are supposed to behave properly, even if others around them do not. For the Jews, righteous behavior is more important than rituals, or ceremonies.

Observance of Religious and Moral Law

Observance of the law is closely related to justice and righteousness. Jews believe that God gave them religious and moral laws to follow. The most important Jewish laws are the Ten Commandments. The commandments require that Jews worship only one God. They also do not allow Jews to do bad things like murder, steal, or lie.

The commandments are only one part of Jewish law. Jews believe that Moses recorded a system of laws, now called Mosaic law, that God had set down for them. Mosaic laws guide many areas of Jews' daily lives, such as how people pray and observe holy days.

READING CHECK **Generalizing** What are the most important beliefs of Judaism?

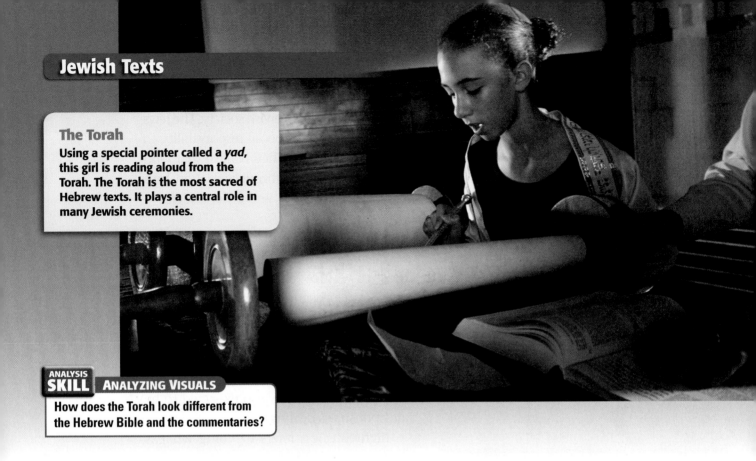

The Torah
Using a special pointer called a *yad*, this girl is reading aloud from the Torah. The Torah is the most sacred of Hebrew texts. It plays a central role in many Jewish ceremonies.

ANALYSIS SKILL **ANALYZING VISUALS**

How does the Torah look different from the Hebrew Bible and the commentaries?

Jewish Texts

The laws and **principles** of Judaism are described in several sacred texts. Among the main texts are the Torah, the Hebrew Bible, and the commentaries.

The Torah

The ancient Jews recorded most of their laws in five books. Together, these books are called the Torah. The **Torah** is the most sacred text of Judaism. In addition to laws, it includes a history of the Jewish people until the death of Moses. Jews believe the contents of the Torah were revealed to Moses by God.

Readings from the Torah are central to Jewish religious services today. Nearly every synagogue (si-nuh-gawg), or Jewish house of worship, has at least one Torah. Out of respect for the Torah, readers do not touch it. They use special pointers to mark their places in the text.

The Hebrew Bible

The Torah is the first of three parts of a group of writings called the Hebrew Bible, or Tanakh (tah-NAHK). The second part is made up of eight books that describe the messages of Hebrew prophets. Prophets are people who are said to receive messages from God to be taught to others.

The final part of the Hebrew Bible is 11 books of poetry, songs, stories, lessons, and history. Many of these stories are told by Jews to show the power of faith.

Also in the final part of the Hebrew Bible are the Proverbs, short expressions of Hebrew wisdom. For example, one Proverb says, "A good name is to be chosen rather than great riches." In other words, it is better to be seen as a good person than to be rich and not respected.

The third part of the Hebrew Bible also includes the Book of Psalms. The Book of Psalms is a collection of short and long songs of praise to God.

The Hebrew Bible

These beautifully decorated pages are from a Hebrew Bible. The Hebrew Bible, sometimes called the Tanakh, includes the Torah and other ancient writings.

The Commentaries

The Talmud is a collection of commentaries and discussions about the Torah and the Hebrew Bible. The Talmud is a rich source of information for discussion and debate. Religious scholars like these young men study the Talmud to learn about Jewish history and laws.

The Commentaries

For centuries **rabbis**, or religious teachers, and scholars have studied the Torah and Jewish laws. Because some laws are hard to understand, scholars write commentaries to explain them. Many explanations can be found in the Talmud (TAHL-moohd), a set of commentaries and lessons for everyday life. The writings of the Talmud were produced between AD 200 and 600. Many Jews consider them second only to the Hebrew Bible in significance to Judaism.

READING CHECK **Analyzing** What texts do Jews consider sacred?

Traditions and Holy Days

Jews feel that understanding their history will help them better follow the Jewish teachings. Their traditions and holy days help Jews connect with their past and celebrate their history.

Hanukkah

One Jewish tradition is celebrated by Hanukkah, which falls in December. It honors a historical event. The ancient Jews wanted to celebrate a victory that had convinced their rulers to let them keep their religion. According to legend, though, the Jews did not have enough lamp oil to celebrate at the temple. Miraculously, the oil they had—enough for only one day— burned for eight full days.

Today Jews celebrate this event by lighting candles in a special candleholder called a menorah (muh-NOHR-uh). Its eight branches represent the eight days through which the oil burned. Many Jews also exchange gifts on each of the eight nights.

Passover

More important to Jews than Hanukkah, Passover is celebrated in March or April. During Passover Jews honor the Exodus, the journey of the Israelites out of slavery.

A Passover Meal

During a special Passover meal called a seder, participants reflect on the events of the Exodus.

ANALYZING VISUALS How can you tell this is a special meal?

High Holy Days

The two most sacred of all Jewish holidays are the High Holy Days. They take place in September or October. The first two days of celebration, Rosh Hashanah (rahsh uh-SHAH-nuh), celebrate the start of a new year in the Jewish calendar.

On Yom Kippur (yohm ki-POOHR), which falls soon afterward, Jews ask God to forgive their sins. Jews consider Yom Kippur to be the holiest day of the entire year. Because it is so holy, Jews do not eat or drink anything all day. They also pray, reflect on the past year, and resolve to improve.

READING CHECK Finding Main Ideas What are the two most important Jewish holidays?

According to Jewish tradition, the Israelites left Egypt so quickly that bakers did not have time to let their bread rise. Therefore, during Passover Jews eat only matzo, a flat, unrisen bread. They also celebrate the holiday with ceremonies.

SUMMARY AND PREVIEW Judaism was the world's first monotheistic religion. Jewish culture and traditions are rooted in the history of the Hebrews and Israelites. Next, you will read about a religion that is related to Judaism—Christianity.

Section 1 Assessment

hmhsocialstudies.com
ONLINE QUIZ

Reviewing Ideas, Terms, and Places

1. **a. Identify** Who first led the Hebrews to **Canaan**?
   b. Evaluate Why was the **Exodus** a significant event in Jewish history?
2. **a. Define** What is **monotheism**?
   b. Explain What is the Jewish view of justice and righteousness?
3. **a. Identify** What are the main sacred texts of Judaism?
   b. Elaborate Why do you think the Commentaries are so significant to many Jews?
4. **a. Identify** What event in their history do the Jews celebrate at Passover?
   b. Elaborate How do you think celebrating traditions and holy days helps Jews connect to their past?

Critical Thinking

5. **Sequencing** Review your notes on the history of the Jewish people. Then draw a diagram like this one and fill in important events from their history in the order they occurred. You may add as many boxes as you need for the information.

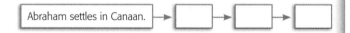

Abraham settles in Canaan.

FOCUS ON WRITING

6. **Noting Main Events in the Origins of Judaism** Look back over this section and imagine what it would have been like to witness some of these events. Identify one or two events that you might describe in your letter.

Interpreting a Route Map

Learn

A route map shows movement from one place to another. Usually, different routes are shown with different colored arrows. Look at the legend to see what the different arrows represent.

Practice

Use the map of Possible Routes of the Exodus to answer the following questions.

1 How many possible Exodus routes does the map show?

2 Where did the Exodus begin?

3 Which possible route would have been the longest?

4 Which route would have passed closest to the Mediterranean Sea?

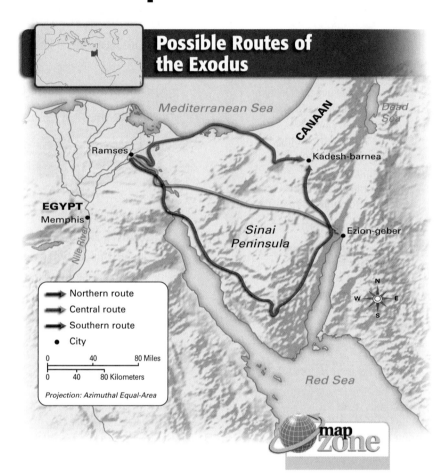

Possible Routes of the Exodus

Legend:
- Northern route
- Central route
- Southern route
- City

0 — 40 — 80 Miles
0 — 40 — 80 Kilometers

Projection: Azimuthal Equal-Area

Apply

Find a map of your city either in an atlas or on the Internet. You will need to draw on the map, so either print it, copy it, or draw a map on your own paper using the information. On the city map, draw the route you take from your home to school. Then draw another route you could take to get to school. Be sure to create a legend to show what your route lines mean.

Origins of Christianity

What You Will Learn...

Main Ideas

1. The life and death of Jesus of Nazareth inspired a new religion called Christianity.
2. Christians believe that Jesus's acts and teachings focused on love and salvation.
3. Jesus's followers taught others about Jesus's life and teachings.
4. Christianity spread throughout the Roman Empire by 400.

The Big Idea

Christianity, a religion based on the life and teachings of Jesus of Nazareth, spread throughout the Roman Empire.

Key Terms and Places

Messiah, *p. 48*
Christianity, *p. 48*
Bible, *p. 48*
Bethlehem, *p. 48*
Resurrection, *p. 49*
disciples, *p. 49*
saint, *p. 52*

hmhsocialstudies.com
TAKING NOTES

Use the graphic organizer online to take notes on Jesus and the spread of Christianity.

If YOU lived there...

You are a fisher in Judea, bringing in the day's catch. As you reach the shore, you see a large crowd. They are listening to a man tell stories. A man in the crowd whispers to you that the speaker is a teacher with some new ideas about religion. You are eager to get your fish to the market, but you are also curious.

What might convince you to stay and listen?

BUILDING BACKGROUND In the first century AD, Roman soldiers occupied Judea, but the Jews living there held firmly to their own beliefs and customs. During that time, one religious teacher began to attract large followings among the people of Judea. That teacher was Jesus of Nazareth.

Jesus of Nazareth

Jesus of Nazareth was the man many people believed was the **Messiah**—a great leader the ancient Jews predicted would come to restore the greatness of Israel. Jesus was a great leader and one of the most influential figures in world history. Jesus's life and teachings form the basis of a religion called **Christianity**. However, we know relatively little about his life. Everything we do know is contained in the **Bible**, the holy book of Christianity.

The Christian Bible is made up of two parts. The first part, the Old Testament, is largely the same as the Hebrew Bible. The second part, the New Testament, is an account of the life and teachings of Jesus and of the early history of Christianity.

The Birth of Jesus

According to the Bible, Jesus was born in a small town called **Bethlehem** (BETH-li-hem) at the end of the first century BC. Jesus's mother, Mary, was married to a carpenter named Joseph. But Christians believe God, not Joseph, was Jesus's father.

As a young man Jesus lived in the town of Nazareth and probably studied with Joseph to become a carpenter. Like many young Jewish men of the time, Jesus also studied the laws and teachings of Judaism. By the time he was about 30, Jesus had begun to travel and teach. Stories of his teachings and actions from this time make up the beginning of the New Testament.

The Crucifixion

As a teacher, Jesus drew many followers with his ideas. But at the same time, his teachings challenged the authority of political and religious leaders. According to the New Testament, they arrested Jesus while he was in Jerusalem in or around AD 30.

Shortly after his arrest, the Romans tried and executed Jesus. He was killed by crucifixion (kroo-suh-FIK-shuhn), a type of execution in which a person was nailed to a cross. In fact, the word *crucifixion* comes from the Latin word for "cross." After he died, Jesus's followers buried him.

The Resurrection

According to Christian beliefs, Jesus rose from the dead and vanished from his tomb three days after he was crucified. Now Christians refer to Jesus's rise from the dead as the **Resurrection** (re-suh-REK-shuhn).

Christians further believe that after the Resurrection, Jesus appeared to some groups of his **disciples** (di-SY-puhls), or followers. Jesus stayed with these disciples for the next 40 days, teaching them and giving them instructions about how to pass on his teachings. Then Jesus rose up into heaven.

Early Christians believed that the Resurrection was a sign that Jesus was the Messiah and the son of God. Some people began to call him Jesus Christ, from the Greek word for Messiah, *Christos*. It is from this word that the words *Christian* and *Christianity* eventually developed.

READING CHECK **Summarizing** What do Christians believe happened after Jesus died?

Jesus of Nazareth

The Christian Bible says that Jesus was born in Bethlehem but grew up in Nazareth. The famous artist Giotto (1266–1336) painted this scene from Jesus's childhood.

ANALYZING VISUALS How does the artist imply that Jesus was important?

Mediterranean Sea

Sea of Galilee

Nazareth

Jordan River

Jerusalem

Bethlehem

Dead Sea

JUDEA

Christian Holidays

For centuries, Christians have honored key events in Jesus's life. Some of these events inspired holidays that Christians celebrate today.

The most sacred holiday for Christians is Easter, which is celebrated each spring. Easter is a celebration of the Resurrection. On Easter Christians usually attend church services. Many people also celebrate by dyeing eggs because eggs are seen as a symbol of new life.

Another major Christian holiday is Christmas. It honors Jesus's birth and is celebrated every December 25. Although no one knows on what date Jesus was actually born, Christians have placed Christmas in December since the 200s. Today people celebrate with church services and the exchange of gifts. Some people reenact scenes of Jesus's birth.

Drawing Conclusions Why do you think people celebrate events in Jesus's life?

Jesus's Acts and Teachings

During his lifetime, Jesus traveled from village to village spreading his message among the Jewish people. As he traveled, he attracted many followers. These early followers later became the first Christians.

Miracles

According to the New Testament, many people became Jesus's followers after they saw him perform miracles. A miracle is an event that cannot normally be performed by a human. For example, the books of the New Testament tell of times when Jesus healed people who were sick or injured. One passage also describes how Jesus once fed an entire crowd with just a few loaves of bread and a few fish. Although there should not have been enough food for everyone, people ate their fill and even had food to spare.

Parables

The Bible says that miracles drew followers to Jesus and convinced them that he was the son of God. Once Jesus had attracted followers, he began to teach them. One way he taught was through parables, or stories that teach lessons about how people should live. Parables are similar to fables, but they usually teach religious lessons. The New Testament includes many of Jesus's parables.

Through his parables, Jesus linked his beliefs and teachings to people's everyday lives. The parables explained complicated ideas in ways that most people could understand. For example, in one parable, Jesus compared people who lived sinfully to a son who had left his home and his family. Just as the son's father would joyfully welcome him home, Jesus said, God would forgive sinners when they turned away from sin.

In another parable, Jesus compared society to a wheat field. In this story, a farmer plants wheat seed, but an enemy comes and plants weeds among the wheat. The farmer lets the weeds and wheat grow in the field together. At harvest time, he gathers the wheat in his barn, but he burns the weeds. Jesus explained this parable by comparing the wheat and weeds to good people and evil people who must live together. However, in the end, Jesus said, the good people would be rewarded and the evil people would be punished.

Jesus's Message

Much of Jesus's message was rooted in older Jewish traditions. For example, he emphasized two rules that were also in the Torah: love God and love other people.

Jesus expected his followers to love all people, not just friends and family. He encouraged his followers to be generous to the poor and the sick. He told people that they should even love their enemies. The way people treated others, Jesus said, showed how much they loved God.

Another important theme in Jesus's teachings was salvation, or the rescue of people from sin. Jesus taught that people who were saved from sin would enter the Kingdom of God when they died. Many of his teachings dealt with how people could reach God's kingdom.

Over the many centuries since Jesus lived, people have interpreted his teachings in different ways. As a result, many different denominations of Christians have developed. A denomination is a group of people who hold mostly the same beliefs. Despite their differences, however, Christians around the world share many basic beliefs about Jesus.

READING CHECK **Summarizing** What were the main ideas in Jesus's message?

The Sermon on the Mount

The Bible says that Jesus attracted many followers. One day he led his followers onto a mountainside to give a religious speech. In this speech, called the Sermon on the Mount, Jesus said that people who love God will be blessed. An excerpt of this sermon appears below.

When Jesus saw the crowds, he went up the mountain; and after he sat down, his disciples came to him. Then he began to speak, and taught them, saying:

"Blessed are the poor in spirit, for theirs is the kingdom of heaven.

"Blessed are those who mourn, for they will be comforted.

"Blessed are the meek, for they will inherit the earth.

"Blessed are those who hunger and thirst for righteousness, for they will be filled.

"Blessed are the merciful, for they will receive mercy.

"Blessed are the pure in heart, for they will see God.

"Blessed are the peacemakers, for they will be called children of God.

"Blessed are those who are persecuted for righteousness' sake, for theirs is the kingdom of heaven.

"Blessed are you when people revile you and persecute you and utter all kinds of evil against you falsely on my account. Rejoice and be glad, for your reward is great in heaven, for in the same way they persecuted the prophets who were before you."

—Matthew 5:1–12, New Revised Standard Version

Scholars believe this location was the site of Jesus's Sermon on the Mount.

ANALYSIS SKILL **ANALYZING INFORMATION**
What kinds of qualities does Jesus say will be rewarded?

The Last Supper

This famous painting by Italian artist Leonardo da Vinci shows Jesus and his Apostles sharing their last meal before Jesus was arrested.

ANALYZING VISUALS What kind of mood do people appear to be in?

Jesus's Followers

Shortly after the Resurrection, the Bible says, Jesus's followers traveled throughout the Roman world telling about Jesus and his teachings. Among the people to pass on Jesus's teachings were 12 chosen disciples called Apostles (uh-PAHS-uhlz) and a man called Paul.

The Apostles

The Apostles were 12 men whom Jesus chose to receive special teaching. During Jesus's lifetime they were among his closest followers and knew him very well. Jesus frequently sent the Apostles to spread his teachings. After the Resurrection, the Apostles continued this task.

One of the Apostles, Peter, became the leader of the group after Jesus died. Peter traveled to a few Roman cities and taught about Jesus in the Jewish communities there. Eventually, he went to live in Rome, where he had much authority among Jesus's followers. In later years after the Christian Church was more organized, many people looked back to Peter as its first leader.

ACADEMIC VOCABULARY

ideals ideas or goals that people try to live up to

The Gospels

Some of Jesus's disciples wrote accounts of his life and teachings. These accounts are called the Gospels. Four Gospels are found in the New Testament of the Bible.

The Gospels were written by men known as Matthew, Mark, Luke, and John. All the men's accounts differ slightly from one another, but together they make up the best source we have on Jesus's life. Historians and religious scholars depend on these stories for information about Jesus's life and teachings. The Gospels tell of miracles Jesus performed. They also contain the parables he told.

Paul

Probably the most important person in the spread of Christianity after Jesus's death was Paul of Tarsus. Although he had never met Jesus, Paul did more to spread Christian beliefs and **ideals** than anyone else. He had so much influence that many people think of him as another Apostle. After Paul died, he was named a **saint**, a person known and admired for his or her holiness.

Like most of Jesus's early followers, Paul was born Jewish. At first he strongly opposed the activities of the Christians. For a time, Paul even worked to prevent followers of Jesus from spreading their message.

According to the New Testament, though, something remarkable happened to Paul one day as he traveled on the road to Damascus. He saw a blinding light and heard the voice of Jesus calling out to him. Soon after that event, Paul became a Christian.

After his conversion, Paul traveled widely, spreading Christian teachings. As you can see on the map, he visited many of the major cities along the eastern coast of the Mediterranean. In addition, he wrote long letters to communities throughout the Roman world. These letters helped explain and elaborate on Jesus's teachings.

In his letters Paul wrote at length about the Christian belief in the Resurrection and about salvation. He also mentioned the idea of the Trinity. The Trinity is a central Christian belief that God is made up of three persons. They are God the Father, Jesus the Son, and the Holy Spirit. This belief holds that, even though there are three persons, there is still only one God.

Paul's teachings attracted both Jews and non-Jews to Christianity in many areas around the Mediterranean. In time, this growing number of Christians helped the Christian Church break away from its Jewish roots. People began to recognize Christianity as a separate religion.

READING CHECK **Finding Main Ideas**
What did Jesus's followers do to help spread Christianity?

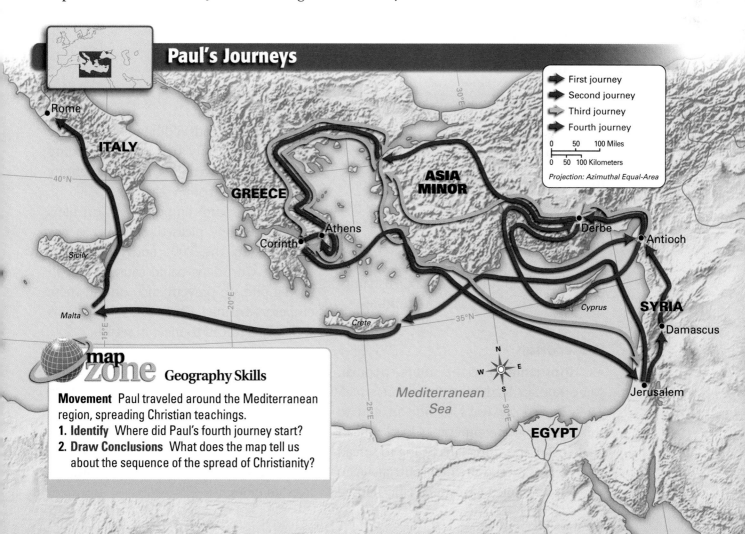

Paul's Journeys

First journey
Second journey
Third journey
Fourth journey

0   50   100 Miles
0   50 100 Kilometers
Projection: Azimuthal Equal-Area

Rome
ITALY
Sicily
Malta
GREECE
Athens
Corinth
Crete
ASIA MINOR
Derbe
Antioch
Cyprus
SYRIA
Damascus
Jerusalem
EGYPT
Mediterranean Sea

map zone Geography Skills

Movement Paul traveled around the Mediterranean region, spreading Christian teachings.
1. **Identify** Where did Paul's fourth journey start?
2. **Draw Conclusions** What does the map tell us about the sequence of the spread of Christianity?

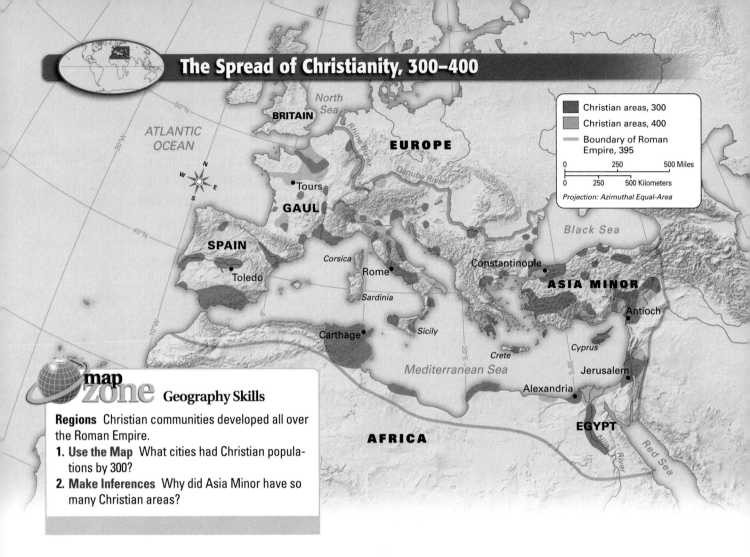

The Spread of Christianity, 300–400

BRITAIN
North Sea
ATLANTIC OCEAN
EUROPE
Rhine River
Tours
GAUL
Danube River
SPAIN
Corsica
Black Sea
Toledo
Rome
Constantinople
ASIA MINOR
Sardinia
Antioch
Carthage
Sicily
Cyprus
Crete
Jerusalem
Mediterranean Sea
Alexandria
AFRICA
EGYPT
Nile River
Red Sea

Christian areas, 300
Christian areas, 400
Boundary of Roman Empire, 395

0 250 500 Miles
0 250 500 Kilometers
Projection: Azimuthal Equal-Area

map zone Geography Skills

Regions Christian communities developed all over the Roman Empire.
1. **Use the Map** What cities had Christian populations by 300?
2. **Make Inferences** Why did Asia Minor have so many Christian areas?

The Spread of Christianity

Early Christians like Paul wanted to share their message about Jesus with the world. To do that, Christians began to write down parts of Jesus's message, including the Gospels. They distributed copies of the Gospels and other writings to strengthen people's faith. Because of their efforts, Christianity spread quickly in Roman communities.

Persecution

As Christianity became more popular, some Roman leaders became concerned. They looked for ways to put an end to this new religion. Sometimes local officals challenged the Christians trying to spread their beliefs. Some of these officials even arrested and killed Christians who refused

to worship the gods of Rome. Many of the leaders of the early Christians, including Peter and Paul, were killed for their efforts in spreading Christian teachings.

Most of Rome's emperors let Christians worship as they pleased. However, a few emperors in the 200s and 300s feared that the Christians could cause unrest in the empire. To prevent such unrest, these emperors banned Christianity. Christians were often forced to meet in secret.

Growth of the Church

Because the early church usually had to meet in secret, it did not have any single leader to govern it. Instead, bishops, or local Christian leaders, led each Christian community. Most of these early bishops lived in cities.

By the late 100s Christians were looking to the bishops of large cities for guidance. These bishops had great influence, even over other bishops. The most honored of all the empire's bishops was the bishop of Rome, or the pope. Gradually, the pope's influence grew and many people in the West came to see him as the head of the whole Christian Church. As the church grew, so did the influence of the pope.

Acceptance of Christianity

As the pope's influence grew, Christianity continued to spread throughout Rome even though it was banned. Then an event changed things for Christians in Rome. The emperor himself became a Christian.

The emperor who became a Christian was Constantine (KAHN-stuhn-teen). According to legend, Constantine was preparing for battle against a rival when he saw a cross in the sky. He thought that this vision meant he would win the battle if he converted to Christianity. Constantine did convert, and he won the battle. As a result of his victory, he became the new emperor of Rome.

As emperor, Constantine removed bans against the practice of Christianity. He also called together a council of Christian leaders from around the empire to try to clarify Christian teachings. Almost 60 years after Constantine died, another emperor banned all non-Christian religious practices in the empire. Christianity eventually spread from Rome all around the world.

FOCUS ON READING
What is the implied main idea of this paragraph?

READING CHECK **Analyzing** What difficulties did early Christians face in practicing and spreading their religion?

SUMMARY AND PREVIEW The life and teachings of Jesus of Nazareth inspired a new religion among the Jews. This religion was Christianity. Next, you will learn about how Christianity and other factors influenced culture in the eastern part of the Roman Empire.

Section 2 Assessment

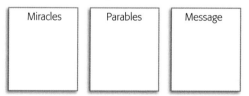
hmhsocialstudies.com
ONLINE QUIZ

Reviewing Ideas, Terms, and Places

1. **a. Define** In Christian teachings, what was the **Resurrection**?
   b. Elaborate Why do you think Christians use the cross as a symbol of their religion?
2. **a. Identify** What did Jesus mean by salvation?
   b. Explain How have differing interpretations of Jesus's teachings affected Christianity?
3. **a. Define** What is a **saint**?
   b. Summarize How did Paul influence early Christianity?
4. **a. Recall** What was the role of bishops in the early Christian Church?
   b. Explain Why were some Roman leaders worried about the growing popularity of Christianity?
   c. Predict What do you think might have happened to Christianity if Constantine had not become a Christian?

Critical Thinking

5. **Making Generalizations** Review your notes on Jesus's acts and teachings. Then make generalizations about the topics shown in the graphic organizer.

Acts and Teachings of Jesus of Nazareth

Miracles	Parables	Message

FOCUS ON WRITING

6. **Identifying Events Related to Christianity** What events from this time can you imagine witnessing? Identify at least one or two events that you might describe in your letter.

The Byzantine Empire

If **YOU** lived there...

You are a trader visiting Constantinople. You have traveled to many cities but have never seen anything so magnificent. The city has huge palaces and stadiums for horse races. In the city center you enter a church and stop, speechless with amazement. Above you is a vast, gold dome lit by hundreds of candles.

How does the city make you feel about its rulers?

BUILDING BACKGROUND The Roman emperor Constantine moved the capital of the empire from Rome east to Constantinople. Power shifted to the eastern part of the empire. Soon, political problems and invasions caused the end of the western Roman Empire.

Emperors Rule from Constantinople

Constantinople was built on the site of an ancient Greek trading city called Byzantium (buh-ZAN-shuhm). Its location between two seas protected the city from attack and let the city control trade between Europe and Asia. Constantinople was in an ideal place to grow in wealth and power.

Justinian

After Rome fell in 476, the emperors of the eastern Roman Empire dreamed of taking it back and reuniting the old Roman Empire. For Justinian (juh-STIN-ee-uhn), an emperor who ruled from 527 to 565, reuniting the empire was a passion. He sent his army to retake Italy. In the end this army conquered not only Italy but also much land around the Mediterranean.

Justinian's other passions were the law and the church. He ordered officials to remove any out-of-date or unchristian laws. He then organized the laws into a legal system called Justinian's Code. By simplifying Roman law, the code helped guarantee fairer treatment for all.

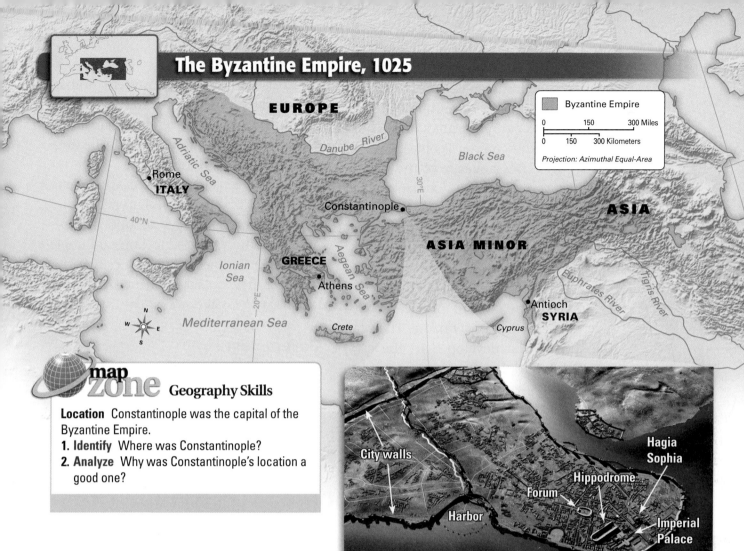

The Byzantine Empire, 1025

EUROPE

Danube River

Black Sea

Rome
ITALY

Adriatic Sea

40°N

Constantinople

ASIA

ASIA MINOR

Ionian
Sea

GREECE

Aegean Sea

Athens

Antioch
SYRIA

Euphrates River

Tigris River

Mediterranean Sea

Crete

Cyprus

Byzantine Empire

0   150   300 Miles
0   150   300 Kilometers
Projection: Azimuthal Equal-Area

map zone Geography Skills

Location Constantinople was the capital of the Byzantine Empire.
1. **Identify** Where was Constantinople?
2. **Analyze** Why was Constantinople's location a good one?

City walls

Harbor

Forum

Hippodrome

Hagia Sophia

Imperial Palace

Constantinople was strategically located where Europe and Asia meet. As a result, the city was in a perfect location to control trade routes between the two continents.

Despite his achievements, Justinian made many enemies. Two groups of these enemies joined together and tried to overthrow him in 532. These groups led riots in the streets. Scared for his life, Justinian prepared to leave Constantinople.

Justinian was stopped from leaving by his wife, Theodora (thee-uh-DOHR-uh). She convinced Justinian to stay in the city. Smart and powerful, Theodora helped her husband rule effectively. With her advice, he found a way to end the riots. Justinian's soldiers killed all the rioters—some 30,000 people—and saved the emperor's throne.

The Empire after Justinian

After the death of Justinian in 565, the eastern empire began to decline. Faced with invasions by barbarians, Persians, and Muslims, later emperors lost all the land Justinian had gained. The eastern empire remained a major power in the world for hundreds of years, but it never regained its former strength.

The eastern Roman Empire finally ended nearly 900 years after the death of Justinian. In 1453 a group called the Ottoman Turks swept in and captured Constantinople. With this defeat the 1,000-year history of the eastern Roman Empire came to an end.

FOCUS ON READING
What is the implied main idea of the last paragraph?

READING CHECK Drawing Conclusions
Why did Justinian reorganize Roman law?

A New Society

In many ways Justinian was the last Roman emperor of the eastern empire. After he died, non-Roman influences took hold throughout the empire. People began to speak Greek, the language of the eastern empire, rather than Latin. Scholars studied Greek, not Roman, philosophy. Gradually, the empire lost its ties to the old Roman Empire, and a new society developed.

The people who lived in this society never stopped thinking of themselves as Romans. But modern historians have given their society a new name. They call the society that developed in the eastern Roman Empire after the west fell the **Byzantine** (BI-zuhn-teen) **Empire**, named after the Greek city of Byzantium.

Outside Influence

One reason eastern and western Roman societies were different was the Byzantines' interaction with other groups. This interaction was largely a result of trade. Because Constantinople's location was ideal for trading between Europe and Asia, it became the greatest trading city in Europe.

Merchants from all around Europe, Asia, and Africa traveled to Constantinople to trade. Over time Byzantine society began to reflect these outside influences as well as its Roman and Greek roots.

Government

The forms of government in the two empires were also different. Byzantine emperors had more power than western

Close-up

The Glory of Constantinople

Constantinople was a crossroads for traders, a center of Christianity, and the capital of an empire. It was a magnificent city filled with great buildings, palaces, and churches. The city's rulers led processions, or ceremonial walks, to show their wealth and power.

This procession went from the church to the royal palace. The procession showed the power and importance of the emperor as head of the church.

emperors did. Eastern emperors also liked to show off their great power. For example, people could not stand while they were in the presence of the eastern emperor. They had to crawl on their hands and knees to talk to him.

The power of an eastern emperor was greater, in part, because the emperor was considered the head of the church as well as the political ruler. The Byzantines thought the emperor had been chosen by God to lead both the empire and the church. In contrast, the emperor in the west was limited to political power. Popes and other bishops were the leaders of the church.

READING CHECK **Contrasting** What were two ways in which eastern and western Roman societies were different?

Byzantine Christianity

Christianity was central to the Byzantines' lives, just as it was to the lives of people in the west. Nearly everyone who lived in the Byzantine Empire was Christian.

To show their devotion to God and the Christian Church, Byzantine artists created beautiful works of religious art. Among the grandest works were **mosaics**, pictures made with pieces of colored stone or glass. Some mosaics sparkled with gold, silver, and jewels.

The procession began at Hagia Sophia, the Byzantines' famous church.

Citizens and visitors crowded the square to see the royal rulers pass by.

ANALYSIS SKILL **ANALYZING VISUALS**

Where did the procession begin and end? What was the significance of this beginning and ending?

59

The Western Roman and Byzantine Empires

In the Western Roman Empire . . .

- Popes and bishops led the church, and the emperor led the government.
- Latin was the main language.

In the Byzantine Empire . . .

- Emperors led the church and the government.
- Greek was the main language.

THE IMPACT TODAY

The Orthodox Church is still the main religion in Russia, Greece, and other parts of Eastern Europe.

Even more magnificent than their mosaics were Byzantine churches, especially Hagia Sophia (HAH-juh soh-FEE-uh). Built by Justinian in the 530s, its huge domes rose high above Constantinople. According to legend, when Justinian saw the church he exclaimed in delight:

> " Glory to God who has judged me worthy of accomplishing such a work as this! O Solomon, I have outdone you! "
>
> –Justinian, quoted in *The Story of the Building of the Church of Santa Sophia*

As time passed, people in the east and west began to interpret and practice Christianity differently. For example, eastern priests could get married, while priests in the west could not. Religious services were performed in Greek in the east. In the west they were held in Latin.

For hundreds of years, church leaders from the east and west worked together peacefully despite their differences. However, the differences between their ideas continued to grow. In time the differences led to divisions within the Christian Church. In the 1000s the split between east and west became official. Eastern Christians formed what became known as the Orthodox Church. As a result, eastern and western Europe were divided by religion.

READING CHECK **Contrasting** What led to a split in the Christian Church?

SUMMARY AND PREVIEW The Roman Empire and the Christian Church both divided into two parts. The Orthodox Church became a major force in the Byzantine Empire. Before long, though, Orthodox Christians encountered members of a religious group they had never met before, the Muslims.

Section 3 Assessment

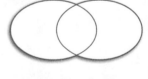
hmhsocialstudies.com
ONLINE QUIZ

Reviewing Ideas, Terms, and Places

1. **a. Describe** Where was **Constantinople** located?
   b. Summarize What were two of Justinian's major accomplishments?
   c. Elaborate What do you think Theodora's role in the government says about women in the eastern empire?
2. **a. Identify** What was one major difference between the powers of emperors in the east and the west?
   b. Explain How did contact with other cultures help change the **Byzantine Empire**?
3. **a. Define** What is a **mosaic**?
   b. Make Generalizations What led to the creation of two different Christian societies in Europe?

Critical Thinking

4. **Comparing and Contrasting** Draw a diagram like this one. Using your notes and the diagram, compare and contrast Christianity in the western Roman Empire with Christianity in the Byzantine Empire.

FOCUS ON WRITING

5. **Choosing Events of the Byzantine Empire** What are the most important events that occurred in the Byzantine Empire? Identify one or two you could write about.

Chapter Review

Geography's Impact

video series
Review the video to answer the closing question:

Why has Istanbul remained a major cultural center throughout its history?

Visual Summary

Use the visual summary below to help you review the main ideas of the chapter.

QUICK FACTS

Jews read the Torah to learn about Jewish history and traditions.

Christianity is based on the life and teachings of Jesus of Nazareth.

Byzantine society was greatly influenced by Christianity.

Reviewing Vocabulary, Terms, and People

Match each "I" statement with the person, place, or thing that might have made the statement.

a. Messiah   **f.** principle

b. Bible   **g.** disciple

c. saint   **h.** Constantinople

d. rabbi   **i.** monotheism

e. Bethlehem   **j.** Torah

1. "I am the town where Jesus of Nazareth was born."
2. "I was the capital of the Byzantine Empire."
3. "I am the holy book of Christianity."
4. "I was a promised leader who was to appear among the Jews."
5. "I am a person known and admired for my holiness."
6. "I am a basic belief, rule, or law."
7. "I am the most sacred text of Judaism."
8. "I am a follower."
9. "I am a Jewish religious teacher."
10. "I am the belief in only one God."

Comprehension and Critical Thinking

SECTION 1 *(Pages 40–46)*

11. **a. Identify** What are the basic beliefs of Judaism?

    b. Analyze What do the various sacred Jewish texts contain?

    c. Elaborate How are Jewish ideas observed in modern western society today?

SECTION 2 *(Pages 48–55)*

12. **a. Describe** According to the Bible, what were the crucifixion and Resurrection?

    b. Analyze Why do you think Jesus's teachings appealed to many people in the Roman Empire?

SECTION 2 *(continued)*

c. Evaluate Why do you think Paul is considered one of the most important people in the history of Christianity?

SECTION 3 *(Pages 56–60)*

13. a. Identify Who were Justinian and Theodora, and what did they accomplish?

b. Contrast In what ways was the Byzantine Empire different from the western Roman Empire?

c. Elaborate Would Constantinople have been an exciting place to visit in the 500s? Why or why not?

Using the Internet

14. Activity: Creating Maps Within 400 years of Jesus's death, Christianity had grown from a small group of Jesus's disciples into the only religion practiced in the Roman Empire. Although 400 years sounds like a long time, to a historian it is practically the blink of an eye. What explains the rapid growth of Christianity? Through the online book, research the key figures, events, and factors in the spread of Christianity. Use what you learn to create an illustrated and annotated map of the spread of Christianity.

↗ hmhsocialstudies.com

Social Studies Skills

Interpreting Route Maps *Use the map of Paul's Journeys in Section 2 to answer the following questions.*

15. How many journeys did Paul take?

16. From where did he start his third journey?

17. On which journeys did Paul visit the cities of Corinth and Athens?

18. What was the last city Paul traveled to?

Map Activity

19. The Jewish and Christian Worlds On a separate sheet of paper, match the letters on the map with their correct labels.

Rome   Constantinople

Jerusalem

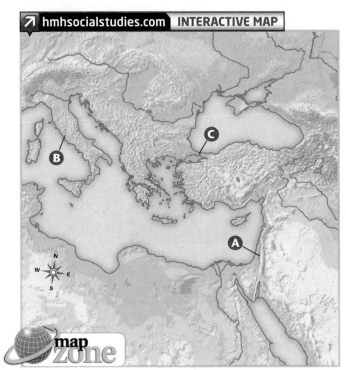

↗ hmhsocialstudies.com   **INTERACTIVE MAP**

FOCUS ON READING AND WRITING

20. Understanding Implied Main Ideas Look back at the beginning of Section 3 of this chapter. For each paragraph under the heading "Justinian," write a statement that you think is the implied main idea of the paragraph.

21. Writing a Letter Your letter is from an eye-witness to the event to a good friend. Look back over your notes and choose one important event for your letter. Your letter should answer the Who? What? Where? How? questions about the event. Write the letter as though you are writing to a good friend and are excited about having seen this event.

Standardized Test Prep

DIRECTIONS: Read questions 1 through 6 and write the letter of the best response. Then read question 7 and write your own well-constructed response.

1 The Jewish holiday that celebrates the start of a new year in the Jewish calendar is
   A Hanukkah.
   B Passover.
   C Rosh Hashanah.
   D Yom Kippur.

2 Many people believe that the Hebrews were the first people to practice
   A monotheism.
   B rituals.
   C religion.
   D law.

3 Which of the following statements about Jesus is false?
   A Some people believed Jesus was the Messiah that Jewish prophets had predicted.
   B Some Roman leaders viewed Jesus as a threat to their power.
   C Jesus failed to attract followers among the Jewish people.
   D Jesus taught people to love God and to be kind to each other.

4 Which of the following statements correctly describes how the Byzantine Empire differed from the western Roman Empire?
   A People practiced Christianity in the Byzantine Empire but not in the western Roman Empire.
   B Byzantine emperors had more power than western emperors did.
   C Popes and bishops were leaders of the church in the Byzantine Empire, while rabbis led the church in the western Roman Empire.
   D The western Roman Empire was known more for its mosaics than the Byzantine Empire was.

" Honor your father and mother, that you may long endure on the land that the Lord your God is assigning to you.

You shall not murder.

You shall not commit adultery.

You shall not steal.

You shall not bear false witness against your neighbor.

You shall not covet your neighbor's house. "

—Exodus 20:12–14

5 The passage above is a selection from the Ten Commandments. Based on this passage, which aspect of Judaism has a basis in the Ten Commandments?
   A celebration of Hanukkah
   B belief in doing what is proper
   C explanation of the Commentaries
   D respect for the Talmud

6 Which of Jesus's followers knew Jesus well and received special teaching?
   A Paul
   B Constantine
   C the Gospels
   D the Apostles

7 **Extended Response** Consider what you have learned in this chapter as well as the selection above from the Ten Commandments. Use this information to write a brief essay explaining one or two ideas and beliefs that are shared by Jews and Christians. Your essay should also explain why you think these two religions share some ideas and beliefs.

CHAPTER 3

History of the Islamic World

AD 550–1650

Essential Question How did Islam develop and spread throughout the world?

What You Will Learn...

Islam, first taught by a man named Muhammad, is now one of the largest religions in the world.

FOCUS ON READING AND WRITING

Sequencing When you read, it is important to keep track of the sequence, or order, in which events happen. Look for dates and other clues to help you figure out the proper sequence. **See the lesson, Sequencing, on page 164.**

Designing a Web Site You have been asked to design a Web site to teach children about Islam and the history of the Muslim people. As you read this chapter, you will collect information about Islam and the Muslim empires. Then you will use that information to design your Web site.

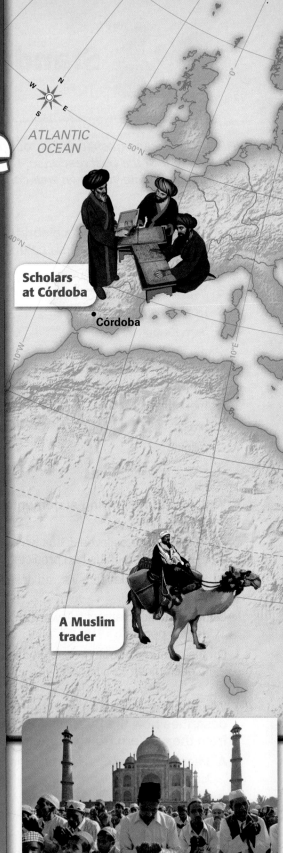

Scholars at Córdoba

• Córdoba

A Muslim trader

Islam One of the world's largest religions, Islam is practiced by people all around the world. These Muslims, or people who practice Islam, are in India.

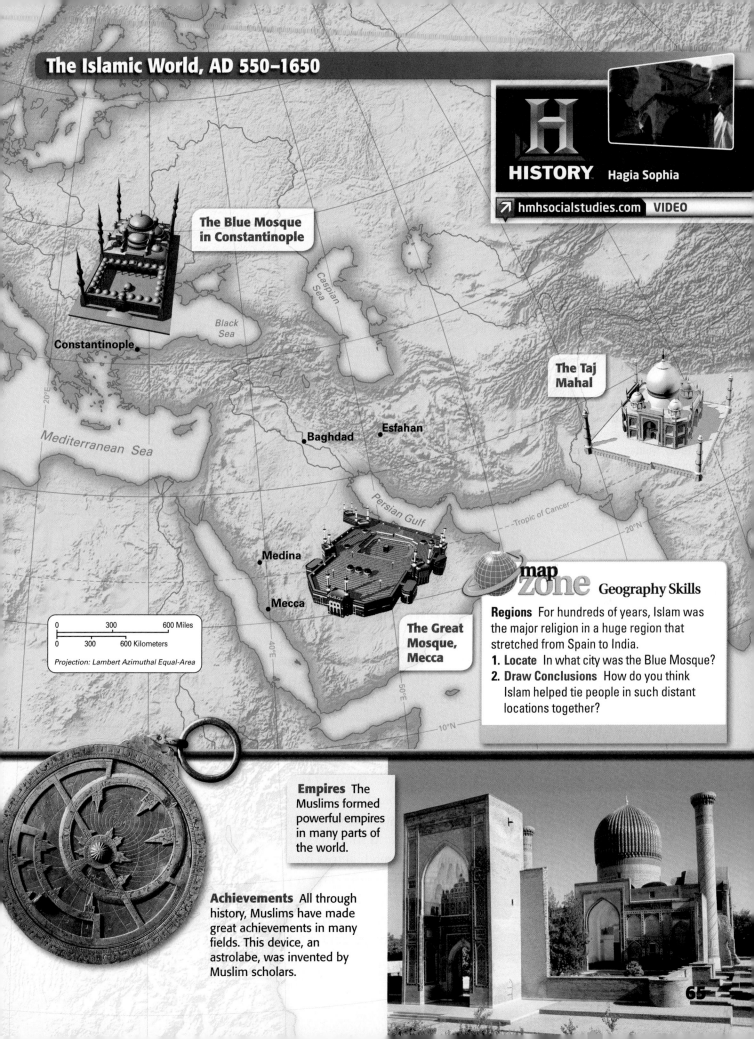

The Islamic World, AD 550–1650

HISTORY Hagia Sophia

↗ hmhsocialstudies.com **VIDEO**

The Blue Mosque in Constantinople

Caspian Sea

Black Sea

Constantinople

Mediterranean Sea

The Taj Mahal

• Baghdad • Esfahan

Persian Gulf

—Tropic of Cancer—

20°N

• Medina

• Mecca

The Great Mosque, Mecca

0   300   600 Miles

0   300   600 Kilometers

Projection: Lambert Azimuthal Equal-Area

20°E

40°E

50°E

10°N

map zone **Geography Skills**

Regions For hundreds of years, Islam was the major religion in a huge region that stretched from Spain to India.
1. **Locate** In what city was the Blue Mosque?
2. **Draw Conclusions** How do you think Islam helped tie people in such distant locations together?

Empires The Muslims formed powerful empires in many parts of the world.

Achievements All through history, Muslims have made great achievements in many fields. This device, an astrolabe, was invented by Muslim scholars.

Origins of Islam

What You Will Learn...

Main Ideas

1. Arabia is mostly a desert land, where two ways of life, nomadic and sedentary, developed.
2. A new religion called Islam, founded by the prophet Muhammad, spread throughout Arabia in the 600s.

The Big Idea

In the harsh desert climate of Arabia, Muhammad, a merchant from Mecca, introduced a major world religion called Islam.

Key Terms and Places

Mecca, *p. 68*
Islam, *p. 68*
Muslim, *p. 68*
Qur'an, *p. 68*
Medina, *p. 69*
mosque, *p. 69*

hmhsocialstudies.com
TAKING NOTES

Use the graphic organizer online to take notes on key places, people, and events in the origins of Islam.

If YOU lived there...

You live in a town in Arabia, in a large merchant family. Your family has grown rich from selling goods brought by traders crossing the desert. Your house is larger than most others in town, and you have servants to wait on you. Although many townspeople are poor, you have always taken such differences for granted. Now you hear that some people are saying the rich should give money to the poor.

How might your family react to this idea?

BUILDING BACKGROUND For thousands of years, traders have crossed the deserts of Arabia to bring goods to market. Scorching temperatures and lack of water have made the journey difficult. However, Arabia not only developed into a thriving trade center, it also became the birthplace of a new religion.

Life in a Desert Land

The Arabian Peninsula, or Arabia, is located in the southwest corner of Asia. It lies near the intersection of Africa, Europe, and Asia. For thousands of years Arabia's location, physical features, and climate have shaped life in the region.

Physical Features and Climate

Arabia lies in a region with hot and dry air. With a blazing sun and clear skies, summer temperatures in the interior parts of the peninsula reach 100°F (38°C) daily. This climate has created a band of deserts across Arabia and northern Africa. Sand dunes, or hills of sand shaped by the wind, can rise to 800 feet (240 m) high and stretch across hundreds of miles!

Arabia's deserts have a very limited amount of water. What water there is exists mainly in scattered oases. An oasis is a wet, fertile area in a desert. Oases have long been key stops along Arabia's overland trade routes.

Two Ways of Life

To live in Arabia's harsh deserts, people developed two main ways of life. Nomads lived in tents and raised herds of sheep, goats, and camels. The animals provided milk, meat, wool, and leather. The camels also carried heavy loads. Nomads traveled with their herds across the desert in search of food and water for their animals.

Among the nomads, water and land belonged to tribes. Membership in a tribe, a group of related people, offered safety from desert dangers.

While nomads moved around, other Arabs lived a more settled life. They made their homes in oases where they could farm. These settlements, particularly the ones along trade routes, became towns.

Towns became centers of trade. There, nomads traded animal products and herbs for goods like cooking supplies and clothes. Merchants sold spices, gold, leather, and other goods brought by caravans.

READING CHECK **Categorizing** What two ways of life were common in Arabia?

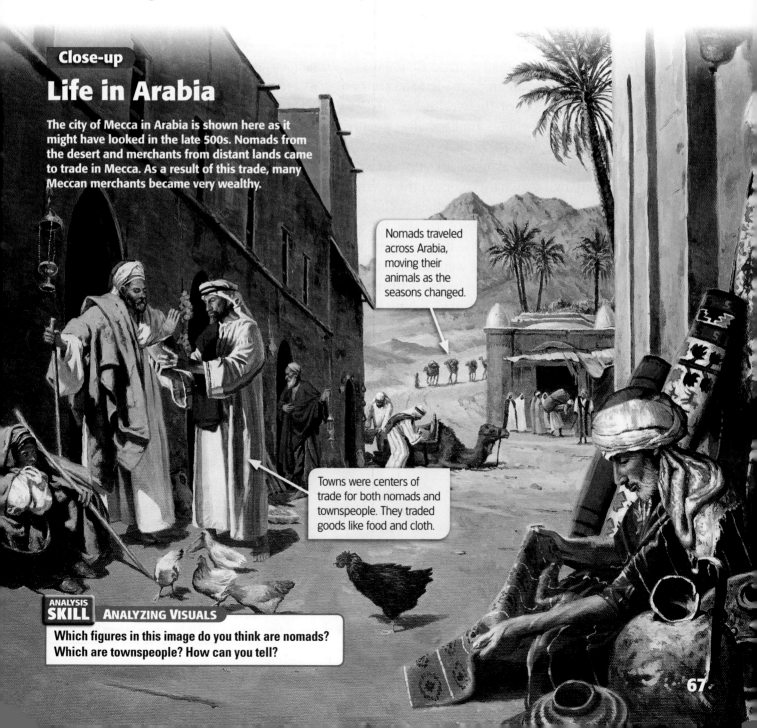

Close-up

Life in Arabia

The city of Mecca in Arabia is shown here as it might have looked in the late 500s. Nomads from the desert and merchants from distant lands came to trade in Mecca. As a result of this trade, many Meccan merchants became very wealthy.

Nomads traveled across Arabia, moving their animals as the seasons changed.

Towns were centers of trade for both nomads and townspeople. They traded goods like food and cloth.

ANALYSIS SKILL **ANALYZING VISUALS**
Which figures in this image do you think are nomads? Which are townspeople? How can you tell?

A New Religion

In early times, Arabs worshipped many gods. That changed, however, when a man named Muhammad brought a new religion to Arabia. Historians know little about Muhammad. What they do know comes from religious writings.

Muhammad Founds Islam

FOCUS ON READING
What clues in this paragraph can help you track the sequence of events?

Muhammad was born into an important family in the city of **Mecca** around 570. As a small child, he traveled with his uncle's caravans. Once he was grown, he managed a caravan business owned by a wealthy woman named Khadijah (ka-DEE-jah). At age 25, Muhammad married Khadijah.

The caravan trade made Mecca a rich city, but most of the wealth belonged to just a few people. Traditionally, wealthy people in Mecca had helped the poor. As Muhammad was growing up, though, many rich merchants ignored the needy.

Concerned about these changes, Muhammad often went to the hills to pray and meditate. One day, when he was about 40 years old, he went to meditate in a cave. According to religious writings, an angel spoke to Muhammad, telling him to "Recite! Recite!" Muhammad asked what he should recite. The angel answered:

"Recite in the name of your Lord who created, created man from clots of blood! Recite! Your Lord is the Most Bountiful One, Who by the pen taught man what he did not know."

—From *The Koran*, translated by N. J. Dawood

Muslims believe that God had spoken to Muhammad through the angel and had made him a prophet, a person who tells of messages from God. The messages that Muhammad received form the basis of the religion called **Islam**. In Arabic, the word *Islam* means "to submit to God."

Muslims, or people who follow Islam, believe that God chose Muhammad to be his messenger to the world. They also believe that Muhammad continued to receive messages from God for the rest of his life. Eventually, these messages were collected in the **Qur'an** (kuh-RAN), the holy book of Islam.

Muhammad's Teachings

In 613 Muhammad began to talk about his messages. He taught that there was only one God, Allah, which means "the God" in Arabic. Like Judaism and Christianity, Islam is monotheistic, or based on the belief in one God. Although people of all three religions believe in one God, their beliefs about God are not the same.

Time Line

Beginnings of Islam

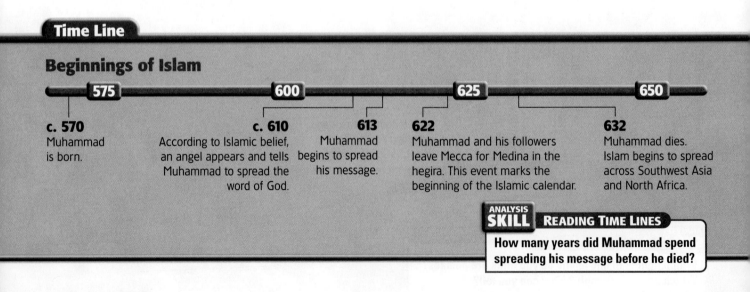

575 — 600 — 625 — 650

c. 570
Muhammad is born.

c. 610
According to Islamic belief, an angel appears and tells Muhammad to spread the word of God.

613
Muhammad begins to spread his message.

622
Muhammad and his followers leave Mecca for Medina in the hegira. This event marks the beginning of the Islamic calendar.

632
Muhammad dies. Islam begins to spread across Southwest Asia and North Africa.

ANALYSIS SKILL   READING TIME LINES

How many years did Muhammad spend spreading his message before he died?

Muhammad's teachings also dealt with how people should live. He taught that all people who believed in Allah were bound together like members of a family. As a result, he said, people should help those who are less fortunate. For example, he thought that people who had money should use that money to help the poor.

Islam Spreads in Arabia

At first Muhammad had few followers. Slowly, more people began to listen to his ideas. As Islam spread, Mecca's rulers grew worried. They threatened Muhammad and even planned to kill him.

A group of people living north of Mecca invited Muhammad to move to their city. So in 622 Muhammad and many of his followers went to **Medina** (muh-DEE-nuh). The name *Medina* means "the Prophet's city" in Arabic. Muhammad's departure from Mecca is called the hegira (hi-JY-ruh), or journey. It is so important a date in the history of Islam that Muslims made 622 the first year of the Islamic calendar.

Muhammad became a spiritual and political leader in Medina. His house became the first **mosque** (MAHSK), or building for Muslim prayer.

As the Muslim community in Medina grew stronger, other Arab tribes began to accept Islam. Conflict with the Meccans, however, increased. In 630, after several years of fighting, the people of Mecca gave in. They accepted Islam as their religion.

Before long, most people in Arabia had accepted Muhammad as their spiritual and political leader and become Muslims. Muhammad died in 632, but the religion he taught would soon spread far beyond the Arabian Peninsula.

READING CHECK **Summarizing** How did Islam spread in Arabia?

Over many centuries, Islam spread from Arabia into other parts of the world. These Muslim children in the African country of Nigeria are studying the Qur'an.

SUMMARY AND PREVIEW In the early 600s Islam was introduced to Arabia by Muhammad. In the next section, you will learn more about the main Islamic teachings and beliefs.

Section 1 Assessment

hmhsocialstudies.com
ONLINE QUIZ

Reviewing Ideas, Terms, and Places

1. **a. Define** What is an oasis?
   b. Make Generalizations Where did towns develop? Why?
   c. Predict Do you think life would have been better for nomads or townspeople in early Arabia? Explain.
2. **a. Identify** What is the **Qur'an**?
   b. Explain According to Islamic belief, what was the source of Islamic teachings?
   c. Elaborate Why did Muhammad move from **Mecca** to **Medina**? What did he accomplish there?

Critical Thinking

3. **Sequencing** Draw a time line like the one below. Using your notes on Muhammad, identify the key dates in his life.

FOCUS ON WRITING

4. **Thinking About Muhammad and Islam** In this section you read about Muhammad and the beginnings of Islam. How might you organize these two topics on your Web site? Write down some ideas.

Islamic Beliefs and Practices

What You Will Learn...

Main Ideas

1. The Qur'an guides Muslims' lives.
2. The Sunnah tells Muslims of important duties expected of them.
3. Islamic law is based on the Qur'an and the Sunnah.

The Big Idea

Sacred texts called the Qur'an and the Sunnah guide Muslims in their religion, daily life, and laws.

Key Terms

jihad, *p. 71*
Sunnah, *p. 71*
Five Pillars of Islam, *p. 72*

hmhsocialstudies.com
TAKING NOTES

Use the graphic organizer online to take notes on the most important beliefs and practices of Islam.

If **YOU** lived there...

Your family owns an inn in Mecca. Usually business is pretty calm, but this week your inn is packed. Travelers have come from all over the world to visit your city. One morning you leave the inn and are swept up in a huge crowd of these visitors. They speak many different languages, but everyone is wearing the same white robes. They are headed to the mosque.

What might draw so many people to your city?

BUILDING BACKGROUND One basic Islamic belief is that everyone who can must make a trip to Mecca sometime during his or her lifetime. More Islamic teachings can be found in Islam's holy books—the Qur'an and the Sunnah.

The Qur'an

During Muhammad's life, his followers memorized his messages and his words and deeds. After Muhammad's death, they collected his teachings and wrote them down to form the book known as the Qur'an. Muslims believe the Qur'an to be the exact word of God as it was told to Muhammad.

Beliefs

The central teaching in the Qur'an is that there is only one God—Allah—and that Muhammad is his prophet. The Qur'an says people must obey Allah's commands. Muslims learned of these commands from Muhammad.

Islam teaches that the world had a definite beginning and will end one day. Muhammad said that on the final day God will judge all people. Those who have obeyed his orders will be granted life in paradise. According to the Qur'an, paradise is a beautiful garden full of fine food and drink. People who have not obeyed God, however, will suffer.

Guidelines for Behavior

Like holy books of other religions, the Qur'an describes Muslim acts of worship, guidelines for moral behavior, and rules for social life.

Some of these guidelines for life are stated **explicitly**. For example, the Qur'an clearly describes how a person should prepare for worship. Muslims must wash themselves before praying so they will be pure before Allah. The Qur'an also tells Muslims what they should not eat or drink. Muslims are not allowed to eat pork or drink alcohol.

Other guidelines for behavior are not stated directly but are **implicit** in the Qur'an. Even though they are not written directly, many of these ideas altered early Arabian society. For example, the Qur'an does not expressly forbid the practice of slavery, which was common in early Arabia. It does, however, imply that slavery should be abolished. Based on this implication, many Muslim slaveholders chose to free their slaves.

Another important subject in the Qur'an has to do with **jihad** (ji-HAHD), which means "to make an effort, or to struggle." Jihad refers to the inner struggle people go through in their effort to obey God and behave according to Islamic ways. Jihad can also mean the struggle to defend the Muslim community, or, historically, to convert people to Islam. The word has also been translated as "holy war."

READING CHECK **Analyzing** Why is the Qur'an important to Muslims?

The Sunnah

The Qur'an is not the only source for the teachings of Islam. Muslims also study the hadith (huh-DEETH), the written record of Muhammad's words and actions. It is also the basis for the Sunnah. The **Sunnah** (SOOH-nuh) refers to the way Muhammad lived, which provides a model for the duties and the way of life expected of Muslims. The Sunnah guides Muslims' behavior.

ACADEMIC VOCABULARY
explicit fully revealed without vagueness

ACADEMIC VOCABULARY
implicit understood though not clearly put into words

The Five Pillars of Islam

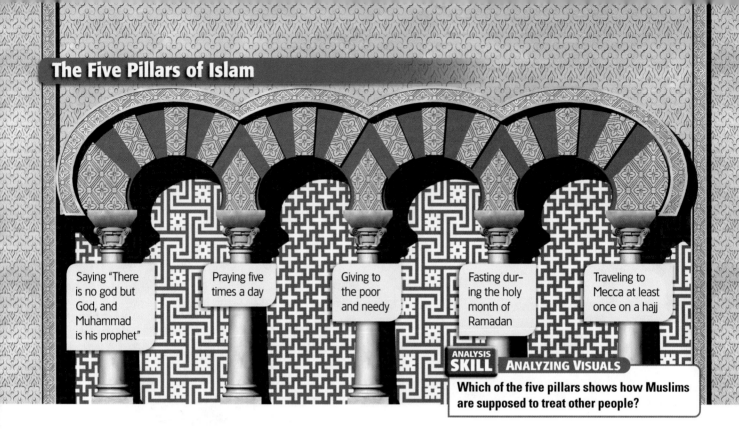

Saying "There is no god but God, and Muhammad is his prophet"

Praying five times a day

Giving to the poor and needy

Fasting during the holy month of Ramadan

Traveling to Mecca at least once on a hajj

ANALYSIS SKILL ANALYZING VISUALS

Which of the five pillars shows how Muslims are supposed to treat other people?

The Five Pillars of Islam

The first duties of a Muslim are known as the **Five Pillars of Islam**, which are five acts of worship required of all Muslims. The first pillar is a statement of faith. At least once in their lives, Muslims must state their faith by saying, "There is no god but God, and Muhammad is his prophet." Muslims say this when they accept Islam. They also say it in their daily prayers.

The second pillar of Islam is daily prayer. Muslims must pray five times a day: before sunrise, at midday, in late afternoon, right after sunset, and before going to bed. At each of these times, a call goes out from a mosque, inviting Muslims to come pray. Muslims try to pray together at a mosque. They believe prayer is proof that someone has accepted Allah.

The third pillar of Islam is a yearly donation to charity. Muslims must pay part of their wealth to a religious official. This money is used to help the poor, build mosques, or pay debts. Helping and caring for others is important in Islam.

The fourth pillar of Islam is fasting—going without food and drink. Muslims fast during the holy month of Ramadan (RAH-muh-dahn). The Qur'an says Allah began his revelations to Muhammad in this month. Throughout Ramadan, most Muslims will not eat or drink anything between dawn and sunset. Muslims believe fasting is a way to show that God is more important than one's own body. Fasting also reminds Muslims of people in the world who struggle to get enough food.

The fifth pillar of Islam is the hajj (HAJ), a pilgrimage to Mecca. All Muslims must travel to Mecca at least once in their lives if they can. The Kaaba, in Mecca, is Islam's most sacred place.

The Sunnah and Daily Life

Besides the five pillars, the Sunnah has other examples of Muhammad's actions and teachings. These form the basis for rules about how to treat others. According to Muhammad's example, people should treat guests with generosity.

72 CHAPTER 3

The Sunnah also provides guidelines for how people should conduct their relations in business and government. For example, one Sunnah rule says that it is bad to owe someone money. Another rule says that people should obey their leaders.

READING CHECK **Generalizing** What do Muslims learn from the Sunnah?

Islamic Law

Together, the Qur'an and the Sunnah are important guides for how Muslims should live. They also form the basis of Islamic law, or Shariah (shuh-REE-uh). Shariah uses both Islamic sources and human reason to judge the rightness of actions a person or community might take. All actions fall on a scale ranging from required to accepted to disapproved to forbidden. Islamic law makes no distinction between religious beliefs and daily life, so Islam affects all aspects of Muslims' lives.

Shariah sets rewards for good behavior and punishments for crimes. It also describes limits of authority. It was the basis for law in Muslim countries until modern times.

Sources of Islamic Beliefs

Qur'an	Sunnah	Shariah
Holy book that includes all the messages Muhammad received from God	Muhammad's example for the duties and way of life expected of Muslims	Islamic law, based on interpretations of the Qur'an and Sunnah

Today, though, most Muslim countries blend Islamic law with legal systems like those in the United States or western Europe.

Islamic law is not found in one book. Instead, it is a set of opinions and writings that have changed over the centuries. As a result, different ideas about Islamic law are found in different Muslim regions.

READING CHECK **Finding Main Ideas** What is the purpose of Islamic law?

SUMMARY AND PREVIEW The Qur'an, the Sunnah, and Shariah teach Muslims how to live. In the next chapter, you will learn more about Muslim culture and the spread of Islam from Arabia to other lands in Europe, Africa, and Asia.

Section 2 Assessment

Reviewing Ideas, Terms, and Places

1. **a. Recall** What is the central teaching of the Qur'an?
   b. Explain How does the Qur'an help Muslims obey God?
2. **a. Recall** What are the **Five Pillars of Islam**?
   b. Make Generalizations Why do Muslims fast during Ramadan?
3. **a. Identify** What is Islamic law called?
   b. Make Inferences How is Islamic law different from law in the United States?
   c. Elaborate What is one possible reason that opinions and writings about Islamic law have changed over the centuries?

Critical Thinking

4. **Categorizing** Draw a chart like the one to the right. Use your notes to list three key teachings from the Qur'an and three teachings from the Sunnah.

Qur'an	Sunnah

FOCUS ON WRITING

5. **Describing Islam** What information would you include on your Web site about the beliefs and practices of Islam? Note how you might organize one page of your Web site about this topic.

The Hajj

Every year, as many as 2 million Muslims make a religious journey, or pilgrimage, to Mecca, Saudi Arabia. This journey, called the hajj, is one of the Five Pillars of Islam—all Muslims are expected to make the journey at least once in their lifetime if they can.

Mecca is the place where Muhammad lived and taught more than 1,300 years ago. As a result, it is the holiest city in Islam. The pilgrims who travel to Mecca each year serve as a living reminder of the connection between history and geography.

On the Road to Mecca

- Before entering Mecca, pilgrims undergo a ritual cleansing and put on special white garments.

- At Mecca, guides help pilgrims through religious rituals.

- One important ritual is the "Standing" on Mount Arafat, near Mecca. Pilgrims stand for hours, praying, at a place where Muhammad is said to have held his last sermon.

- Pilgrims then participate in a three-day ritual of "Stoning," in which they throw pebbles at three pillars.

- Finally, pilgrims complete their journey by returning to the Grand Mosque in Mecca, where a great feast is held.

Europe and the Americas Many countries in Europe and the Americas have a Muslim population. These pilgrims are from Germany.

Africa Pilgrims also come from Africa. These pilgrims are from Nigeria, just one of the African countries that is home to a large Muslim population.

Southeast Asia These pilgrims are from Indonesia, in Southeast Asia. Like all pilgrims, they wear simple white garments that symbolize the equality and unity of all Muslims.

Persian Gulf

● **MECCA**

SAUDI ARABIA

Red Sea

Southwest Asia Pilgrims from Southwest Asia live closest to Mecca. Because of their close relative location, some are able to make the hajj more than once.

Arabian Sea

GEOGRAPHY SKILLS | **INTERPRETING MAPS**

1. **Movement** What are some of the places from which Muslims begin their journey to Mecca?
2. **Place** Why is Mecca the holiest city in Islam?

Muslim Empires

If **YOU** lived there...

You are a farmer living in a village on the coast of India. For centuries, your people have raised cotton and spun its fibers into a soft fabric. One day, a ship arrives in the harbor carrying Muslim traders from far away. They bring interesting goods you have never seen before. They also bring new ideas.

What ideas might you learn from the traders?

What You Will Learn...

Main Ideas

1. Muslim armies conquered many lands into which Islam slowly spread.
2. Trade helped Islam spread into new areas.
3. Three Muslim empires controlled much of Europe, Asia, and Africa from the 1400s to the 1800s.

The Big Idea

After the early spread of Islam, three large Muslim empires formed—the Ottoman, Safavid, and Mughal empires.

Key Terms and Places

caliph, *p. 76*
tolerance, *p. 78*
Baghdad, *p. 78*
Córdoba, *p. 78*
janissaries, *p. 78*
Istanbul, *p. 78*
Esfahan, *p. 80*

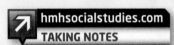
hmhsocialstudies.com
TAKING NOTES

Use the graphic organizer online to take notes on the spread of Islam and three large Muslim empires.

BUILDING BACKGROUND For years traders traveled from Arabia to markets far away. As they traveled, they picked up new goods and ideas, and they introduced these to the people they met. Some of the new ideas the traders spread were Islamic ideas.

Muslim Armies Conquer Many Lands

After Muhammad's death his followers quickly chose Abu Bakr (uh-boo BAK-uhr), one of Muhammad's first converts, to be the next leader of Islam. He was the first **caliph** (KAY-luhf), a title that Muslims use for the highest leader of Islam. In Arabic, the word *caliph* means "successor." As Muhammad's successors, the caliphs had to follow the prophet's example. This meant that they had to rule according to the Qur'an. Unlike Muhammad, however, the early caliphs were not religious leaders.

Beginnings of an Empire

Abu Bakr directed a series of battles to unite Arabia. By his death in 634, he had made Arabia into a unified Muslim state. With Arabia united, Muslim leaders turned their attention elsewhere. Their armies, strong after their battles in Arabia, won many stunning victories. They defeated the Persian and Byzantine empires, which were weak from many years of fighting.

When the Muslims conquered lands, they set certain rules for non-Muslims living there. For example, some non-Muslims could not build churches in Muslim cities or dress like Muslims. However, Christians and Jews could continue to practice their own religion. They were not forced to convert to Islam.

Growth of the Empire

Many early caliphs came from one family, the Umayyad (oom-EYE-yuhd) family. The Umayyads moved the capital to Damascus, in Muslim-conquered Syria, and continued to expand the empire. They took over lands in Central Asia and in northern India. The Umayyads also gained control of trade in the eastern Mediterranean and conquered parts of North Africa.

The Berbers, the native people of North Africa, resisted Muslim rule at first. After years of fighting, however, many Berbers converted to Islam.

In 711 a combined Arab and Berber army invaded Spain and quickly conquered it. Next, the army moved into what is now France, but it was stopped by a Christian army near the city of Tours (TOOR). Despite this defeat, Muslims called Moors ruled parts of Spain for the next 700 years.

A new Islamic dynasty, the Abbasids (uh-BAS-idz), came to power in 749. They reorganized the government to make it easier to rule such a large region.

READING CHECK **Analyzing** What role did armies play in spreading Islam?

Trade Helps Islam Spread

Islam gradually spread through areas the Muslims conquered. Trade also helped spread Islam. Along with their goods, Arab merchants took Islamic beliefs to India, Africa, and Southeast Asia. Though Indian kingdoms remained Hindu, coastal trading cities soon had large Muslim communities. In Africa, many leaders converted to Islam. As a result, societies often had both African and Muslim customs. Between 1200 and 1600, Muslim traders carried Islam even farther east. Muslim communities grew up in what are now Malaysia and Indonesia.

Trade also brought new products to Muslim lands. For example, Arabs learned from the Chinese how to make paper and use gunpowder. New crops such as cotton, rice, and oranges arrived from India, China, and Southeast Asia.

Many Muslim merchants traveled to African market towns, too. They wanted African products such as ivory, cloves, and slaves. In return they offered fine white pottery called porcelain from China, cloth goods from India, and iron from Europe and Southwest Asia. Arab traders grew wealthy from trade between regions.

FOCUS ON READING

As you read this page, look for words that give clues to the sequence of events.

THE IMPACT TODAY

Indonesia now has the world's largest Muslim population.

The City of Córdoba

By the early 900s, Córdoba, Spain, was one of the wealthiest cities in Europe and a center of Islamic learning. Rich examples of Islamic architecture can still be seen in the city.

A Mix of Cultures

As Islam spread, Arabs came into contact with people who had different beliefs and lifestyles than they did. Muslims generally practiced **tolerance**, or acceptance, with regard to the people they conquered. For example, Muslims did not ban all other religions in their lands. Because they shared some beliefs with Muslims, Christians and Jews in particular kept many of their rights. They did, however, have to pay a special tax. Christians and Jews were also forbidden from converting anyone to their religions.

Many people conquered by the Arabs converted to Islam. These people often adopted other parts of Arabic culture, including the Arabic language. The Arabs, in turn, adopted some customs from the people they conquered. This cultural blending changed Islam from a mostly Arab religion into a religion that included many other cultures. However, the Arabic language and shared religion helped unify the different groups of the Islamic world.

Growth of Cities

The growing cities of the Muslim world reflected the blending of cultures. Trade had brought people together and created wealth, which supported great cultural development in Muslim cities.

Baghdad, in what is now Iraq, became the capital of the Islamic Empire in 762. Trade and farming made Baghdad one of the world's richest cities. The caliphs there supported science and the arts. The city was a center of culture and learning.

Córdoba (KAWR-doh-bah), a great city in Spain, became another showplace of Muslim civilization. By the early 900s Córdoba was the largest and most advanced city in western Europe.

> **READING CHECK** **Finding the Main Idea** How did trade affect the spread of Islam?

Three Muslim Empires

The great era of Arab Muslim expansion lasted until the 1100s. Afterward, three non-Arab Muslim groups built large, powerful empires that took control of much of Europe, Asia, and Africa.

The Ottoman Empire

In the mid-1200s Muslim Turkish warriors known as Ottomans began to take territory from the Christian Byzantine Empire. They eventually ruled land from eastern Europe to North Africa and Arabia.

The key to the empire's expansion was the Ottoman army. The Ottomans trained Christian boys from conquered towns to be soldiers. These slave soldiers, called **janissaries**, converted to Islam and became fiercely loyal warriors. The Ottomans also benefitted from their use of new weapons, especially gunpowder.

In 1453 Ottomans led by Mehmed II used huge cannons to conquer the city of Constantinople. With the city's capture, Mehmed defeated the Byzantine Empire. He became known as the Conqueror. Mehmed made Constantinople, which the Ottomans called **Istanbul**, his capital. He also turned the Byzantines' great church, Hagia Sophia, into a mosque.

After Mehmed's death, another ruler, or sultan, continued his conquests. This sultan expanded the empire to the east through the rest of Anatolia, another name for Asia Minor. His armies also conquered Syria and Egypt. The holy cities of Mecca and Medina then accepted Ottoman rule.

The Ottoman Empire reached its height under Suleyman I (soo-lay-MAHN), "the Magnificent." During his rule from 1520 to 1566, the Ottomans took control of the eastern Mediterranean and pushed farther into Europe, areas they would control until the early 1800s.

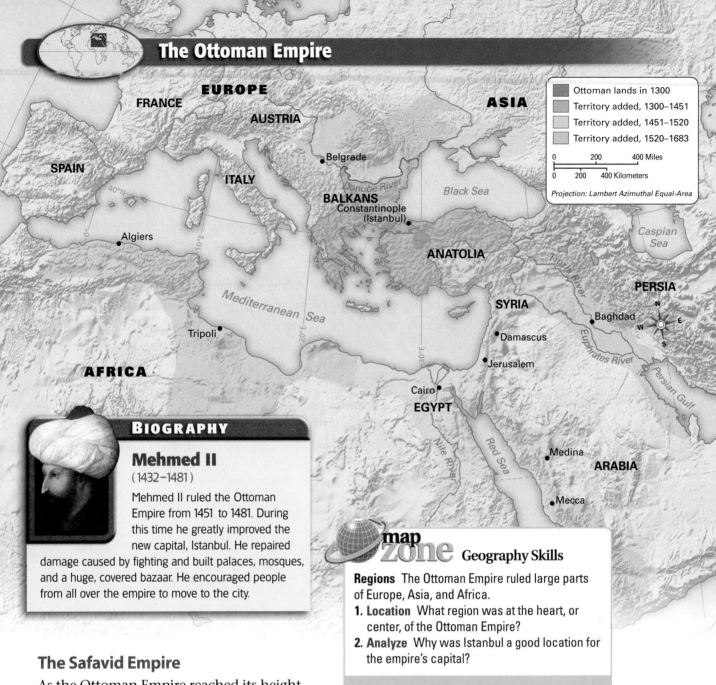

The Ottoman Empire

EUROPE

FRANCE

AUSTRIA

SPAIN

ITALY

Belgrade

Danube River

BALKANS
Constantinople
(Istanbul)

Black Sea

ASIA

ANATOLIA

PERSIA

Algiers

Mediterranean Sea

Baghdad

Caspian
Sea

Tripoli

SYRIA

Damascus

Euphrates River

Tigris River

Jerusalem

Persian Gulf

AFRICA

Cairo

EGYPT

Nile River

Red Sea

Medina

ARABIA

Mecca

Legend:
- Ottoman lands in 1300
- Territory added, 1300–1451
- Territory added, 1451–1520
- Territory added, 1520–1683

0   200   400 Miles
0   200   400 Kilometers

Projection: Lambert Azimuthal Equal-Area

BIOGRAPHY

Mehmed II
(1432–1481)

Mehmed II ruled the Ottoman Empire from 1451 to 1481. During this time he greatly improved the new capital, Istanbul. He repaired damage caused by fighting and built palaces, mosques, and a huge, covered bazaar. He encouraged people from all over the empire to move to the city.

map zone Geography Skills

Regions The Ottoman Empire ruled large parts of Europe, Asia, and Africa.

1. **Location** What region was at the heart, or center, of the Ottoman Empire?
2. **Analyze** Why was Istanbul a good location for the empire's capital?

The Safavid Empire

As the Ottoman Empire reached its height, a group of Persian Muslims, the Safavids (sah-FAH-vuhds), was gaining power to the east, in the area of present-day Iran. Before long, the Safavids came into conflict with the Ottomans and other Muslims.

The conflict arose from an old dispute among Muslims about who should be caliph. In the mid-600s, Islam split into two groups. The two groups were the Shia (SHEE-ah) and the Sunni (SOO-nee). Shia Muslims thought only Muhammad's descendants could become caliphs. The Sunni did not think caliphs had to be related to Muhammad. The Ottomans were Sunni, and the Safavid leaders were Shia.

The Safavid Empire began in 1501 when a strong Safavid leader named Esma'il (is-mah-EEL) conquered Persia. He took the ancient Persian title of shah, or king.

Esma'il made Shiism—the beliefs of the Shia—the official religion of the empire. But he wanted to spread Shiism farther.

THE IMPACT TODAY

Most Muslims today belong to the Sunni branch of Islam.

He tried to gain more Muslim lands and convert more Muslims to Shiism. He fought the Uzbek people, but he suffered a major defeat by the Ottomans in 1514.

In 1588 the greatest Safavid leader, 'Abbas, became shah. He strengthened the military and gave his soldiers gunpowder weapons. Copying the Ottomans, 'Abbas trained foreign slave boys to be soldiers. Under 'Abbas's rule the Safavids defeated the Uzbeks and took back land that had been lost to the Ottomans.

The Safavids blended many Persian and Muslim traditions. They grew wealthy from trade and built glorious mosques in their capital, **Esfahan** (es-fah-HAHN). The Safavid Empire lasted until the mid-1700s.

The Mughal Empire

East of the Safavid Empire, in northern India, lay the Mughal (MOO-guhl) Empire. The Mughals were Turkish Muslims from Central Asia. Their empire was established by a leader named Babur (BAH-boohr), or "tiger." He tried for years to build an empire in Central Asia. When he did not succeed there, he decided to create an empire in northern India instead. The result was the Mughal Empire, created in 1526.

In the mid-1500s an emperor named Akbar conquered many new lands and worked to strengthen the government of the empire. He also instituted a tolerant religious policy. Akbar believed members of all religions could live and work together.

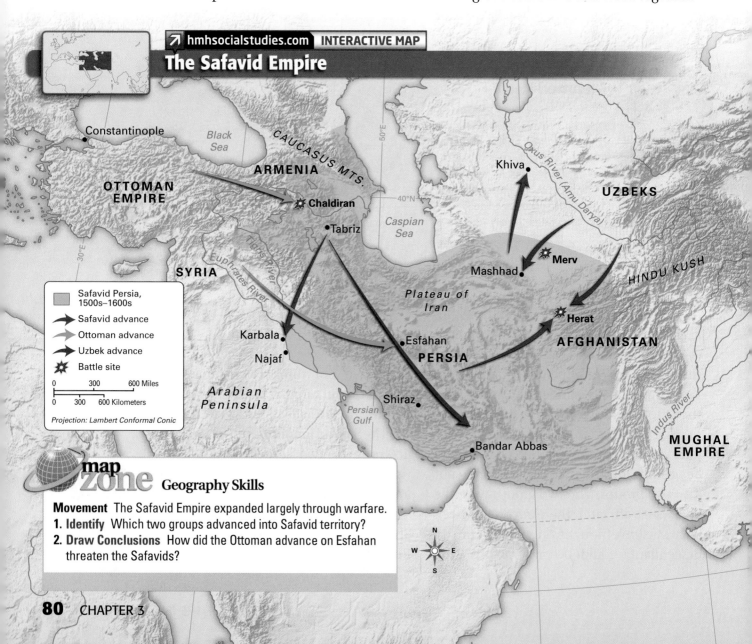

↗ hmhsocialstudies.com **INTERACTIVE MAP**

The Safavid Empire

Safavid Persia, 1500s–1600s
➤ Safavid advance
➤ Ottoman advance
➤ Uzbek advance
✦ Battle site

0   300   600 Miles
0   300   600 Kilometers

Projection: Lambert Conformal Conic

map zone **Geography Skills**

Movement The Safavid Empire expanded largely through warfare.
1. **Identify** Which two groups advanced into Safavid territory?
2. **Draw Conclusions** How did the Ottoman advance on Esfahan threaten the Safavids?

Akbar's tolerance allowed Muslims and Hindus in the empire to live in peace. In time, cooperation between the two groups helped create a unique Mughal culture. It blended Persian, Islamic, and Hindu elements. The Mughals became known for their monumental works of architecture. One famous example of this architecture is the Taj Mahal, a tomb built in the 1600s by emperor Shah Jahan for his wife. Its graceful domes and towers are a symbol of India today.

In the late 1600s, an emperor reversed Akbar's tolerant policies. He destroyed many Hindu temples, and violent revolts broke out. The Mughal Empire fell apart.

READING CHECK **Analyzing** How did the Ottomans gain land for their empire?

SUMMARY AND PREVIEW Islam spread beyond Arabia through warfare and trade. The Ottomans, Safavids, and Mughals built empires and continued the spread of Islam. In Section 4, you will learn about the cultural achievements of the Islamic world.

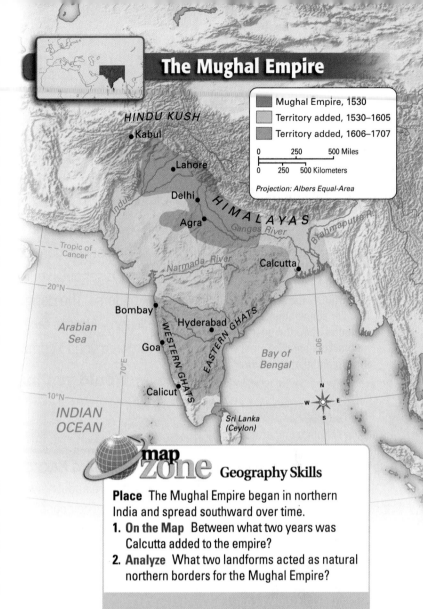

The Mughal Empire

Mughal Empire, 1530
Territory added, 1530–1605
Territory added, 1606–1707

0   250   500 Miles
0   250   500 Kilometers

Projection: Albers Equal-Area

HINDU KUSH
• Kabul
• Lahore
Delhi •
Agra • HIMALAYAS
Ganges River
Tropic of Cancer
Narmada River
Calcutta •
20°N
Bombay •
Arabian Sea
Hyderabad •
Goa • WESTERN GHATS EASTERN GHATS
Bay of Bengal
70°E
90°E
10°N
Calicut •
INDIAN OCEAN
Sri Lanka (Ceylon)

map zone Geography Skills

Place The Mughal Empire began in northern India and spread southward over time.
1. **On the Map** Between what two years was Calcutta added to the empire?
2. **Analyze** What two landforms acted as natural northern borders for the Mughal Empire?

Section 3 Assessment

hmhsocialstudies.com
ONLINE QUIZ

Reviewing Ideas, Terms, and Places

1. **a. Define** What is a **caliph**?
   b. Evaluate Do you think the rules that Muslims made for conquered non-Muslims were fair? Why or why not?
2. **a. Identify** Name three places Islam spread to through trade.
   b. Explain How did trade help spread Islam?
   c. Elaborate What was life in **Córdoba** like?
3. **a. Recall** Who were the **janissaries**?
   b. Contrast How did Sunni and Shia beliefs about caliphs differ?
   c. Evaluate Which of the Muslim empires do you think made the greatest achievements? Why?

Critical Thinking

4. **Comparing and Contrasting** Draw a chart like the one below. Use your notes to compare and contrast the Ottoman, Safavid, and Mughal empires.

	Ottomans	Safavids	Mughals
Leaders			
Location			
Religious policy			

FOCUS ON WRITING

5. **Collecting Information About Empires** You will need one web page on Muslim empires. Note one or two points you will make about each empire.

Cultural Achievements

What You Will Learn...

Main Ideas

1. Muslim scholars made lasting contributions to the fields of science and philosophy.
2. In literature and the arts, Muslim achievements included beautiful poetry, memorable short stories, and splendid architecture.

The Big Idea

Muslim scholars and artists made important contributions to science, art, and literature.

Key Terms

Sufism, *p. 83*
minarets, *p. 85*
calligraphy, *p. 85*

hmhsocialstudies.com
TAKING NOTES

Use the graphic organizer online to take notes on the achievements and advances the Muslims made in various fields.

If **YOU** lived there...

You are a servant in the court of a powerful Muslim ruler. Your life at court is comfortable, though not one of luxury. Now the ruler is sending your master to explore unknown lands and distant kingdoms. The dangerous journey will take him across seas and deserts. He can take only a few servants with him. He has not ordered you to come but has given you a choice.

Would you join the expedition? Why or why not?

BUILDING BACKGROUND Muslim explorers traveled far and wide to learn about new places. They used what they learned to make maps. Their contributions to geography were just one way Muslim scholars made advancements in science and learning.

Science and Philosophy

The empires of the Islamic world made great advances in many fields—astronomy, geography, philosophy, math, and science. Scholars at Baghdad and Córdoba translated ancient writings on these subjects into Arabic. Scholars all over the Arabic world then used these ancient writings as the bases for their own works.

Islamic Achievements

Astronomy

Knowledge of astronomy allowed Muslim scientists to invent the astrolabe. This device made it possible for sailors to navigate using the stars. Before this, sailors had to stay within sight of shore or risk getting lost at sea.

Astronomy

Many Muslim cities had observatories. In these observatories, Muslim scientists worked to increase their knowledge of astronomy. Their study of the sky had practical benefits as well. For example, scientists used astronomy to improve their understanding of time, which let them build better clocks. They also improved the astrolabe, a device that allowed people to calculate their location on Earth.

Geography

Studying astronomy also helped Muslims explore the world. As people learned to use the stars to calculate time and location, merchants and explorers began to travel widely. The explorer Ibn Battutah traveled to Africa, India, China, and Spain in the 1320s. As a result of such travels, Muslim geographers made more accurate maps than were available before.

Philosophy

Many great thinkers lived in the Muslim world. Some studied **classical** writings and, like the ancient Greeks, believe in the importance of reason. Other philosophies taught that religion was more important than science. One of these philosophies was **Sufism** (SOO-fi-zuhm), which taught people they could find God's love by having a personal relationship with God.

Math

Muslim scholars also made advances in mathematics. For example, in the 800s they combined the ancient Indian system of numbers—including the use of zero—with Greek mathematical ideas. The results of these Muslim advances still affect how we think of math today. The number system we use is based on ancient Muslim writings. In addition, the field of algebra, an advanced type of mathematics, was first developed by Muslim scholars.

Medicine

The greatest of all Muslim achievements may have come in medicine. They based their medical skills on ancient Greek and Indian knowledge and added many new discoveries of their own.

Muslim doctors started the world's first pharmacy school to teach people how to make medicine. They built hospitals and learned to cure many serious diseases, such as smallpox. A Muslim doctor known in the West as Avicenna (av-uh-SEN-uh) recorded medical knowledge in an encyclopedia. It was used throughout Europe until the 1600s and is one of the most famous books in the history of medicine.

READING CHECK Drawing Conclusions
How did Muslims influence the fields of science and medicine?

THE IMPACT TODAY
We still call the numerals 0, 1, 2, 3, 4, 5, 6, 7, 8, and 9 Arabic or Hindu-Arabic numerals.

ACADEMIC VOCABULARY
classical referring to the cultures of ancient Greece or Rome

Geography
Muslim travelers collected much information about the world, some of which was used to make this map. New and better maps led to even more travel and a greater understanding of the world's geography.

Medicine
Muslim doctors made medicines from plants like this mandrake plant, which was used to treat pain and illnesses. They developed better ways to prevent, diagnose, and treat many diseases.

The Blue Mosque

The Blue Mosque in Istanbul was built in the early 1600s for an Ottoman sultan. It upset many people at the time it was built because they thought its six minarets—instead of the usual four—were an attempt to make it as great as the mosque in Mecca.

Domes are a common feature of Islamic architecture. Huge columns support the center of this dome, and more than 250 windows let light into the mosque.

The mosque gets its name from its beautiful blue Iznik tiles.

Tall towers called minarets are found outside many mosques.

The most sacred part of a mosque is the mihrab, the niche that points the way to Mecca. This man is praying facing the mihrab.

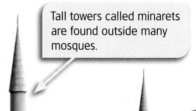

ANALYSIS SKILL | **ANALYZING VISUALS**

Why do you think the decoration of the Blue Mosque is so elaborate?

84   CHAPTER 3

Literature and the Arts

In addition to scientific achievements, the Muslims made great advances in the arts. Some of these artistic advances can be seen in literature and the visual arts.

Literature

Literature, especially poetry, was popular in the Muslim world. Much of this poetry was influenced by Sufism. Sufi poets often wrote about their loyalty to God. One of the most famous Sufi poets was Omar Khayyám (oh-mahr ky-AHM). In a book of poems known as the *Rubáiyát*, he wrote about faith, hope, and other emotions.

Muslims also enjoyed reading short stories. Many stories are collected in *The Thousand and One Nights*. This collection includes tales about legendary characters such as Sinbad, Aladdin, and Ali Baba.

Visual Arts

Of the visual arts, architecture was the most important in the Muslim world. Rich Muslim rulers used their wealth to have beautiful mosques built to honor God and inspire religious followers. Many mosques feature large domes and graceful **minarets**, tall towers from where Muslims are called to prayer.

Muslim architects also built palaces, marketplaces, and libraries. Many of these buildings have complicated domes and arches, colored bricks, and decorated tiles.

Although most Muslim buildings were highly decorated, most Muslim art does not show any people or animals. Muslims think only God can create humans and animals or their images. Instead, Muslim artists created complex geometric patterns. Muslim artists also turned to **calligraphy**, or decorative writing. They made sayings from the Qur'an into works of art to decorate mosques and other buildings.

Muslim art and literature combined Islamic influences with regional traditions of the places Muslims conquered. This mix of Islam with cultures from Asia, Africa, and Europe gave literature and the arts a unique style and character.

READING CHECK **Generalizing** What were two Muslim artistic achievements?

SUMMARY AND PREVIEW The Muslims made great advances in science and art. In the next chapter, you'll learn about an area where many of these advances were made—the Eastern Mediterranean.

Section 4 Assessment

hmhsocialstudies.com
ONLINE QUIZ

Reviewing Ideas, Terms, and Places

1. **a. Identify** Who traveled to India, Africa, China, and Spain and contributed his knowledge to the study of geography?
   b. Explain How did Muslim scholars help preserve learning from the ancient world?
   c. Rank In your opinion, what was the most important Muslim scientific achievement? Why?
2. **a. Describe** What function do **minarets** serve in mosques?
   b. Explain How did Muslim artists create art without showing humans or animals?

Critical Thinking

3. **Analyzing** Using your notes, complete a chart like the one below. For each category in the first column, list one important achievement or advance the Muslims made.

Category	Achievement or Advance
Astronomy	
Geography	
Math	
Medicine	
Philosophy	

FOCUS ON WRITING

4. **Describing Muslim Achievements and Advances** Review your notes on key Muslim achievements and advances in science, philosophy, literature, and the arts. Now decide what information about each of these topics you will include on your Web site.

Outlining

Learn

The chapters in your textbooks are full of facts and ideas. Sometimes keeping track of all the information that you read can be overwhelming. At these times, it may help you to construct an outline of what you are reading.

An outline lists the main ideas of a chapter and the details that support those main ideas. The most important ideas are labeled with Roman numerals (I, II, III, and so on). Supporting ideas are listed below the main ideas, indented and labeled with capital letters (A, B, C, and so on). Less important details are indented farther and labeled with numbers (1, 2, 3) and lowercase letters (a, b, c). By arranging the ideas in an outline, you can see which are most important and how various ideas are related.

Practice

To the right is a partial outline of the discussion titled Literature and the Arts in Section 4 of this chapter. Study the outline and then answer the following questions.

1 What are the major ideas on this outline? How are they marked?

2 What details were listed to support the first main idea?

3 How are the heads on the outline related to the heads in the text of the discussion?

Literature and the Arts
I. Literature
  A. Poetry
  B. Short Stories
    1. *The Thousand and One Nights*
    2. Stories about Sinbad, Aladdin, Ali Baba
II. Visual Arts
  A. Architecture
    1. Mosques
      a. Large domes
      b. Minarets
    2. Palaces, marketplaces, libraries
  B. Art
    1. No people or animals
    2. Complex geometric patterns
    3. Calligraphy

Apply

Read back over the discussion titled Science and Philosophy in Section 4 of this chapter. Create an outline of this discussion. Before you write your outline, decide what you will use as your main heads. Then fill in the details below each of the heads.

Chapter Review

Geography's Impact
video series
Review the video to answer the closing question:
Why might the pilgrimage to Mecca mean so much to the Muslims who go there?

Visual Summary

Use the visual summary below to help you review the main ideas of the chapter.

QUICK FACTS

Islam was first taught by Muhammad. Its teachings are found in the Qur'an and the Sunnah.

From Arabia, Islam spread into many parts of the world. Muslims ruled great empires in Asia, Europe, and Africa.

Muslim scholars and artists made great achievements in science, medicine, math, philosophy, and the arts.

Reviewing Vocabulary, Terms, and Places

For each statement below, write T if it is true and F if it is false. If the statement is false, write the correct term that would make the sentence a true statement.

1. Muslims gather to pray at the **Five Pillars of Islam**.

2. Traders often traveled in **caravans** to take their goods to markets.

3. An **Islam** is a person who submits to God and follows the teachings of Muhammad.

4. According to Islamic belief, God's messages to Muhammad during his lifetime make up the **Sunnah**.

5. A **caliph** is a journey to a sacred place.

6. A **minaret** is a tower from where Muslims are called to prayer.

7. **Janissaries** converted to Islam and became fierce warriors in the Ottoman army.

8. The hajj is a pilgrimage to Islam's most sacred city, **Baghdad**.

Comprehension and Critical Thinking

SECTION 1 *(pages 66–69)*

9. **a. Recall** According to Muslim belief, how was Islam revealed to Muhammad?

   b. Analyze How did Muhammad encourage people to treat each other?

   c. Evaluate What are some possible benefits to a nomadic lifestyle, and what are some possible benefits to a town lifestyle?

SECTION 2 *(pages 70–73)*

10. **a. Define** What is the hajj?

    b. Contrast Both the Qur'an and the Sunnah have guided Muslims' behavior for centuries. Apart from discussing different topics, how do these two differ?

    c. Predict Which of the Five Pillars of Islam do you think would be the most difficult to perform? Why?

SECTION 3 (pages 76–81)

11. a. Identify Who was Abu Bakr, and why is he important in the history of Islam?

b. Analyze Why did the Safavids come into conflict with the Ottomans?

c. Evaluate In your opinion, was conquest or trade more effective in spreading Islam? Why?

SECTION 4 (pages 82–85)

12. a. Describe What are two elements often found in Muslim architecture?

b. Draw Conclusions How did having a common language help scholars in the Islamic world?

c. Elaborate Why might a ruler want to use his or her wealth to build a mosque?

Map Activity

13. The Islamic World On a separate sheet of paper, match the letters on the map with their correct labels.

Mecca	Medina	Red Sea
Persian Gulf	Arabian Sea	

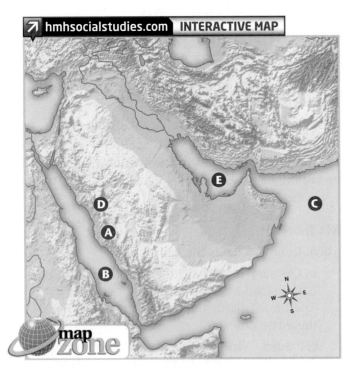

Social Studies Skills

14. Outlining Find the discussion titled The Five Pillars of Islam in Section 2 of this chapter. If you were going to outline this discussion, what would you use as your main ideas?

Using the Internet

15. Activity: Researching Muslim Achievements Muslim advances in science, math, and art were spread around the world both by explorers and by traders. Through the online book, learn about some of these advances. Choose an object created by Muslim scholars in the 600s or 700s and write a paragraph that explains its roots and how it spread to other cultures. End your paragraph with a discussion of how the object is used in modern times.

 hmhsocialstudies.com

FOCUS ON READING AND WRITING

16. Sequencing Arrange the following list of events in the order in which they happened. Then write a brief paragraph describing the events, using clue words such as *after, then,* and *later* to show the proper sequence.

- Muhammad moves to Medina.
- Muhammad begins to teach about Islam.
- Muhammad works as a merchant.
- Muhammad becomes a political leader.

17. Creating Your Web Site You have now collected information on Muhammad, the religion of Islam, major Muslim empires, and Muslim achievements. Create a home page and one Web page on each of these topics. You can write about your topics in paragraph form or in a list of bullet points. You may design the pages either online or on sheets of paper. Remember that your audience is children, so you should keep the sentences simple.

Standardized Test Prep

DIRECTIONS: Read questions 1 through 7 and write the letter of the best response. Then read question 8 and write your own well-constructed response.

1 **During the month of Ramadan, Muslims**
  A fast.
  B do not pray.
  C travel to Medina.
  D hold feasts.

2 **The teachings of Muhammad are found mainly in the Qur'an and the**
  A Commentaries.
  B Sunnah.
  C Analects.
  D Torah.

3 **Which Muslim empire was located in India?**
  A Ottoman Empire
  B Mughal Empire
  C Safavid Empire
  D Córdoba Empire

4 **Muslim scholars are credited with developing**
  A geometry.
  B algebra.
  C calculus.
  D physics.

5 **The most sacred city in Islam is**
  A Baghdad.
  B Mecca.
  C Medina.
  D Esfahan.

Travels in Asia and Africa

"From Tabuk the caravan travels with great speed night and day, for fear of this desert. Halfway through is the valley of al-Ukhaydir . . . One year the pilgrims suffered terribly here from the samoom-wind; the water-supplies dried up and the price of a single drink rose to a thousand dinars, but both seller and buyer perished. Their story is written on a rock in the valley."

—Ibn Battutah, from *The Travels*

6 **From the passage above, you can conclude that the climate near Tabuk is**
  A mild and sunny.
  B cold and wet.
  C hot and dry.
  D cool and pleasant.

7 **Which of the following people was known as a great traveler and geographer?**
  A Abu Bakr
  B 'Abbas
  C Omar Khayyám
  D Ibn Battutah

8 **Extended Response** Look back at Section 3 of this chapter and read the discussion of the Ottoman and Safavid empires again. Write a paragraph that notes one way in which the Ottoman Empire and the Safavid Empire were similar. Then describe two ways in which they were different.

The Eastern Mediterranean

Essential Question How has religion shaped the development of the nations of the Eastern Mediterranean?

? **What You Will Learn...**

In this chapter you will learn about the countries of the Eastern Mediterranean region—their physical geography, history, government, economy, and culture.

FOCUS ON READING AND WRITING

Setting a Purpose Good readers often set a purpose before they read. Ask yourself, "Why am I reading this chapter?" For example, you might want to learn about the geography of a country. Keeping your purpose in mind will help you focus on what is important. **See the lesson, Setting a Purpose, on page 165.**

Writing a Description As you read this chapter, you will collect information about the lands and people in this region. Later you will write a description for readers who have not visited the region.

EUROPE

Istanbul

Sea of Marmara

40°N

Izmir

Gediz

Menderes

Aegean Sea

- ✧ National capital
- • Other cities
- ▨ Some areas controlled by the Palestinian Authority

0   50   100 Miles

0   50   100 Kilometers

Projection: Lambert Azimuthal Equal-Area

Mediterranean Sea

EGYPT

Geography The Jordan River valley in Israel provides fertile soils for farming.

The Eastern Mediterranean: Political

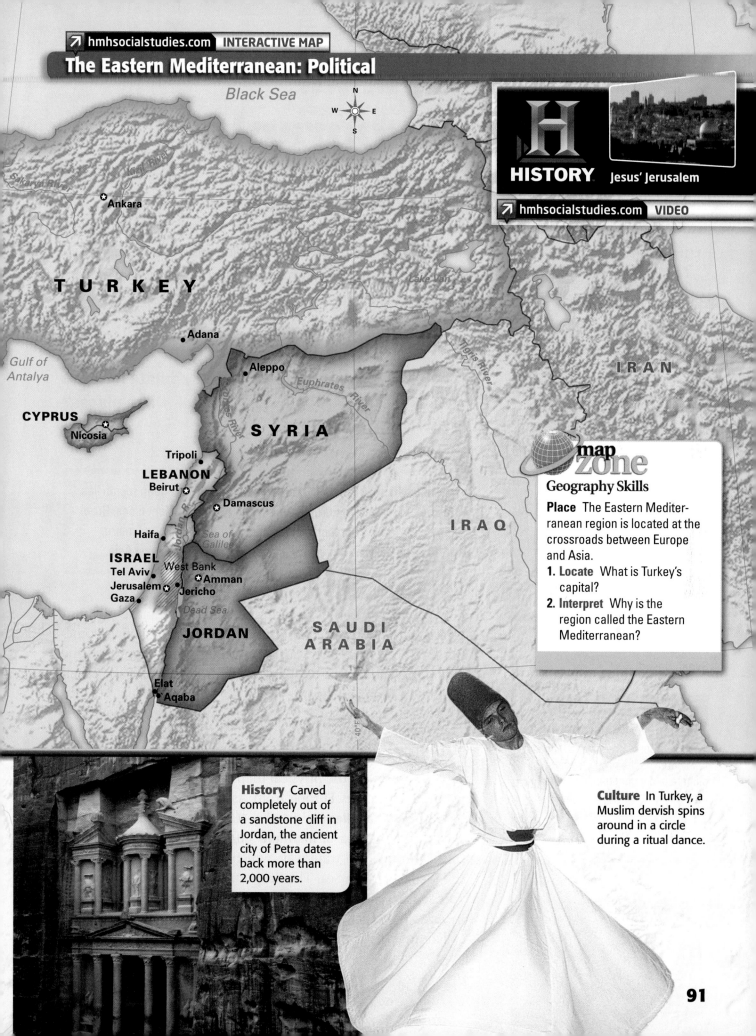

Black Sea

N
W   E
S

Sakarya River

● Ankara

T U R K E Y

Tigris River

Lake Van

Gulf of
Antalya

● Adana

Aleppo ●

Euphrates River

I R A N

CYPRUS
● Nicosia

S Y R I A

Tripoli ●

LEBANON
Beirut ●

● Damascus

Tigris River

Haifa ●

Sea of
Galilee

I R A Q

ISRAEL
Tel Aviv ●
Jerusalem ●
Gaza ●

West Bank
● Amman
Jericho

Dead Sea

JORDAN

**S A U D I
A R A B I A**

Elat ●
● Aqaba

map zone

Geography Skills

Place The Eastern Mediterranean region is located at the crossroads between Europe and Asia.

1. **Locate** What is Turkey's capital?
2. **Interpret** Why is the region called the Eastern Mediterranean?

History Carved completely out of a sandstone cliff in Jordan, the ancient city of Petra dates back more than 2,000 years.

Culture In Turkey, a Muslim dervish spins around in a circle during a ritual dance.

91

Physical Geography

What You Will Learn...

Main Ideas

1. The Eastern Mediterranean's physical features include the Bosporus, the Dead Sea, rivers, mountains, deserts, and plains.
2. The region's climate is mostly dry with little vegetation.
3. Important natural resources in the Eastern Mediterranean include valuable minerals and the availability of water.

The Big Idea

The Eastern Mediterranean, a region with a dry climate and valuable resources, sits in the middle of three continents.

Key Terms and Places

Dardanelles, *p. 92*
Bosporus, *p. 92*
Jordan River, *p. 93*
Dead Sea, *p. 93*
Syrian Desert, *p. 94*

hmhsocialstudies.com
TAKING NOTES

Use the graphic organizer online to take notes on the physical features, climate and vegetation, and natural resources of the region.

If YOU lived there...

You live in Izmir, Turkey, on the Aegean Sea, but are traveling into the far eastern part of the country called eastern Anatolia. At home you are used to a warm, dry Mediterranean climate. You are surprised by the colder and wetter climate you're experiencing. Two mountain ranges come together here, and you notice that the peaks are covered with snow.

How does geography affect climate in these two places?

BUILDING BACKGROUND The Eastern Mediterranean region lies at the crossroads of Europe, Africa, and Asia. In ancient times, Greek colonists settled here, and it was later part of the Roman Empire. Geographically, however, it is almost entirely in Southwest Asia.

The countries of the Eastern Mediterranean make up part of a larger region called Southwest Asia. This region is sometimes referred to as the Middle East. Europeans first called the region the Middle East to distinguish it from the Far East, which included China and Japan.

Physical Features

As you can see on the physical map on the next page, a narrow waterway separates Europe from Asia. This waterway is made up of the **Dardanelles** (dahrd-uhn-ELZ), the **Bosporus** (BAHS-puh-ruhs), and the **Sea of Marmara** (MAHR-muh-ruh). Large ships travel through the waterway, which connects the Black Sea to the Mediterranean Sea. The Bosporus also splits the country of Turkey into two parts, a small part lies in Europe and the rest in Asia. The Asian part of Turkey includes the large peninsula called Anatolia (a-nuh-TOH-lee-uh).

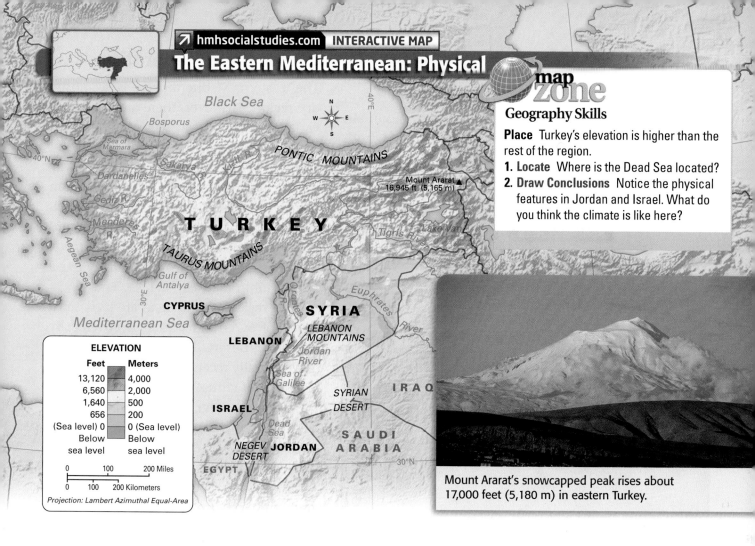

The Eastern Mediterranean: Physical

map zone

Geography Skills

Place Turkey's elevation is higher than the rest of the region.
1. **Locate** Where is the Dead Sea located?
2. **Draw Conclusions** Notice the physical features in Jordan and Israel. What do you think the climate is like here?

ELEVATION

Feet	Meters
13,120	4,000
6,560	2,000
1,640	500
656	200
(Sea level) 0	0 (Sea level)
Below sea level	Below sea level

Projection: Lambert Azimuthal Equal-Area

Mount Ararat's snowcapped peak rises about 17,000 feet (5,180 m) in eastern Turkey.

Rivers and Lakes

The **Jordan River** begins in Syria and flows south through Israel and Jordan. The river finally empties into a large lake called the **Dead Sea**. As its name suggests, the Dead Sea contains little life. Only bacteria lives in the lake's extremely salty water. The world's saltiest lake, its surface is 1,312 feet (400 m) below sea level—the lowest point on any continent.

Mountains and Plains

As you can see on the map, two mountain systems stretch across Turkey. The Pontic Mountains run east–west along the northern edge. The Taurus Mountains run east–west along the southern edge.

Heading south from Turkey and into Syria lies a narrow plain. The Euphrates River flows southeast from Turkey through the plains to Syria and beyond.

Dead Sea

Because of its high salt content, swimmers do not sink in the Dead Sea.

ANALYZING VISUALS
What appears on the shore of the Dead Sea?

93

Farther inland lies plateaus, hills, and valleys. A rift valley that begins in Africa extends northward into Syria. Hills rise on both sides of the rift. Two main mountain ridges run north–south. One runs from southwestern Syria through western Jordan. The other, closer to the coast, runs through Lebanon and Israel.

READING CHECK **Summarizing** What are the region's main physical features?

Satellite View

The Bosporus is a strait that divides the city of Istanbul, Turkey.

Istanbul and the Bosporus

Throughout history, geography has almost always determined the location of a city. Istanbul, Turkey, which sits between Europe and Asia, is no exception. In this satellite image the city of Istanbul appears light brown and white. The body of water that cuts through the city is a strait called the Bosporus. It separates the Sea of Marmara in the south with the Black Sea in the north. Historically, the Bosporus has served as a prized area for empires that have controlled the city. Today, the strait is a major shipping route.

Drawing Conclusions Why do you think the Bosporus was seen as a strategic location?

Climate and Vegetation

The Eastern Mediterranean is a mostly dry region. However, there are important variations. As you can see on the map on the next page, Turkey's Black Sea coast and the Mediterranean coast all the way to northern Israel have a Mediterranean climate. Much of interior Turkey experiences a steppe climate. Central Syria and lands farther south have a desert climate. A small area of northeastern Turkey has a humid subtropical climate.

The region's driest areas are its deserts. Much of Syria and Jordan is covered by the **Syrian Desert**. This desert of rock and gravel usually receives less than five inches (12.7 cm) of rainfall a year. Another desert, the Negev (NE-gev), lies in southern Israel. Here the temperatures can reach as high as 114°F (46°C), and annual rainfall totals barely two inches.

In such dry conditions, only shrubs grow scattered throughout the region's deserts. However, in other areas vegetation is plentiful. In Israel, more than 2,800 species of plants thrive throughout the country's various environments.

READING CHECK **Generalizing** What are climates like in the Eastern Mediterranean?

Natural Resources

Because the Eastern Mediterranean is so dry, water is a valuable resource. The people of this region are mostly farmers. The region lacks oil resources, but does have valuable minerals.

Land and Water

In this dry region the limited availability of water limits how land is used. Commercial farms can only grow crops where rain or irrigation provides enough water.

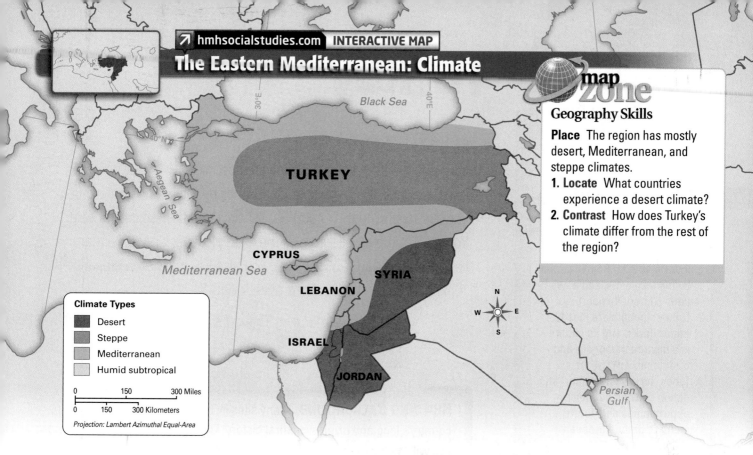

The Eastern Mediterranean: Climate

Geography Skills

Place The region has mostly desert, Mediterranean, and steppe climates.
1. **Locate** What countries experience a desert climate?
2. **Contrast** How does Turkey's climate differ from the rest of the region?

Climate Types
- Desert
- Steppe
- Mediterranean
- Humid subtropical

0   150   300 Miles
0   150   300 Kilometers

Projection: Lambert Azimuthal Equal-Area

In drier areas, subsistence farming and livestock herding are common. In the desert areas, available water supports a few nomadic herders, but no farming.

Mineral Resources

The region's resources include many minerals, including sulfur, mercury, and copper. Syria, Jordan, and Israel all produce phosphates—mineral salts that contain the element phosphorus. Phosphates are used to make fertilizers. This region also produces asphalt—the dark tarlike material used to pave streets.

READING CHECK **Drawing Conclusions** How do people use the region's mineral resources?

SUMMARY AND PREVIEW In this section you learned about the physical geography of the Eastern Mediterranean. Next, you will learn about Turkey.

Section 1 Assessment

Reviewing Ideas, Terms, and Places

1. **a. Describe** What makes the **Dead Sea** unusual?
   b. Explain What physical features separate Europe and Asia?
2. **a. Recall** What desert covers much of Syria and Jordan?
   b. Make Generalizations What is the climate of the Eastern Mediterranean like?
3. **a. Identify** What mineral resource is produced by Syria, Jordan, and Israel?
   b. Draw Conclusions Why must farmers in the region rely on irrigation?

Critical Thinking

4. **Summarizing** Using your notes, summarize the physical geography of Israel and Turkey. Use this chart to organize your notes.

Physical Features	
Turkey	Israel

FOCUS ON WRITING

5. **Describing the Physical Geography** What physical features would you include in your description? How would you describe the climate? Note your ideas.

Turkey

If YOU lived there...

Your cousins from central Turkey are coming to visit your hometown, Istanbul. You think your city is both beautiful and interesting. You like to stroll in the Grand Bazaar and smell the spices for sale. You admire the architecture of the Blue Mosque, whose walls are lined with thousands of tiny tiles. You also like to visit the elegant Topkapi Palace, where sultans once lived.

What sights will you show your cousins?

BUILDING BACKGROUND Many sites in Turkey reflect the country's long and diverse cultural history. Throughout the country you will find the ruins of ancient Greek temples and Roman palaces. You can also see magnificent early Christian buildings and art, as well as the palaces and mosques of Ottoman rulers.

What You Will Learn...

Main Ideas

1. Turkey's history includes invasion by the Romans, rule by the Ottomans, and a twentieth-century democracy.
2. Turkey's people are mostly ethnic Turks, and its culture is a mixture of modern and traditional.
3. Today, Turkey is a democratic nation seeking economic opportunities as a future member of the European Union.

The Big Idea

Although Turkey has historically been more Asian than European, its leaders are seeking to develop closer economic ties to Europe.

Key Terms and Places

Ankara, *p. 98*
Istanbul, *p. 99*
secular, *p. 99*

hmhsocialstudies.com
TAKING NOTES

Use the graphic organizer online to take notes on Turkey.

Close-up
Early Farming Village

The village of Çatal Hüyük in modern Turkey is one of the earliest farming villages discovered. Around 8,000 years ago, the village was home to about 5,000–6,000 people living in more than 1,000 houses. Villagers farmed, hunted and fished, traded with distant lands, and worshipped gods in special shrines.

Villagers used simple channels to move water to their fields.

Wheat, barley, and peas were some of the main crops grown outside the village.

History

Around 8,000 years ago the area that is now Turkey was home to one of the world's earliest farming villages. For centuries invasions from powerful empires shaped the region. By the 1920s Turkey was a democratic nation.

Invasions

When the Romans invaded the area, they captured the city of Byzantium and later renamed it Constantinople. Its location at the crossroads between Europe and Asia made Constantinople an important trading port. After the fall of Rome, Constantinople became the capital of the Byzantine Empire.

In the AD 1000s a nomadic people from central Asia called the Seljuk Turks invaded the area. In 1453 another Turkish people, the Ottoman Turks, captured the city of Constantinople and made it the capital of their Islamic empire.

The Ottoman Empire

During the 1500s and 1600s the Ottoman Empire was very powerful. The empire controlled territory in northern Africa, southwestern Asia, and southeastern Europe.

In World War I the Ottomans fought on the losing side. When the war ended, they lost most of their territory.

Houses were made of wood covered with mud. Since they didn't have doors, people entered on ladders through rooftop openings.

Inside their houses, villagers made the earliest-known wooden bowls and cups, pottery, and mirrors.

Some houses were built as shrines and had small statues of goddesses and large sculpted bulls' heads.

ANALYSIS SKILL ANALYZING VISUALS

How did farmers get water to their fields?

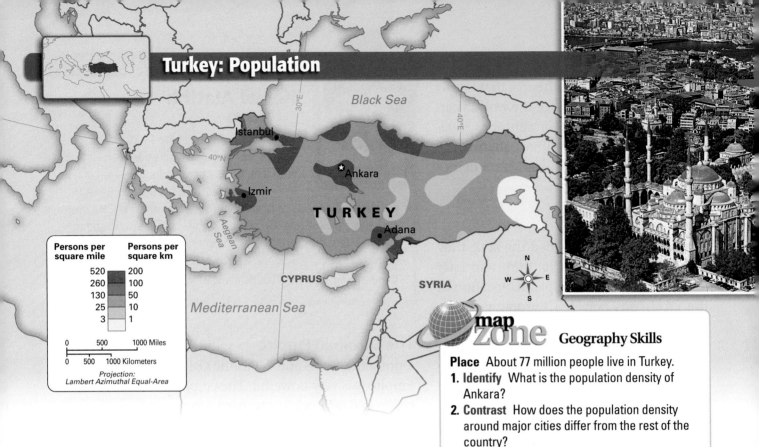

Turkey: Population

map zone **Geography Skills**

Place About 77 million people live in Turkey.
1. **Identify** What is the population density of Ankara?
2. **Contrast** How does the population density around major cities differ from the rest of the country?

Military officers then took over the government, led by a war hero, Mustafa Kemal. He later adopted the name Kemal Atatürk, which means Father of Turks. Atatürk created the democratic nation of Turkey and moved the capital to **Ankara** from Constantinople, which was renamed Istanbul.

Modern Turkey

Atatürk believed Turkey needed to modernize and adopt Western **methods** in order to be a strong nation. For example, he banned the fez, the traditional hat of Turkish men, and required that they wear European-style hats. Reforms urged women to stop wearing traditional veils. Women were also encouraged to vote, work, and hold office. Other ways Atatürk modernized Turkey included replacing the Arabic alphabet with the Latin alphabet, and adopting the metric system.

READING CHECK **Finding Main Ideas** How did Atatürk modernize Turkey?

People and Culture

Most of Turkey's people are mostly ethnic Turks. Kurds are the largest minority and make up 20 percent of the population.

Turkey's culture today is a reflection of some of Kemal Atatürk's changes. He created a cultural split between Turkey's urban middle class and rural villagers. The lifestyle and attitudes of middle-class Turks have much in common with those of the European middle class. In contrast, most rural Turks are more traditional. Islam strongly influences their attitudes on matters such as the role of women.

Turkish cooking features olives, vegetables, cheese, yogurt, and bread. Kebabs—grilled meats on a skewer—are a favorite Turkish dish.

READING CHECK **Contrasting** How are urban Turks different from rural Turks?

With about 10 million people, Istanbul, shown here, is Turkey's largest city.

Turkey Today

Turkey's government meets in the capital of Ankara, but **Istanbul** is Turkey's largest city. Istanbul's location will serve as an economic bridge to Europe as Turkey plans to join the European Union.

Government

Turkey's legislature is called the National Assembly. A president and a prime minister share executive power.

Although most of its people are Muslim, Turkey is a secular state. **Secular** means that religion is kept separate from government. For example, the religion of Islam allows a man to have up to four wives. However, by Turkish law a man is permitted to have just one wife. In recent years Islamic political parties have attempted to increase Islam's role in Turkish society.

Economy and Resources

As a member of the European Union, Turkey's economy and people would benefit by increased trade with Europe. Turkey's economy includes modern factories as well as village farming and craft making.

Among the most important industries are textiles and clothing, cement, and electronics. About 30 percent of Turkey's labor force works in agriculture. Grains, cotton, sugar beets, and hazelnuts are major crops.

Turkey is rich in natural resources, which include oil, coal, and iron ore. Water is also a valuable resource in the region. Turkey has spent billions of dollars building dams to increase its water supply. On one hand, these dams provide hydroelectricity. On the other hand, some of these dams have restricted the flow of river water into neighboring countries.

READING CHECK **Finding Main Ideas** What kind of government does Turkey have?

SUMMARY AND PREVIEW In this section you learned about Turkey's history, people, government, and economy. Next, you will learn about Israel.

Section 2 Assessment

Reviewing Ideas, Terms, and Places

1. **a. Recall** What city did both the Romans and Ottoman Turks capture?
   b. Explain In what ways did Atatürk try to modernize Turkey?
2. **a. Recall** What ethnic group makes up 20 percent of Turkey's population?
   b. Draw Conclusions What makes Turkey **secular**?
   c. Elaborate Why do you think Turkey wants to be a member of the European Union?

Critical Thinking

3. **Summarizing** Using the information in your notes, summarize Turkey's history and Turkey today.

Turkey's History	Turkey Today

FOCUS ON WRITING

4. **Describing Turkey** A description of Turkey might include details about its people, culture, government, and economy. Take notes on the details you think are important and interesting.

Israel

If YOU lived there...

When you were only six years old, your family moved to Israel from Russia. You are learning Hebrew in school, but your parents and grandparents still speak Russian at home. When you first moved here, your parents worked in an office building, but you now live on a farm where you grow oranges and tomatoes.

What do you like about living in Israel?

History

Do you know that Israel is often referred to as the Holy Land? Some people call Israel the Holy Land because it is home to sacred sites for three major religions—Judaism, Christianity, and Islam. According to the Bible, many events in Jewish history and in the life of Jesus happened in Israel.

The Holy Land

The Israelites, the descendants of the Hebrews and ancestors of the Jews, first established the kingdom of Israel about 1000 BC. It covered roughly the same area as the modern state of Israel. In the 60s BC the Roman Empire conquered the region, which was called Judea. After several Jewish revolts, the Romans forced many Jews to leave the region and renamed it Palestine in AD 135. This dispersal of the Jewish population is known as the **Diaspora**.

Muslims conquered Palestine in the mid-600s. However, from the late 1000s to the late 1200s, Christians from Europe launched a series of invasions of Palestine called the Crusades. The Crusaders captured the city of **Jerusalem** in 1099. In time the Crusaders were pushed out of the area. Palestine then became part of the Ottoman Empire. After World War I, it came under British control.

What You Will Learn...

Main Ideas

1. Israel's history includes the ancient Hebrews and the creation of the nation of Israel.
2. In Israel today, Jewish culture is a major part of daily life.
3. The Palestinian Territories are areas within Israel controlled partly by Palestinian Arabs.

The Big Idea

Israel and the Palestinian Territories are home to Jews and Arabs who continue to struggle over the region's land.

Key Terms and Places

Diaspora, *p. 100*
Jerusalem, *p. 100*
Zionism, *p. 101*
kosher, *p. 102*
kibbutz, *p. 102*
Gaza, *p. 103*
West Bank, *p. 103*

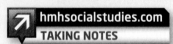
hmhsocialstudies.com
TAKING NOTES

Use the graphic organizer online to take notes on Israel and the Palestinian Territories.

Creation of Israel

Zionism, a nationalist movement calling for Jews to establish a Jewish state in their ancient homeland, began in Europe in the late 1800s. Tens of thousands of Jews from around the world began moving to the region.

In 1947 the United Nations voted to divide Palestine, then under British control, into Jewish and Arab states. While Arab countries rejected this plan, the Jews accepted it, and a year later created the State of Israel. Arab armies then invaded Israel. In a very short war, the Israelis defeated the Arabs.

After Israel's victory, many Palestinians fled to neighboring Arab countries. Israel and Arab countries have fought each other in several wars since then. Disputes between the two sides continue today.

READING CHECK **Summarizing** What two groups played a large role in Israel's history?

Israel Today

Jews from all over the world, including many who fled from Arab lands, have settled in Israel hoping to find peace and stability. Yet, they have faced continual conflicts with neighboring countries. Despite these problems, Israelis have built a modern, democratic country.

Primary Source

HISTORIC DOCUMENT
The Dead Sea Scrolls

Written by Jews about 2,000 years ago, the Dead Sea Scrolls include prayers, commentaries, letters, and passages from the Hebrew Bible. Hidden in caves near the Dead Sea, these scrolls were not found until 1947. Here are two passages from a prayer written on one of the scrolls.

❝ With knowledge shall I sing out my music, only for the glory of God, my harp, my lyre for His holiness established; the flute of my lips will I lift, His law its tuning fork. **❞**

❝ When first I begin campaign or journey, His name shall I bless; when first I set out or turn to come back; when I sit down or rise up, when I spread my bed, then shall I rejoice in Him. **❞**

ANALYSIS SKILL **ANALYZING PRIMARY SOURCES**

What does this prayer from the Dead Sea Scrolls reveal about the people who wrote it?

Government and Economy

Israel has a prime minister and a parliament—the Knesset. There are several major political parties and many smaller ones.

Israel's government has built a strong military. At age 18 most Israeli men and women must serve at least one year.

FOCUS ON READING
What do you want to find out about Israel today?

Jerusalem

The city of Jerusalem is sacred to three world religions—Judaism, Islam, and Christianity.

101

Israel's economy is modern and diverse. Items like high-technology equipment and cut diamonds are important exports. Israel has increased food production by irrigating farmland. Israel's economy also benefits from the millions of visitors who come to Israel to see the country's historic sites.

Cities, Diversity, and Languages

Most of Israel's population lives in cities. Jerusalem, the capital, and Tel Aviv are Israel's largest cities.

About 75 percent of Israel's population is Jewish. The rest of the country's people are mostly Arab. About three-fourths of Israeli Arabs are Muslim, but some are Christian. Israel's Jewish population includes Jews from all parts of the world. Many arrive not knowing Hebrew, one of Israel's official languages. To assist these new citizens, the government provides language classes. Israeli Arabs speak Arabic, Israel's other official language.

Culture and Rural Settlements

Israeli Jewish culture is rich in holidays and special foods. For Jews, the Sabbath, from sunset Friday until sundown Saturday, is a holy day. Yom Kippur, a very important Jewish holiday, is celebrated in the fall. Passover, in the spring, celebrates the Israelites' escape from captivity in ancient Egypt.

Because Judaism is a way of life, religious laws address every aspect of daily life, including what Jews should eat. These laws are ancient and appear in the Hebrew Bible. **Kosher**, which means "fit" in Hebrew, is the term used for food allowed under Jewish dietary laws. Jews eating a kosher diet do not eat pork or shellfish. They also do not mix meat and milk products.

About 100,000 Israeli Jews live in rural settlements. Each settlement, or **kibbutz** (ki-BOOHTS), is a large farm where people share everything in common. Israeli Jews live in more than 250 kibbutzim.

READING CHECK **Generalizing** What is Jewish culture in Israel like?

THE WORLD ALMANAC
Facts about Countries

Origin of Israel's Jewish Population

- ■ Non-Jewish
- ■ Jewish

Israel 51.3%
Non-Jewish 23.6%
Europe, the Americas, the Pacific 17.4%
Asia 3.2%
Africa 4.5%

↗ hmhsocialstudies.com

Jews from all over the world have settled in Israel. The graph above shows the percentages of Jews who migrated from different places. Non-Jews in Israel include Arabs who are Muslims, Christians, and Druze. This photo shows a Jewish teenager celebrating his bar mitzvah—a ceremony that acknowledges 13-year-old Jewish boys as adults in the community.

ANALYZING VISUALS According to the graph, what part of the world did the highest percentage of Israel's Jewish population emigrate from?

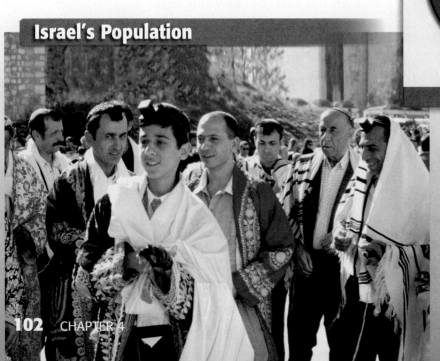

Israel's Population

The Palestinian Territories

In 1967 during the Six-Day War, Israel captured areas from Jordan and Egypt inhabited by Palestinian Arabs—Gaza, the West Bank, and East Jerusalem. Since then, Jews and Arabs have fought over the right to live in these areas.

Gaza

Gaza is a small, crowded piece of coastal land where more than a million Palestinians live. The area has almost no resources. However, citrus fruit is grown in irrigated fields. Unemployment is a problem for the Palestinians living in Gaza. In 2005, Israel withdrew from Gaza, which is now under Palestinian control.

West Bank

The **West Bank** is much larger than Gaza and has a population of about 2.4 million. It is mostly rural, but the territory has three large cities—Nablus, Hebron, and Ramallah. The West Bank's economy is mostly based on agriculture. Farmers rely on irrigation to grow their crops.

Since Israel took control of the West Bank, 280,000 Israelis moved into settlements there. Israelis and Palestinians dispute the territory. Peace agreements have tried to divide the land fairly. This conflict over land and terrorist attacks against Israel are the greatest sources of tension between Arabs and Israelis.

East Jerusalem

Other disputed land includes Israel's capital, Jerusalem. Control of Jerusalem is a difficult and emotional issue for Jews, Muslims, and Christians. The city has sites that are holy to all three religions. Areas of the old city are divided into Jewish, Muslim, and Christian neighborhoods.

Palestinians claim East Jerusalem as their capital. However, Israel annexed East

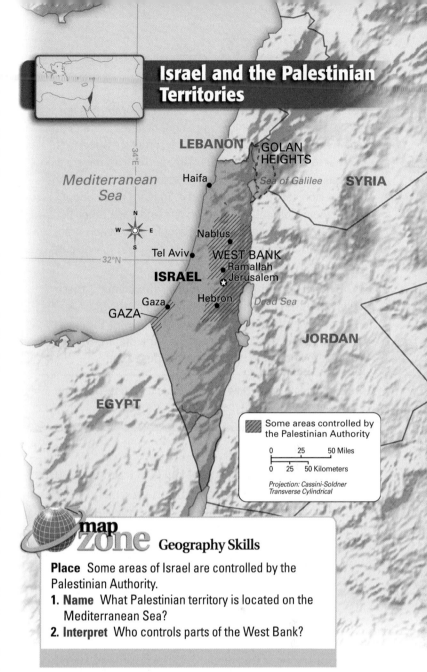

Israel and the Palestinian Territories

Geography Skills

Place Some areas of Israel are controlled by the Palestinian Authority.
1. **Name** What Palestinian territory is located on the Mediterranean Sea?
2. **Interpret** Who controls parts of the West Bank?

Jerusalem in 1980. Even before this, the Israeli government had moved its capital to Jerusalem from Tel Aviv. Most foreign countries have chosen not to recognize this transfer.

The Future of the Territories

In the 1990s Israel agreed to turn over parts of the territories to the Palestinians. In return, the Palestinian Authority agreed to recognize Israel and renounce terrorism. In 2005 the Israelis transferred Gaza to the Palestinian Authority.

hmhsocialstudies.com

ANIMATED GEOGRAPHY Explore the Holy Sites of Jerusalem.

Israeli Teens for Peace

Peace between Israeli Jews and Palestinian Arabs has not been easy in the past. Moreover, some believe peace in the region might be impossible ever to accomplish. But don't tell that to a group of 2,000 Jewish and Arab teenagers who are making a difference in Israel. These teens belong to an organization called Seeds of Peace. To learn more about each other's cultures and thus understand each other better, these teens meet regularly. For example, Jews teach Arabs Hebrew and Arabs teach Jews Arabic. They also participate in community service projects.

By bridging the gap between their two cultures, these teens hope they can one day live peacefully together. A Palestinian boy in the group expressed his hope for the future. He explained, "I realize that peace is not a dream when you truly get to know who you are making peace with."

Drawing Conclusions How are Jewish and Arab teenagers in Israel working toward peace?

The future of the peace process is uncertain. Some Palestinian groups have continued to commit acts of terrorism. Jewish Israelis fear they would be open to attack if they withdrew from the territories.

READING CHECK **Analyzing** Why have the Palestinian Territories been a source of conflict?

SUMMARY AND PREVIEW In this section you learned about Israel's history, people, government and economy, and the future of the Palestinian Territories. In the next section you will learn about the history and culture of Israel's neighbors—Syria, Lebanon, and Jordan.

Section 3 Assessment

hmhsocialstudies.com
ONLINE QUIZ

Reviewing Ideas, Terms, and Places

1. **a. Define** What is the **Diaspora**?
   b. Explain How did **Zionism** help create the nation of Israel?
2. **a. Recall** What is food allowed under Jewish dietary laws called?
   b. Draw Conclusions Why have Israeli leaders built up a strong military?
   c. Elaborate Why do you think Jews from around the world migrate to Israel?
3. **a. Identify** Which territory is fully controlled by Palestinians and which is partly controlled?
   b. Make Inferences How might, or might not, giving land to the Palestinians help or not help achieve peace in Israel?

Critical Thinking

4. **Categorizing** Use the chart below to separate your notes on Israel into categories.

Israel Today

Government	
Economy	
Diversity and Languages	
Jewish Culture	

FOCUS ON WRITING

5. **Describing Israel** What features make Israel unique? Take notes on how you might describe these features for your readers.

Social Studies Skills

Analyzing a Cartogram

Learn

For statistical information like population figures, geographers sometimes create a special map called a cartogram. A cartogram displays information about countries by the size shown for each country. In contrast, a political map like the one on the right reflects countries' actual physical size. Here are some guidelines for reading and analyzing a cartogram.

- Read the title of the map to determine the subject area covered.

- Compare the political map to the cartogram. Notice how some countries are much different in size on the cartogram compared to the map.

- Read the cartogram's legend and think about what the information means.

Practice

1 Which country has the largest population?

2 How is the size of Saudi Arabia's land area different from the size of its population?

3 Using the cartogram legend, what is the approximate population of Lebanon?

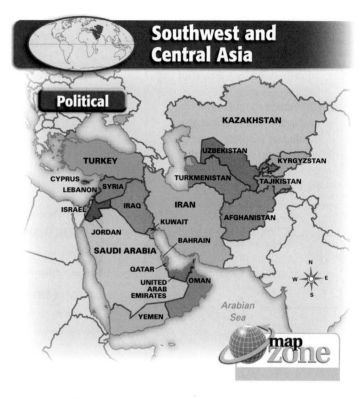

Southwest and Central Asia

Political

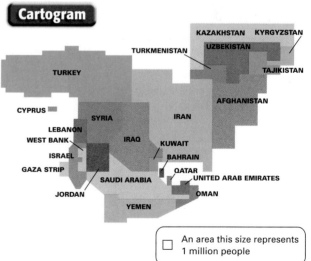

Cartogram

☐ An area this size represents 1 million people

Apply

Draw your own cartogram using the gross domestic product, or GDP, of each country in Southwest and Central Asia. Use a reference source or the Internet to find these statistics. Then determine the scale for sizing each country by GDP. For example, you might use one square unit of area per $10 billion or $100 billion. Countries with a high GDP should appear larger than countries with a low GDP.

Syria, Lebanon, and Jordan

What You Will Learn...

Main Ideas

1. Syria, once part of the Ottoman Empire, is an Arab country ruled by a powerful family.
2. Lebanon is recovering from civil war and its people are divided by religion.
3. Jordan has few resources and is home to Bedouins and Palestinian refugees.

The Big Idea

Syria, Lebanon, and Jordan are Arab nations coping with religious diversity.

Key Terms and Places

Damascus, *p. 106*
Beirut, *p. 108*
Bedouins, *p. 108*
Amman, *p. 109*

hmhsocialstudies.com
TAKING NOTES

Use the graphic organizer online to take notes on Syria, Lebanon, and Jordan.

If YOU lived there...

You live in Beirut, Lebanon. Your grandparents often tell you about the years before civil wars destroyed the heart of Beirut. The city then had wide boulevards, parks, and elegant shops. It was popular with tourists. Even though much of Beirut has been rebuilt, you find it hard to imagine what the city used to look like.

What hopes do you have for your country?

BUILDING BACKGROUND The histories of Lebanon, Syria, and Jordan have been tangled together since the countries gained independence in the 1940s. Syria is a large nation with a strong military. Syria has often dominated Lebanon's political life. Other conflicts in the region have also spilled over into Lebanon.

Look again at the map at the beginning of this chapter. Notice that Syria, Lebanon, and Jordan all border Israel. Because of their location near Israel, these countries have been involved in conflicts in the region. In addition, Syria, Lebanon, and Jordan also share a similar history, religion, and culture.

Syria

The capital of Syria, **Damascus**, is believed to be the oldest continuously inhabited city in the world. For centuries it was a leading regional trade center. Syria became part of the Ottoman Empire in the 1500s. After World War I, France controlled Syria. Syria finally became independent in the 1940s.

History and Government

From 1971 to 2000, the Syrian government was led by a dictator, Hafiz al-Assad. As president, Assad increased the size of Syria's military. He wanted to match Israel's military strength and protect his rule from his political enemies within Syria. After Assad's death in 2000, his son, Bashar, was elected president. One of Bashar al-Assad's main goals was to improve Syria's economy.

Syria has a socialist government, which owns the country's oil refineries, larger electrical plants, railroads, and some factories. Syria's key manufactured goods are textiles, food products, and chemicals. Agriculture remains important. Syria has only small deposits of oil and natural gas. It is rich in iron ore, basalt, and phosphates.

Syria's People

Syria's population of more than 20 million is about 90 percent Arab. The other 10 percent includes Kurds and Armenians. About 74 percent of Syrians are Sunni Muslim. About 16 percent are Druze and Alawites, members of small religious groups related to Islam. About 10 percent of Syrians are Christian. There are also small Jewish communities in some cities.

READING CHECK Analyzing How is Syria's economy organized?

Lebanon

Lebanon is a small, mountainous country on the Mediterranean coast. It is home to several different groups of people. At times these different groups have fought.

Lebanon's History and People

During the Ottoman period, many religious and ethnic minority groups settled in Lebanon. After World War I, France controlled Lebanon and Syria. Lebanon finally gained independence in the 1940s. Even so, some aspects of French culture influenced Lebanese culture. For example, in addition to Arabic, many Lebanese also speak French.

Lebanon's people are overwhelmingly Arab, but they are divided by religion. Most Lebanese are either Muslim or Christian. Each of those groups is divided into several smaller groups. Muslims are divided into Sunni, Shia, and Druze.

The Maronites are the largest of the Christian groups in the country. Over time, however, Muslims have become Lebanon's majority religious group.

FOCUS ON READING
Look at the headings under Lebanon to set your purpose for reading these paragraphs.

Ancient Syria

In Syria today, ruins of an ancient Roman trading center still stand. The Romans called the city Palmyra, meaning "city of palm trees."

People of Syria, Lebanon, and Jordan

The people of Syria, Lebanon, and Jordan share many cultural traits. For example, most people living in this region are Arab and practice Islam.

ANALYZING VISUALS What can you see in these photos that tells you about daily life in the region?

Syria In Syria drinking tea is an important part of Arab culture. Many Syrians, like this carpet seller, drink tea every day with family and friends.

Conflict and Civil War

After independence, Christians and Muslims shared power in Lebanon. Certain government positions were held by different religious groups. For example, the president was always a Maronite. However, over time tensions between Christians and Muslims mounted.

In the 1970s civil war broke out. Lebanon's Muslims, including many Palestinian refugees, fought against Christians. Syria, Israel, and other countries became involved in the conflict. During the fighting, many people died and the capital, **Beirut**, was badly damaged. Warfare lasted until 1990.

After 1990, Syria continued to maintain a strong influence in Lebanon. In fact, Syrian troops stayed in Lebanon until they were pressured to leave in 2005. In 2006, cross border attacks by Lebanese guerrillas against Israel led to fighting between the two countries.

READING CHECK Drawing Conclusions
What has caused divisions in Lebanese society?

Jordan

Jordan's short history has been full of conflict. The country has few resources and several powerful neighbors.

Jordan's History and Government

The country of Jordan was created after World War I. The British controlled the area and named an Arab prince as the monarch of the new country. In the 1940s the country became fully independent.

At the time of its independence, Jordan's population was small. Most Jordanians lived a nomadic or semi-nomadic life. Hundreds of thousands of Palestinian Arab refugees fled Israel and came to live in Jordan. From 1952 to 1999 Jordan was ruled by King Hussein. The king enacted some democratic reforms in the 1990s.

Jordan's People and Resources

Many of Jordan's people are **Bedouins**, or Arabic-speaking nomads who mostly live in the deserts of Southwest Asia. Jordan produces phosphates, cement, and potash. Tourism and banking are becoming impor-

Lebanon After more than two decades of civil war, Lebanon's people are rebuilding their capital, Beirut. The city's people now enjoy a new public square.

Jordan Jordan's people value education and equal rights for women. Jordanian teenagers like these girls are required to attend school until age 15.

tant industries. Jordan depends on economic aid from the oil-rich Arab nations and the United States. **Amman**, the capital, is Jordan's largest city. Jordanian farmers grow fruits and vegetables and raise sheep and goats. A shortage of water is a crucial resource issue for Jordan.

READING CHECK **Summarizing** How did King Hussein affect Jordan's history?

SUMMARY AND PREVIEW In this section you learned about the history, government, and people of Syria, Lebanon, and Jordan. In the next chapter you will learn about Iraq and Iran and the countries of the Arabian Peninsula—Saudi Arabia, Kuwait, Bahrain, Qatar, the United Arab Emirates, Yemen, and Oman.

Section 4 Assessment

Reviewing Ideas, Terms, and Places

1. **a. Recall** What is the capital of Syria?
   b. Explain What does Syria's government own?
   c. Elaborate Why did Hafiz al-Assad want to increase the size of Syria's military?
2. **a. Identify** What European country ruled Lebanon after World War I?
   b. Analyze How was **Beirut** damaged?
   c. Elaborate What is the history of political divisions between religious groups in Lebanon's government?
3. **a. Define** Who are the **Bedouins**?
   b. Summarize Who provides economic aid to Jordan?

Critical Thinking

4. **Comparing and Contrasting** Use your notes to identify similarities and differences among the people in the three countries.

	Similarities	Differences
Syria		
Lebanon		
Jordan		

FOCUS ON WRITING

5. **Describing Syria, Lebanon, and Jordan** If you could only include two details about these countries, what would they be?

from
Red Brocade

by Naomi Shihab Nye

Drinking tea with guests is a traditional Arab custom.

GUIDED READING

WORD HELP

pine nuts a small sweet edible seed of some pine trees

brocade a heavy fabric of silk, cotton, or wool woven with a raised design, often using metallic threads

mint a plant with aromatic leaves that grows in northern temperate regions and is often used for flavoring

❶ Arabs are a cultural group that speak Arabic. They live mostly in Southwest Asia and North Africa.

❷ When entertaining, Arabs often sit on pillows on the floor.

About the Poem *In "Red Brocade," Arab-American writer Naomi Shihab Nye tells about an Arab custom. As a part of this custom, strangers are given a special welcome by those who meet them at the door. Since the poet is Arab-American, she is suggesting that we go "back to that" way of accepting new people.*

AS YOU READ Identify the special way that Arab people in Southwest Asia greet strangers at their door.

The Arabs ❶ used to say,
When a stranger appears at your
    door,
feed him for three days
before asking who he is,
where he's come from,
where he's headed.
That way, he'll have strength
enough to answer.
Or, by then you'll be
such good friends
you don't care.

Let's go back to that.
Rice? Pine nuts?

Here, take the red brocade
    pillow. ❷
My child will serve water
to your horse.

No, I was not busy when you
    came!
I was not preparing to be busy.
That's the armor everyone put
    on to pretend they had a purpose
in the world.

I refuse to be claimed.
Your plate is waiting.
We will snip fresh mint
into your tea.

Connecting Literature to Geography

1. Describing What details in the second verse show us that the Arab speaker is extending a warm welcome to the stranger?

2. Comparing and Contrasting Do you think this poem about greeting a stranger at the door would be different if it had taken place in another region of the world? Explain your answer.

Chapter Review

Geography's Impact
video series
Review the video to answer the closing question:
Why do you think the conflict in Jerusalem today is difficult to solve?

Visual Summary

Use the visual summary below to help you review the main ideas of the chapter.

QUICK FACTS

The eastern Mediterranean is a dry region, and water is a key resource.

The region's history includes conflict between three major religions.

Most people living in the eastern Mediterranean are Arab Muslims.

Reviewing Vocabulary, Terms, and Places

Fill in the blanks with the correct term or place from this chapter.

1. The_____ is the lowest point on any continent and the world's saltiest body of water.

2. A desert located in southern Israel is called the_____.

3. A_____is a way of doing something.

4. Turkey's largest city is_____.

5. _____means that religion is kept separate from government.

6. The dispersal of the Jewish population is known as_____.

7. A_____is a large farm where people share everything in common.

8. _____is Lebanon's capital that was badly damaged during the country's civil war.

Comprehension and Critical Thinking

SECTION 1 *(Pages 92–95)*

9. **a. Describe** How is the Eastern Mediterranean considered a part of the Middle East?

   b. Draw Conclusions How would the region's dry climates affect where people lived?

   c. Predict What would happen if the region's people did not have access to water?

SECTION 2 *(Pages 96–99)*

10. **a. Recall** How was control of Constantinople important?

    b. Make Inferences How did modernization change Turkey?

    c. Elaborate Why do you think Turkey wants to be a member of the European Union?

SECTION 3 *(Pages 100–104)*

11. **a. Define** What is Zionism?

SECTION 3 (continued)

b. Make Inferences Why does Israel need a strong military?

c. Elaborate How has Israel's history affected the country today?

SECTION 4 (Pages 106–109)

12. a. Identify What is the capital of Syria? Why is it historically significant?

b. Analyze Why did Lebanon have a civil war?

c. Evaluate How do you think Jordan survives with so few resources?

Using the Internet

13. Creating an Exhibit Jerusalem is a city rich in tradition, history, and culture dating back thousands of years. Through the online book, travel back in time to historic Jerusalem. Explore its history, archaeology, buildings, daily life, food, and more. Then create a museum exhibit to highlight the artifacts, information, and stories you encounter in your journey through Jerusalem's past. Some things you may want to include are artifacts, models, time lines, maps, small placards providing information, and an exhibit guide for viewers.

↗ **hmhsocialstudies.com**

Social Studies Skill

Analyzing a Cartogram *Use the cartogram and political map of Southwest and Central Asia on this chapter's Social Studies Skills page to answer the following questions.*

14. Why do you think Turkey's size on the political map is similar to its size on the cartogram?

15. How does the cartogram show the high population density of Israel and the Palestinian Territories?

16. From looking at the cartogram, is the population density of Kazakhstan, high or low? Explain your answer.

Map Activity

17. The Eastern Mediterranean On a separate sheet of paper, match the letters on the map with their correct labels.

Bosporus   Negev

Jordan River   Euphrates River

Dead Sea

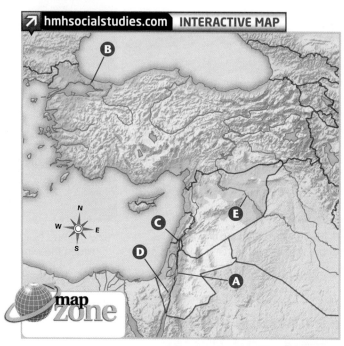

↗ **hmhsocialstudies.com** INTERACTIVE MAP

FOCUS ON READING AND WRITING

Setting a Purpose *Use the information in this chapter to answer the following questions.*

18. How does setting a purpose before you read help you become a better reader?

19. How is your purpose in reading this chapter different from your purpose when you read a newspaper comic strip?

20. How can looking at headings and main idea statements help you set a purpose for reading?

21. Writing a Description Look over your notes and choose one Eastern Mediterranean country to describe. Organize your notes by topic—physical features, people, culture and government. Then, write a one-to-two-paragraph description of the country. Include information you think would be interesting to someone who knows nothing about the country. Add details that will help your readers picture the country.

Standardized Test Prep

DIRECTIONS: Read questions 1 through 7 and write the letter of the best response. Then read question 8 and write your own well-constructed response.

1 The climate of most of Israel, Jordan, and Syria is

A desert.

B steppe.

C humid subtropical.

D Mediterranean.

2 Turkey's government wants to be more like countries on what continent?

A Asia

B South America

C Australia

D Europe

3 Jews and Palestinian Arabs make up most of what country's population?

A Jordan

B Israel

C Turkey

D Lebanon

4 What city is sacred to Jews, Muslims, and Christians?

A Istanbul

B Tel Aviv

C Jerusalem

D Damascus

5 Most people living in Syria, Lebanon, and Jordan are

A Arabs.

B Jews.

C European.

D Christians.

Turkey: Physical Geography

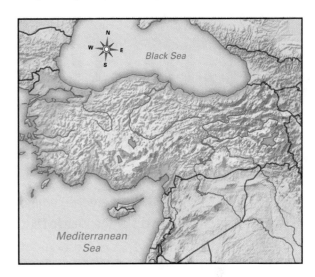

6 Based on the map above, what physical features surround most of Turkey?

A mountains

B seas

C plateaus

D lakes

7 Many of Jordan's people are

A Bedouins.

B Lebanese.

C Jewish.

D Turkish.

8 **Extended Response** Based on the map above and your knowledge of the region, write a brief essay explaining how Turkey's location has influenced its history and the country today.

The Arabian Peninsula, Iraq, and Iran

Essential Question What are the common cultural and geographic characteristics of the Islamic Middle East?

What You Will Learn...

In this chapter you will learn about the Arabian Peninsula. You will also learn about the history and people of Iraq and Iran.

FOCUS ON READING AND WRITING

Re-Reading Sometimes a single reading is not enough to fully understand a passage of text. If you feel like you do not fully understand something you have read, it may help to re-read the passage more slowly. **See the lesson, Re-Reading, on page 166.**

Creating a Geographer's Log You are a geographer taking a journey of discovery through the Arabian Peninsula, Iraq, and Iran. As you travel from place to place, create a geographer's log, a written record of what you see on your journey.

Mediterranean Sea

AFRICA

- ✪ National capital
- ● Other cities

```
0        150        300 Miles
0    150    300 Kilometers
```
Projection: Lambert Conformal Conic

map zone

Geography Skills

Place The countries of the Arabian Peninsula, Iraq, and Iran are centered around the Persian Gulf.
1. **Locate** What is the capital of Saudi Arabia?
2. **Analyze** Approximately how many miles would you have to travel from Baghdad to Kuwait City?

Culture Islam is a major part of the culture in every country in the region. These women pray at a mosque in Mecca, Saudi Arabia.

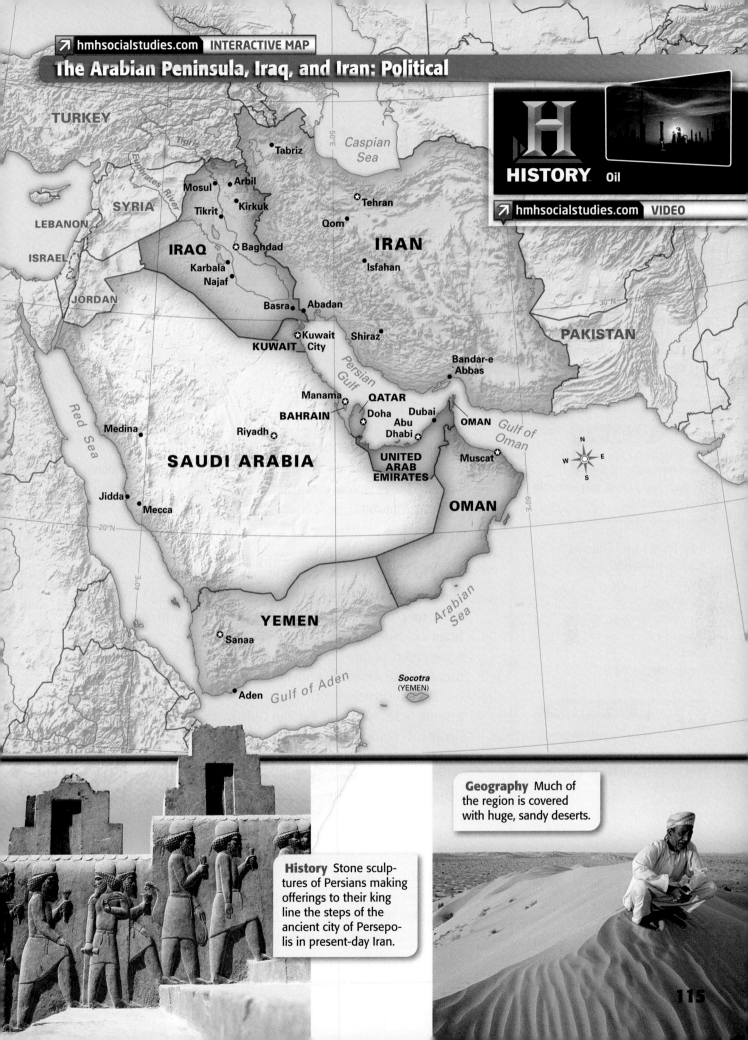

The Arabian Peninsula, Iraq, and Iran: Political

HISTORY Oil

↗ hmhsocialstudies.com | VIDEO

TURKEY

SYRIA

LEBANON

ISRAEL

JORDAN

Tigris

Euphrates River

Mosul

Arbil

Tikrit

Kirkuk

IRAQ

Baghdad

Karbala

Najaf

Basra

Tabriz

Caspian Sea

50°E

Tehran

Qom

IRAN

Isfahan

Abadan

30°N

PAKISTAN

Shiraz

Bandar-e Abbas

KUWAIT

Kuwait City

Persian Gulf

Manama

BAHRAIN

QATAR

Doha

Abu Dhabi

Dubai

OMAN

Gulf of Oman

Red Sea

Medina

Riyadh

SAUDI ARABIA

Jidda

Mecca

20°N

40°E

UNITED ARAB EMIRATES

Muscat

60°E

OMAN

N
W   E
S

YEMEN

Sanaa

Arabian Sea

Aden

Gulf of Aden

Socotra (YEMEN)

Geography Much of the region is covered with huge, sandy deserts.

History Stone sculptures of Persians making offerings to their king line the steps of the ancient city of Persepolis in present-day Iran.

Physical Geography

What You Will Learn...

Main Ideas

1. Major physical features of the Arabian Peninsula, Iraq, and Iran are desert plains and mountains.
2. The region has a dry climate and little vegetation.
3. Most of the world is dependent on oil, a resource that is exported from this region.

The Big Idea

The Arabian Peninsula, Iraq, and Iran make up a mostly desert region with very valuable oil resources.

Key Terms and Places

Arabian Peninsula, *p. 116*
Persian Gulf, *p. 116*
Tigris River, *p. 116*
Euphrates River, *p. 116*
oasis, *p. 118*
wadis, *p. 119*
fossil water, *p. 119*

hmhsocialstudies.com
TAKING NOTES

Use the graphic organizer online to take notes on the region's physical geography.

If YOU lived there...

You are in a plane flying over the vast desert areas of the Arabian Peninsula. As you look down, you see some tents of desert nomads around trees of an oasis. Sometimes you can see a truck or a line of camels crossing the dry, rocky terrain. A shiny oil pipeline stretches for miles in the distance.

What is life like for people in the desert?

BUILDING BACKGROUND Iran, Iraq, and the countries of the Arabian Peninsula are part of a region sometimes called the "Middle East." This region lies at the intersection of Africa, Asia, and Europe. Much of the region is dry and rugged.

Physical Features

Did you know that not all deserts are made of sand? The **Arabian Peninsula** has the largest sand desert in the world. But it also has huge expanses of desert covered with bare rock or gravel. These wide desert plains are a common landscape in the region that includes the Arabian Peninsula, Iraq, and Iran.

The countries of this region appear on the map in sort of a semicircle, with the **Persian Gulf** in the center. The Arabian Peninsula is also bounded by the Gulf of Oman, the Arabian Sea, and the Red Sea. The Caspian Sea borders Iran to the north.

The region contains four main landforms: rivers, plains, plateaus, and mountains. The **Tigris** (TY-gruhs) and **Euphrates** (yooh-FRAY-teez) rivers flow across a low, flat plain in Iraq. They join together before they reach the Persian Gulf. The Tigris and Euphrates are what are known as exotic rivers, or rivers that begin in humid regions and then flow through dry areas. The rivers create a narrow fertile area, which in ancient times was called Mesopotamia, or the "land between the rivers." The Arabian Peninsula has no permanent rivers.

The vast, dry expanse of the Arabian Peninsula is covered by plains in the east. The peninsula's desert plains are covered with sand in the south and volcanic rock in the north. As you can see on the map, the surface of the peninsula rises gradually from the Persian Gulf to the Red Sea. Near the Red Sea the landscape becomes one of plateaus and mountains, with almost no coastal plain. The highest point on the peninsula is in the mountains of Yemen.

Plateaus and mountains also cover most of Iran. In fact, Iran is one of the world's most mountainous countries. In the west, the land climbs sharply to form the Zagros Mountains. The Elburz Mountains and the Kopet-Dag lie in the north. Historically, this mountainous landscape has kept towns there isolated from each other.

FOCUS ON READING After you read this paragraph, re-read it to make sure you understand Iran's landscape.

READING CHECK **Summarizing** What are the major physical features of this area?

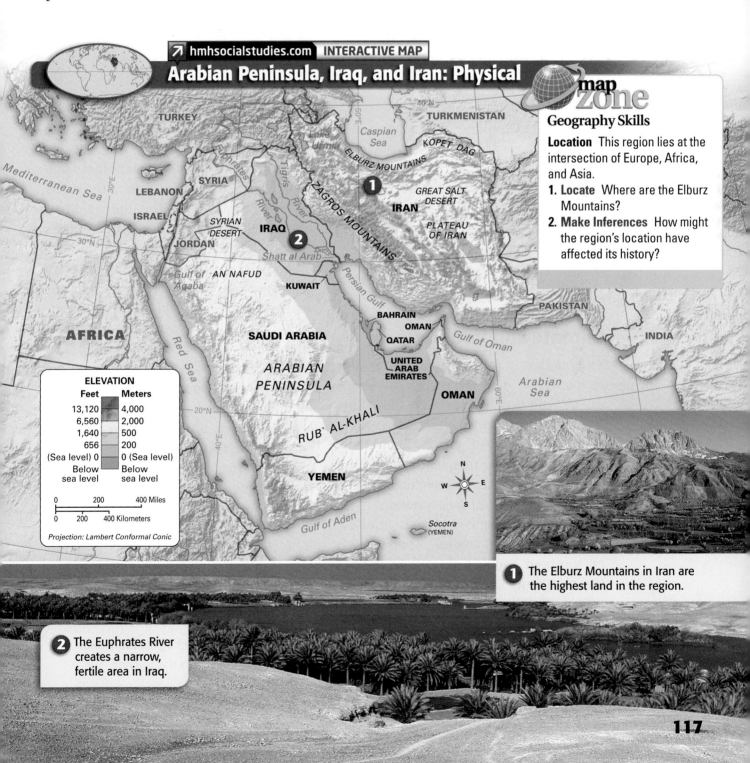

↗ hmhsocialstudies.com **INTERACTIVE MAP**

Arabian Peninsula, Iraq, and Iran: Physical

Geography Skills

Location This region lies at the intersection of Europe, Africa, and Asia.

1. **Locate** Where are the Elburz Mountains?
2. **Make Inferences** How might the region's location have affected its history?

TURKEY
Caspian Sea
Lake Urmia
TURKMENISTAN
KOPET DAG
ELBURZ MOUNTAINS
Mediterranean Sea
SYRIA
LEBANON
ISRAEL
ZAGROS MOUNTAINS
GREAT SALT DESERT
IRAN ❶
PLATEAU OF IRAN
SYRIAN DESERT
IRAQ ❷
JORDAN
Shatt al Arab
Gulf of Aqaba
AN NAFUD
KUWAIT
Persian Gulf
PAKISTAN
INDIA
AFRICA
Red Sea
BAHRAIN
OMAN
QATAR
SAUDI ARABIA
UNITED ARAB EMIRATES
Gulf of Oman
Arabian Sea
ARABIAN PENINSULA
OMAN
RUB' AL-KHALI
YEMEN
Gulf of Aden
Socotra (YEMEN)

ELEVATION

Feet	Meters
13,120	4,000
6,560	2,000
1,640	500
656	200
(Sea level) 0	0 (Sea level)
Below sea level	Below sea level

0   200   400 Miles
0   200   400 Kilometers

Projection: Lambert Conformal Conic

❶ The Elburz Mountains in Iran are the highest land in the region.

❷ The Euphrates River creates a narrow, fertile area in Iraq.

117

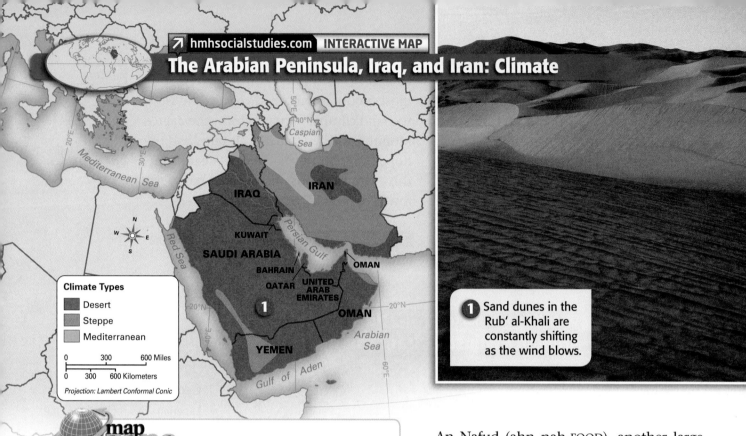

The Arabian Peninsula, Iraq, and Iran: Climate

Climate Types

- Desert
- Steppe
- Mediterranean

0   300   600 Miles
0   300   600 Kilometers

Projection: Lambert Conformal Conic

1 Sand dunes in the Rub' al-Khali are constantly shifting as the wind blows.

map zone Geography Skills

Regions Most of this region has a desert climate.
1. **Identify** Which countries have only desert climates?
2. **Interpret** Look back at the physical map. How do landforms in the region influence climate?

Climate and Vegetation

As you have already read, most of this region has a desert climate. The desert can be both very hot and very cold. In the summer, afternoon temperatures regularly climb to over 100°F (38°C). During the night, however, the temperature may drop quickly. Nighttime temperatures in the winter sometimes dip below freezing.

The world's largest sand desert, the Rub' al-Khali (ROOB ahl-KAH-lee), covers much of southern Saudi Arabia. *Rub' al-Khali* means "Empty Quarter," a name given to the area because there is so little life there. Sand dunes in the desert can rise to 800 feet (245 m) high and stretch for nearly 200 miles! In northern Saudi Arabia is the

An Nafud (ahn nah-FOOD), another large desert. These deserts are among the driest places in the world. The Rub' al-Khali receives an average of less than 4 inches (10 cm) of rainfall each year.

Some plateau and mountain areas do get winter rains or snow. These higher areas generally have semiarid steppe climates. Some mountain peaks receive more than 50 inches (130 cm) of rain per year.

Rainfall supports vegetation in some parts of the region. Trees are common in mountain regions and in scattered desert oases. An **oasis** is a wet, fertile area in a desert that forms where underground water bubbles to the surface. Most desert plants have adapted to survive without much rain. For example, the shrubs and grasses that grow on the region's dry plains have roots that either grow deep or spread out far to capture as much water as possible. Still, some places in the region are too dry or too salty to support any vegetation.

READING CHECK Finding the Main Idea
What climate dominates this region?

Resources

Water is one of the region's two most valuable resources. However, this resource is very scarce. In some places in the desert, springs provide water. At other places, water can come from wells dug into dry streambeds called **wadis**. Modern wells can reach water deep underground, but the groundwater in these wells is often fossil water. **Fossil water** is water that is not being replaced by rainfall. Wells that pump fossil water will eventually run dry.

While water is scarce, the region's other important resource, oil, is plentiful. Oil exports bring great wealth to the countries that have oil fields. Most of the oil fields are located near the shores of the Persian Gulf. However, although oil is plentiful now, it cannot be replaced once it is taken from Earth. Too much drilling for oil now may cause problems in the future because most countries of the region are not rich in other resources. Iran is an exception with its many mineral deposits.

READING CHECK **Summarizing** What are the region's important resources?

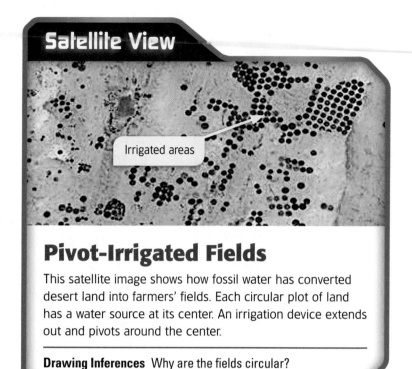

Satellite View

Irrigated areas

Pivot-Irrigated Fields

This satellite image shows how fossil water has converted desert land into farmers' fields. Each circular plot of land has a water source at its center. An irrigation device extends out and pivots around the center.

Drawing Inferences Why are the fields circular?

SUMMARY AND PREVIEW The Arabian Peninsula, Iraq, and Iran form a desert region with significant oil resources. Next, you will learn more about the countries of the Arabian Peninsula.

Section 1 Assessment

hmhsocialstudies.com
ONLINE QUIZ

Reviewing Ideas, Terms, and Places

1. **a. Describe** Where was Mesopotamia?
   b. Explain Where are the region's mountains?
   c. Elaborate Why do you think the **Tigris** and **Euphrates** rivers were so important in history?

2. **a. Recall** What parts of the region receive the most rainfall?
   b. Explain How have desert plants adapted to their environment?

3. **a. Define** What is **fossil water**?
   b. Make Inferences How do you think resources in the region influence where people live?
   c. Predict What might happen to the oil-rich countries if their oil was used up or if people found a new energy source to replace oil?

Critical Thinking

4. **Comparing and Contrasting** Using your notes and a graphic organizer like the one here, note physical characteristics unique to each area. Then list characteristics shared by all three areas.

Arabian Peninsula	Iraq	Iran
All		

FOCUS ON WRITING

5. **Describing Physical Geography** Take notes on the physical features, climate and vegetation, and resources that you could record in your log. What would you see and feel if you were in this region?

The Arabian Peninsula

What You Will Learn...

Main Ideas

1. Islamic culture and an economy greatly based on oil influence life in Saudi Arabia.
2. Most other Arabian Peninsula countries are monarchies influenced by Islamic culture and oil resources.

The Big Idea

Most countries of the Arabian Peninsula share three main characteristics: Islamic religion and culture, monarchy as a form of government, and valuable oil resources.

Key Terms

Shia, *p. 120*
Sunni, *p. 120*
OPEC, *p. 121*

hmhsocialstudies.com

TAKING NOTES

Use the graphic organizer online to take notes on the countries of the Arabian Peninsula.

If **YOU** lived there...

You are a financial adviser to the ruler of Oman. Your country has been making quite a bit of money from oil exports. However, you worry that your economy is too dependent on oil. You think Oman's leaders should consider expanding the economy. Oman is a small country, but it has beautiful beaches, historic palaces and mosques, and colorful markets.

How would you suggest expanding the economy?

BUILDING BACKGROUND Oman and all the countries of the Arabian Peninsula have valuable oil resources. In addition to oil, these countries share two basic characteristics: Islamic religion and monarchy as a form of government. The largest country, and the one with the most influence in the region, is Saudi Arabia.

Saudi Arabia

Saudi Arabia is by far the largest of the countries of the Arabian Peninsula. It is also a major religious and cultural center and has one of the region's strongest economies.

People and Customs

Nearly all Saudis are Arabs and speak Arabic. Their culture is strongly influenced by Islam, a religion founded in Saudi Arabia by Muhammad. Islam is based on submitting to God and on messages Muslims believe God gave to Muhammad. These messages are written in the Qur'an, the holy book of Islam.

Nearly all Saudis follow one of two main branches of Islam. **Shia** Muslims believe that true interpretation of Islamic teaching can only come from certain religious and political leaders called imams. **Sunni** Muslims believe in the ability of the majority of the community to interpret Islamic teachings. About 85 percent of Saudi Muslims are Sunni.

$$y = -2x(x^2 - 2x + 4) + 3x^3$$

Muslim Contributions to Math

During the early centuries of the Middle Ages, European art, literature, and science declined. However, during this same period, Muslim scholars made important advances in literature, art, medicine, and mathematics.

Our familiar system of numerals, which we call Arabic, was first created in India. However, it was Muslim thinkers who introduced that system to Europe. They also developed algebra and made advances in geometry. Muslims used math to advance the study of astronomy and physics. Muslim geographers calculated distances between cities, longitudes and latitudes, and the direction from one city to another. Muslim scientists even defined ratios and used mathematics to explain the appearance of rainbows.

Drawing Inferences Why do we need math to study geography?

Islam influences Saudi Arabia's culture in many ways. For example, in part because Islam requires modesty, Saudi clothing keeps arms and legs covered. Men usually wear a long, loose shirt. They often wear a cotton headdress held in place with a cord. Saudi women traditionally wear a black cloak and veil in public, although some now wear Western-style clothing.

Saudi laws and customs limit women's activities. For example, a woman rarely appears in public without her husband or a male relative. Also, women are not allowed to drive cars. However, women can own and run businesses in Saudi Arabia.

Government and Economy

Saudi Arabia is a monarchy. Members of the Saud family have ruled Saudi Arabia since 1932. Most government officials are relatives of the king. The king may ask members of his family, Islamic scholars, and tribal leaders for advice on decisions.

The country has no elected legislature. Local officials are elected, but only men are allowed to vote.

Saudi Arabia's economy is based on oil. In fact, Saudi Arabia has the world's largest reserves, or supplies, of oil and is the world's leading exporter of oil. Because it controls so much oil, Saudi Arabia is an influential member of the Organization of Petroleum Exporting Countries, or OPEC. **OPEC** is an international organization whose members work to influence the price of oil on world markets by controlling the supply.

Oil has brought wealth to Saudi Arabia. The country has a sizable middle class, and the government provides free health care and education to its citizens. Even so, Saudi Arabia faces economic challenges. For example, it must import much of its food because freshwater needed for farming is scarce. The country uses desalination plants to remove salt from seawater, but this requires an extremely expensive **procedure**.

ACADEMIC VOCABULARY

procedure a series of steps taken to accomplish a task

FOCUS ON READING

After you read this paragraph, re-read it to make sure you understand Saudi Arabia's economic challenges.

Another economic challenge for Saudi Arabia is its high unemployment rate. One reason for the lack of jobs is the high population growth rate. About 38 percent of Saudis are younger than 15. Another reason for unemployment is that many young Saudis choose to study religion instead of the technical subjects their economy requires.

READING CHECK **Finding Main Ideas** What religion influences Saudi Arabia's culture?

Other Countries of the Arabian Peninsula

Saudi Arabia shares the Arabian Peninsula with six smaller countries. Like Saudi Arabia, these countries are all influenced by Islam. Also like Saudi Arabia, most have monarchies and economies based on oil.

Kuwait

Oil was discovered in Kuwait in the 1930s. Since then it has made Kuwait very rich. In 1990 Iraq invaded Kuwait to try to control its oil, starting the Persian Gulf War. The United States and other countries defeated Iraq, but the war caused major destruction to Kuwait's oil fields.

Although Kuwait's government is dominated by a royal family, the country did elect a legislature in 1992. Only men from certain families—less than 15 percent of Kuwait's population—had the right to vote in these elections. However, Kuwait recently gave women the right to vote.

Bahrain and Qatar

Bahrain is a group of islands in the Persian Gulf. It is a monarchy with a legislature. Bahrain is a rich country. Most people there live well in big, modern cities. Oil made Bahrain wealthy, but in the 1990s the country began to run out of oil. Now banking and tourism are major industries.

Qatar occupies a small peninsula in the Persian Gulf. Like Bahrain, Qatar is ruled by a powerful monarch. In 2003 men and women in Qatar voted to approve a new constitution that would give more power to elected officials. Qatar is a wealthy country. Its economy relies on its oil and natural gas.

Oil Wealth

Big, modern cities such as Dubai, UAE, were built with money from oil exports. Many people in the region's cities can afford to buy luxury items.

ANALYZING VISUALS What kind of luxury items is this man selling?

The United Arab Emirates

The United Arab Emirates, or UAE, consists of seven tiny kingdoms. Profits from oil and natural gas have created a modern, comfortable lifestyle for the people of the UAE. Partly because it is so small, the UAE depends on foreign workers. In fact, it has more foreign workers than citizens.

Oman and Yemen

Oman covers most of the southeastern part of the Arabian Peninsula. Oman's economy is also based on oil. However, Oman does not have the great oil wealth of Kuwait or the UAE. Therefore, the government is attempting to develop new industries.

Yemen is located on the southwestern part of the Arabian Peninsula. The country has an elected government, but it has suffered from corruption. Oil was not discovered in Yemen until the 1980s. Oil and coffee generate much of the national income, but Yemen is still the poorest country on the Arabian Peninsula.

READING CHECK **Summarizing** How has oil affected the countries of the Arabian Peninsula?

Yemen

Yemen's architecture is an important part of its culture. These buildings are more than 2,000 years old.

SUMMARY AND PREVIEW Islam is a major influence on the people and culture of Saudi Arabia and the other countries of the Arabian Peninsula. The other major influence in the region is oil. Oil has brought wealth to most countries on the peninsula. In the next section you will learn about Iraq, a neighboring country with similar influences.

Section 2 Assessment

hmhsocialstudies.com
ONLINE QUIZ

Reviewing Ideas, Terms, and Places

1. **a. Define** What is **OPEC**?
   b. Compare and Contrast How are **Sunni** and **Shia** Muslims similar, and how are they different from each other?
   c. Elaborate What do you think Saudi Arabia would be like if it did not have such huge oil reserves?
2. **a. Identify** What resource is the most important to the economies of countries on the Arabian Peninsula?
   b. Analyze How does its small size affect the United Arab Emirates?
   c. Predict How might Yemen change now that oil is a major part of its economy?

Critical Thinking

3. **Summarizing** Look at your notes on the countries of the Arabian Peninsula. Then copy the graphic organizer here and for each topic, write a one-sentence summary about the region.

	Summary
Culture	
Government	
Economy	

FOCUS ON WRITING

4. **Writing About the Arabian Peninsula** If you were traveling through these lands, what would you see or experience? Write some notes in your log.

Oil in Saudi Arabia

Essential Elements

The World in Spatial Terms
Places and Regions
Physical Systems
Human Systems
Environment and Society
The Uses of Geography

Background Try to imagine your life without oil. You would probably walk or ride a horse to school. You would heat your home with coal or wood. You would never fly in a plane, walk in rubber-soled shoes, or even drink out of a plastic cup.

Our society depends on oil. However, oil is a nonrenewable resource. This means that supplies are limited, and we may one day run out of oil. In fact, the United States no longer produces enough oil to satisfy its own needs. We now depend on foreign countries, such as Saudi Arabia, for oil.

Oil Reserves in Saudi Arabia

Saudi Arabia has the world's largest supply of oil. This important resource, found naturally in the environment, has had a huge impact on Saudi Arabia's society.

Before the discovery of oil there in the 1930s, Saudi Arabia was a poor country. But income from oil exports has given the government money to invest in improvements such as new apartments, communications systems, airports, oil pipelines, and roads.

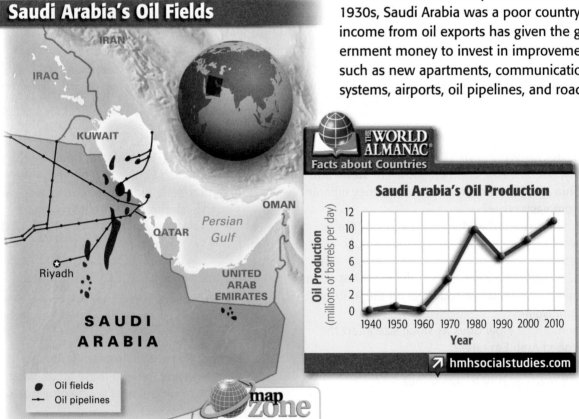

Saudi Arabia's Oil Fields

IRAN
IRAQ
KUWAIT
OMAN
Persian Gulf
QATAR
Riyadh
UNITED ARAB EMIRATES
SAUDI ARABIA

- Oil fields
- Oil pipelines

map zone

THE WORLD ALMANAC
Facts about Countries

Saudi Arabia's Oil Production

Oil Production (millions of barrels per day)

12
10
8
6
4
2
0

1940 1950 1960 1970 1980 1990 2000 2010
Year

hmhsocialstudies.com

Saudi Arabia's oil is pumped through pipelines to tankers that ship the oil around the world. The oil industry has made Saudi Arabia a rich country.

THE WORLD ALMANAC®
Facts about Countries

Saudi Arabia's Exports

Oil Products 91%

Other 9%

↗ hmhsocialstudies.com

For example, in 1960 Saudi Arabia had only about 1,000 miles (1,600 km) of roads. By 2005 it had over 94,000 miles (152,000 km) of roads. These improvements have helped modernize Saudi Arabia's economy.

Oil exports have also affected Saudi society. Rising incomes have given many people there more money to spend on consumer goods. New stores and restaurants have opened, and new schools have been built throughout the country. Education is now available to all citizens. Increased education means the literacy rate has increased also—from about 3 percent when oil was discovered to about 85 percent today. Health care there has also improved.

The oil industry has also increased Saudi Arabia's importance in the world. Since it is a member of the Organization of Petroleum Exporting Countries (OPEC), Saudi Arabia influences the price of oil on the world market. Countries around the world want to have good relations with Saudi Arabia because of its vast oil reserves.

What It Means Today Saudi Arabia's government has a lot of money. This wealth has come almost entirely from the sale of oil. However, since the world's oil supplies are limited, Saudi Arabia's economy may be at risk in the future. Many countries are beginning to research other types of energy that can one day be used in place of oil. Until then, the many countries buying oil from Saudi Arabia will continue to pump wealth into Saudi society.

Geography for Life Activity

1. How has oil changed Saudi Arabia's society?

2. What are some advantages and disadvantages for a society that relies on oil?

3. **Other Types of Energy** Research other types of energy we can get from the environment. Based on your findings, do you think other types of energy will replace oil in the near future? Why or why not?

THE ARABIAN PENINSULA, IRAQ, AND IRAN **125**

Iraq

If YOU lived there...

You are a student in a school in Iraq's capital, Baghdad. During the war, your school and its library were badly damaged. Since then, you and your friends have had few books to read. Now your teachers and others are organizing a project to rebuild your library. They want to include books from all countries of the world as well as computers so students can use the Internet.

What would you like to have in the new library?

What You Will Learn...

Main Ideas

1. Iraq's history includes rule by many conquerors and cultures, as well as recent wars.
2. Most of Iraq's people are Arabs, and Iraqi culture includes the religion of Islam.
3. Iraq today must rebuild its government and economy, which have suffered from years of conflict.

The Big Idea

Iraq, a country with a rich culture and natural resources, faces the challenge of rebuilding after years of conflict.

Key Terms and Places

embargo, *p. 127*
Baghdad, *p. 129*

hmhsocialstudies.com
TAKING NOTES

Use the graphic organizer online to take notes on Iraq's history and on Iraq today.

BUILDING BACKGROUND In spite of its generally harsh climate, the area that is now Iraq was one of the ancient cradles of civilization. Mesopotamia—the "land between the rivers"—was part of the "Fertile Crescent." Thousands of years ago, people there developed farming, domesticated animals, and organized governments.

History

Did you know that the world's first civilization was located in Iraq? Thousands of years ago people known as Sumerians settled in Mesopotamia—a region that is part of Iraq today. The country's recent history includes wars and a corrupt leader.

Early Civilization

Throughout Mesopotamia's history, different cultures and empires conquered the region. As you can see on the map on the next page, the Sumerians settled in southern Mesopotamia. By about 3000 BC, the Sumerians built the world's first known cities there. The Persians then conquered Mesopotamia in the 500s BC. By 331 BC Alexander the Great made it part of his empire. In the AD 600s Arabs conquered Mesopotamia, and the people gradually converted to Islam.

In the 1500s Mesopotamia became part of the Ottoman Empire. During World War I Great Britain took over the region. The British set up the kingdom of Iraq in 1932 and placed a pro-British ruler in power. In the 1950s a group of Iraqi army officers overthrew this government.

Saddam Takes Power

In 1968, after several more changes in Iraq's government, the Baath (BAHTH) Party took power. In 1979, a Baath leader named Saddam Hussein became Iraq's president. Saddam Hussein was a harsh ruler. He controlled Iraq's media, restricted personal freedoms, and killed an unknown number of political enemies.

Invasions of Iran and Kuwait

Under Saddam's leadership, Iraq invaded Iran in 1980. The Iranians fought back, and the Iran-Iraq War dragged on until 1988. Both countries' economies were seriously damaged, and many people died.

In 1990 Iraq invaded Kuwait, Iraq's oil-rich neighbor to the south. This event shocked and worried many world leaders. They were concerned that Iraq might gain control of the region's oil. In addition, they worried about Iraq's supply of weapons of mass destruction, including chemical and biological weapons.

War and Its Effects

In 1991, an alliance of countries led by the United States forced the Iraqis out of Kuwait. This six week event was called the Persian Gulf War. Saddam, who remained in power after the war, would not accept all the United Nations' (UN) terms for peace. In response, the UN placed an **embargo**, or limit on trade, on Iraq. As a result, Iraq's economy suffered.

Soon after the fighting ended, Saddam faced two rebellions from Shia Muslims and Kurds. He brutally put down these uprisings. In response, the UN forced Iraq to end all military activity. The UN also required that Iraq allow inspectors into the country. They wanted to make sure that Saddam had destroyed the weapons of mass destruction. Iraq later refused to cooperate completely with the UN.

Ten years after the Persian Gulf War, the terrorist attacks of September 11, 2001, led to new tensions between the United States and Iraq. U.S. government officials believed that Iraq aided terrorists. In March 2003, President George W. Bush ordered U.S. forces to attack Iraqi targets. Within a few weeks the Iraqi army was defeated and Saddam's government was crushed. Saddam went into hiding, but U.S. soldiers later found Saddam hiding in an underground hole in Iraq. Saddam was arrested, tried, and executed for his crimes.

READING CHECK **Summarizing** What are some key events in Iraq's history?

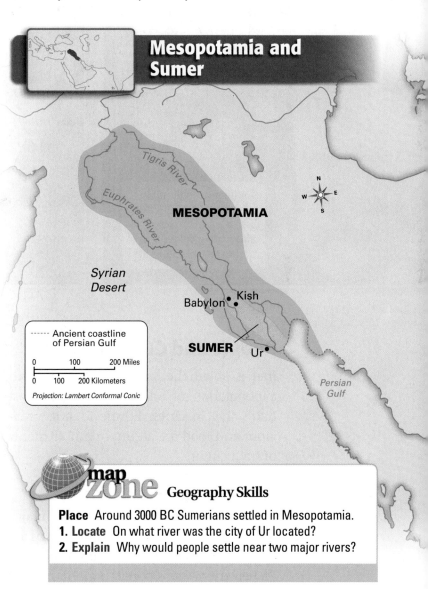

Mesopotamia and Sumer

map zone Geography Skills

Place Around 3000 BC Sumerians settled in Mesopotamia.
1. **Locate** On what river was the city of Ur located?
2. **Explain** Why would people settle near two major rivers?

With the help of the United States, Iraqis are rebuilding their country.

ANALYZING VISUALS How is the United States helping Iraq's people today?

U.S. soldiers in Iraq search for suspected terrorists.

An Iraqi woman holds up her ink-stained finger in a sign of victory after voting in Iraq's first democratic elections.

A U.S. soldier passes out school supplies to Iraqi schoolchildren.

People and Culture

Iraq is about the size of California, with a population of about 29 million. Most Iraqis live in cities. Ethnic identity, religion, and food are all important elements of Iraqi culture.

Ethnic Groups

Most of Iraq's people belong to two major ethnic groups—Arabs and Kurds. Arabs are the largest group and make up more than 75 percent of Iraq's population. Iraqi Arabs speak the country's official language, Arabic. The smaller group, the Kurds, make up some 15 to 20 percent of the population. The Kurds are mostly farmers and live in a large region of northern Iraq. Most Iraqi Kurds speak Kurdish in addition to Arabic.

Religion

Like ethnic identity, religion plays a large role in the lives of most Iraqis. Nearly all Iraqis, both Arab and Kurdish, are Muslim. Within Iraq, the two different branches of Islam—Shia and Sunni—are practiced. About 60 percent of Iraqis are Shia and live in the south. Some 35 percent of Iraqis are Sunnis and live in the north.

READING CHECK **Summarizing** What ethnic groups do most Iraqis belong to?

Iraq Today

Despite years of war, Iraq is slowly rebuilding. However, the country faces many challenges, such as ongoing fighting.

Rebuilding Baghdad

Iraq's capital, **Baghdad**, was severely damaged in the overthrow of Saddam's government. For example, the city's 6 million people lost electricity and running water. To help the city's residents, U.S. military and private contractors worked with the Iraqis to restore electricity and water and to rebuild homes, businesses, and schools. However, violence in Baghdad continued, disrupting efforts to rebuild.

Government and Economy

In January 2005 Iraqis participated in democracy for the first time. Millions of Iraqis went to the polls to elect members to the National Assembly. One of the Assembly's first tasks was to create a new constitution. Deep divisions among Iraqis led to fierce internal fighting, however, and threatened the new government's stability.

Iraqis also began trying to rebuild their once strong economy. In the 1970s Iraq was the world's second-largest oil exporter. Time will tell if Iraq can again be a major oil producer.

Oil isn't Iraq's only resource. From earliest times, Iraq's wide plains and fertile soils have produced many food crops. Irrigation from the Tigris and Euphrates rivers allows farmers to grow barley, cotton, and rice.

After decades of a harsh government and wars, Iraq's future remains uncertain. As the United States military transfers control back to the Iraqis, the country's government faces huge challenges in creating a free and prosperous society.

READING CHECK **Drawing Conclusions** What happened to Iraq's oil industry?

FOCUS ON READING
Do you understand everything you just read? If not, try re-reading the paragraphs that you do not understand.

SUMMARY AND PREVIEW In this section, you have learned about Iraq's ancient history, rich culture, and efforts to rebuild. Next, you will learn about Iran, which also has an ancient history but is otherwise quite different from Iraq.

Section 3 Assessment
hmhsocialstudies.com
ONLINE QUIZ

Reviewing Ideas, Terms, and Places

1. **a. Recall** Where was the world's first civilization located?
   b. Sequence What events led to the **embargo** on Iraq by the United Nations?
2. **a. Identify** What are two major ethnic groups in Iraq?
   b. Contrast What is one difference between Shia Muslims and Sunni Muslims?
3. **a. Describe** How was **Baghdad** damaged by war?
   b. Draw Conclusions What natural resource may help Iraq's economy recover?
   c. Predict What kind of country do you think Iraq will be in five years?

Critical Thinking

4. **Summarizing** Use your notes on Iraq today to fill in this table by summarizing what you have learned about Baghdad and Iraq's government and economy.

Baghdad	Government	Economy

FOCUS ON WRITING

5. **Writing about Iraq** Add details about Iraq's people, culture, and the country today to your notes. What sights have you seen that you might record in your log?

Iran

What You Will Learn...

Main Ideas

1. Iran's history includes great empires and an Islamic republic.
2. In Iran today, Islamic religious leaders restrict the rights of most Iranians.

The Big Idea

Islam is a huge influence on government and daily life in Iran.

Key Terms and Places

shah, *p. 131*
revolution, *p. 131*
Tehran, *p. 131*
theocracy, *p. 132*

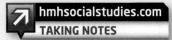

hmhsocialstudies.com
TAKING NOTES

Use the graphic organizer online to take notes on Iran's history and life in the country today.

If **YOU** lived there...

You are a student in Tehran, the capital of Iran. In school, you are taught that the way of life in the West—countries of Europe and the Americas—is bad. News reports and newspapers are filled with negative propaganda about Western countries. Yet you know that some of your friends secretly listen to Western popular music and watch American television programs that they catch using illegal satellite dishes at home. This makes you very curious about Western countries.

What would you like to know about life in other countries?

BUILDING BACKGROUND Like Iraqis, Iranians have a proud and ancient history. While most people living in the Arabian Peninsula and Iraq are Arabs, the majority of Iranians are Persian. They have a distinct culture and language.

History

The early history of the country we now call Iran includes the Persian Empire and a series of Muslim empires. Iran's recent history includes an Islamic revolution. Today Iran is an Islamic republic, which limits the rights of many Iranians.

Persian Empire

Beginning in the 500s BC, the Persian Empire ruled the region around present-day Iran. For centuries Persia was a great center of art and learning. The Persian Empire was known for its spectacular paintings, carpets, metalwork, and architecture. In the empire's capital, Persepolis, walls and statues throughout the city glittered with gold, silver, and precious jewels.

The Persian Empire was later conquered by several Muslim empires. Muslims converted the Persians to Islam, but most people retained their Persian culture. They built beautiful mosques with colorful tiles and large domes.

The Shah and Islamic Revolution

In 1921 an Iranian military officer took power and encouraged change in Iran's government. He claimed the old Persian title of **shah**, or king. In 1941 the shah's son took control. This shah became an ally of the United States and Great Britain and tried to modernize Iran. His programs were unpopular with many Iranians.

In 1978 Iranians began a revolution. A **revolution** is a drastic change in a country's government and way of life. By 1979, Iranians overthrew the shah and set up an Islamic republic. This type of government follows strict Islamic law.

Soon after Iran's Islamic Revolution began, relations with the United States broke down. A mob of students attacked the U.S. Embassy in Iran's capital, **Tehran**. With the approval of Iran's government, the students took Americans working at the embassy hostage. More than 50 Americans were held by force for over a year.

READING CHECK **Drawing Conclusions** How did Iran's history lead to the Islamic Revolution?

Iran Today

Iranian culture differs from many other cultures of Southwest Asia. Unlike most of the Arab peoples living in the region, more than half of all Iranians are Persian. They speak Farsi, the Persian language.

People and Culture

With about 66 million people, Iran has one of the largest populations in Southwest Asia. Iran's population is very young. The average age in Iran is about 27 years old. It is also ethnically diverse. Iranian ethnic groups other than the Persian majority include Azerbaijanis, Kurds, Arabs, and Turks.

Most Iranians belong to the Shia branch of Islam. Only about 10 percent are Sunni Muslim. The rest of Iran's people practice Christianity, Judaism, or other religions.

In addition to the Islamic holy days, Iranians celebrate Nowruz—the Persian New Year. Iranians tend to spend this holiday outdoors. As a part of this celebration, they display goldfish in their homes to symbolize life.

FOCUS ON READING
Re-read the paragraphs under The Shah and Islamic Revolution to better understand important parts of Iran's recent history.

Yazd, Iran

In the ancient city of Yazd, spectacular tilework covers the dome of an Islamic mausoleum built in the 1300s.

Iranian culture also includes close-knit families and respect for elders. Most family gatherings in Iran are centered around Persian food, which includes rice, bread, vegetables, fruits, lamb, and tea.

Economy and Government

Huge oil reserves, which are among the largest in the world, make Iran a wealthy country. In addition to oil, the production of beautiful woven carpets contributes to Iran's economy. The country's strong agricultural sector employs nearly one-third of the Iranian workforce.

The current government of Iran is a **theocracy**—a government ruled by religious leaders. These religious leaders, or *ayatollahs*, control Iran's government. The head of the *ayatollahs,* or supreme leader, has unlimited power. Even though religious leaders control Iran, its government has an elected president and parliament.

Life in Iran and the United States

Iran	United States
Daily Life	**Daily Life**
■ An Iranian woman has to cover her head and most of her body with clothing in public.	■ Americans are free to wear any type of clothing.
■ Iranians are forbidden to view most Western Web sites, and Internet use is monitored by the government.	■ Americans are free to surf the Internet and view most Web sites.
■ Boys and girls have separate schools, and they can not be alone with each other without adult supervision.	■ Boys and girls can attend the same school.
Government	**Government**
■ Iran is a theocracy.	■ The United States is a democracy.
■ A supreme religious leader rules Iran.	■ A president is the leader of our country.
■ Only candidates approved by the government can run for political office.	■ Any U.S. citizen can run for political office.
Basic Rights	**Basic Rights**
■ Freedom of speech, religion, and the press is limited.	■ Freedom of speech, religion, and the press is allowed.

Iranian teenagers can shop for computers, but a girl must wear clothing that covers most of her body.

Unlike Iranians, Americans are free to speak in public. Here a teenager speaks on the steps of the Texas State Capitol in Austin.

Contrasting In what ways does Iran's government differ from the U.S. government?

Iran's government has supported many hard-line policies. For example, it has called for the destruction of Israel. It has also supported terrorist groups in other countries. With a newly elected president in 1997, some signs indicated that Iran's government might adopt democratic reforms. This government attempted to improve Iran's economy and rights for women.

However, in 2005 Iranians moved away from democratic reforms by electing Mahmoud Ahmadinejad (mah-MOOD ah-mah-di-nee-ZHAHD) president. He wants Iranians to follow strict Islamic law. After the election, a reporter asked the new president if he had any plans for reforms. He responded, "We did not have a revolution in order to have a democracy."

More recently, international debate arose over Iran's expansion of its nuclear program. The United States and some of its allies feared that Iran was building nuclear weapons, which could threaten world security. Iran claimed it was using nuclear technology to create energy.

READING CHECK **Analyzing** What are Iran's government and people like?

BIOGRAPHY

Shirin Ebadi
(1947–   )

Iranians hoping for more democratic reforms were encouraged in 2003 when Shirin Ebadi received the Nobel Peace Prize. Ebadi is a lawyer, judge, and author. However, her work attempting to improve human rights in Iran has at times made her unpopular with the country's government leaders. Ebadi's goals include to attain better conditions for women, children, and refugees.

Drawing Inferences Why would Iran's government be opposed to Ebadi's human rights efforts?

SUMMARY AND PREVIEW In this section you learned about Iran's history, people, culture, economy, and government. In the next chapter, you will learn about the countries of Central Asia that lie to the north and east of Iran.

Section 4 Assessment

Reviewing Ideas, Terms, and Places

1. **a. Define** What is a **revolution**?
   b. Explain What was the Persian Empire known for?
   c. Elaborate What changes were made in Iran after the Islamic Revolution?
2. **a. Recall** What kind of leaders have authority over their people in a **theocracy**?
   b. Compare In what ways does Iran's culture differ from cultures in other countries of Southwest Asia?
   c. Predict How do you think the United States and other nations will deal with Iran's nuclear weapons program?

Critical Thinking

3. **Finding Main Ideas** Use your notes on Iran today to fill in this diagram with the main ideas of Iran's people, culture, economy, and government.

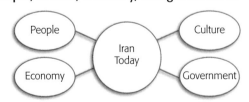

FOCUS ON WRITING

4. **Writing About Iran** Record details about Iran in your log. What types of things would you see if you were traveling around Iran?

Analyzing Tables and Statistics

Learn

Tables provide an organized way of presenting statistics, or data. The data are usually listed side by side for easy reference and comparison. Use the following guidelines to analyze a table:

- Read the table's title to determine its subject.

- Note the headings and labels of the table's columns and rows. This will tell you how the data are organized.

- Locate statistics where rows and columns intersect by reading across rows and down columns.

- Use critical thinking skills to compare and contrast data, identify relationships, and note trends.

Literacy Rates in Southwest Asia			
	Literacy Rate (%)		
Country	Male	Female	Total
Iran	83.5	70.4	77
Iraq	84.1	64.2	74.1
Oman	86.8	73.5	81.4
Qatar	89.1	88.6	89
Saudi Arabia	84.7	70.8	78.8

Source: Central Intelligence Agency, *World Factbook 2010*

Practice

Use the table here to answer the following questions.

1. Which country has the highest total literacy rate? Which country has the lowest?

2. Which country has the largest difference between the literacy rate among men and the literacy rate among women?

3. What inference, or educated guess, can you make about education in these countries?

Apply

Using the Internet, an encyclopedia, or an almanac, locate information on the population density, birthrate, and death rate for each country listed in the table above. Then create your own table to show this information.

Chapter Review

Geography's Impact
video series
Review the video to answer the closing question:
Why is it important for countries to prepare for possible oil shortages?

Visual Summary

Use the visual summary below to help you review the main ideas of the chapter.

QUICK FACTS

Deserts cover much of the Arabian Peninsula. The region also has a lot of valuable oil reserves.

Many people in Iraq, such as this woman, enjoy more freedoms now that the country has a new government.

Iran is a theocracy. Islam is an important part of the country's government and culture.

Reviewing Vocabulary, Terms, and Places

Match the words in the columns with the correct definitions listed below.

1. wadis

2. revolution

3. embargo

4. procedure

5. fossil water

6. OPEC

7. shah

8. theocracy

a. the Persian title for a king

b. dry streambeds

c. a limit on trade

d. a series of steps taken to accomplish a task

e. water that is not being replaced by rainfall

f. an organization whose members try to influence the price of oil on world markets

g. a drastic change in a country's government

h. a government ruled by religious leaders

Comprehension and Critical Thinking

SECTION 1 *(Pages 116–119)*

9. a. Identify Through what country do the Tigris and Euphrates rivers flow?

b. Analyze Based on the landforms and climate, where do you think would be the best place in the region to live? Explain your answer.

c. Evaluate Do you think oil or water is a more important resource in the region? Explain your answer.

SECTION 2 *(Pages 120–123)*

10. a. Describe What kind of government does Saudi Arabia have?

b. Analyze In what ways does religion affect Saudi Arabia's culture and economy?

c. Elaborate What challenges might countries on the Arabian Peninsula face in attempting to create new industries in addition to oil?

SECTION 3 (Pages 126–129)

11. a. Recall What is the region of Mesopotamia known for?

b. Draw Conclusions Why did Iraq invade Kuwait in 1990?

c. Elaborate How did war damage Baghdad?

SECTION 4 (Pages 130–133)

12. a. Describe What occurred at the U.S. Embassy in Tehran after the Islamic Revolution?

b. Compare and Contrast How is Iran similar to or different from the United States?

c. Predict Do you think Iran's government will ever become more democratic? Why or why not?

Social Studies Skills

Analyzing Tables and Statistics *Use the Facts about Countries table at the beginning of the unit to answer the following questions.*

13. What is the population of Iraq?

14. What country is the smallest?

15. How many TVs per thousand people are there in Qatar?

Using the Internet

16. Activity: Charting Democracy Some countries face challenges as they work to promote a more democratic form of government. Iraq, for example, has struggled as it has begun to develop its own form of democracy. How does democracy in Iraq, or elections in Saudi Arabia and Lebanon, affect the people of those countries? How do the media, literature, and arts in those areas reflect life in a democratic society? In what ways does democracy in Southwest Asia differ from democracy in the United States? Through the online book, create a chart or diagram that compares democratic life in the United States with democratic life in Iraq and other countries of Southwest Asia.

Map Activity

17. The Arabian Peninsula, Iraq, and Iran On a separate sheet of paper, match the letters on the map with their correct labels.

Rub' al-Khali	Tehran, Iran
Persian Gulf	Riyadh, Saudi Arabia
Tigris River	Euphrates River

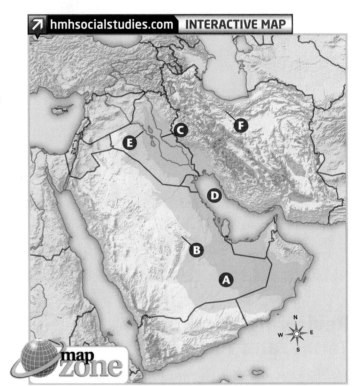

hmhsocialstudies.com   INTERACTIVE MAP

FOCUS ON READING AND WRITING

18. Re-Reading Read the passage titled Resources in Section 1. After you read, write down the main ideas of the passage. Then go back and re-read the passage carefully. Identify at least one thing you learned from the passage when you re-read it and add the new information to your list of main ideas.

19. Creating a Geographer's Log Imagine that you began your journey in Saudi Arabia. Write the name of the country at the top of your log. Under the country's name, record details about what you saw as you traveled through the country. Then choose another country and do the same until you have created an entry in your log for each country. Look at your notes to help you remember what you saw. Be sure to include descriptions of the land and people.

Standardized Test Prep

DIRECTIONS: Read questions 1 through 7 and write the letter of the best response. Then read question 8 and write your own well-constructed response.

1 **Dry streambeds in the desert are known as**

A wadis.

B salty rivers.

C exotic rivers.

D disappearing rivers.

2 **What kind of government does Saudi Arabia have?**

A monarchy

B legislature

C democracy

D republic

3 **Iraq's official language is**

A Persian.

B Arabic.

C French.

D Kurdish.

4 **Saddam Hussein is the former president of**

A Saudi Arabia.

B Iraq.

C Oman.

D Iran.

5 **Iran's government is a theocracy ruled by**

A Islamic religious leaders.

B priests.

C Christian ministers.

D democratic leaders.

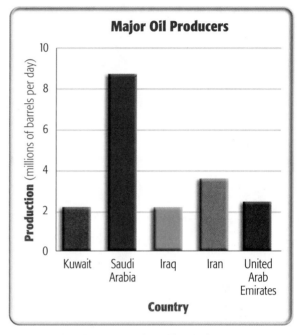

Major Oil Producers

Source: Central Intelligence Agency, *The World Factbook 2005*

6 **Based on the graph above, about how many barrels of oil per day does Saudi Arabia produce?**

A 9

B 9 thousand

C 9 million

D 9 billion

7 **Based on the graph above, which country produces the second largest amount of oil in the region?**

A United Arab Emirates

B Iran

C Iraq

D Kuwait

8 **Extended Response** Based on the graph above and your knowledge of the region, write a paragraph explaining the influence oil has on the region. Identify at least two ways in which oil affects the region.

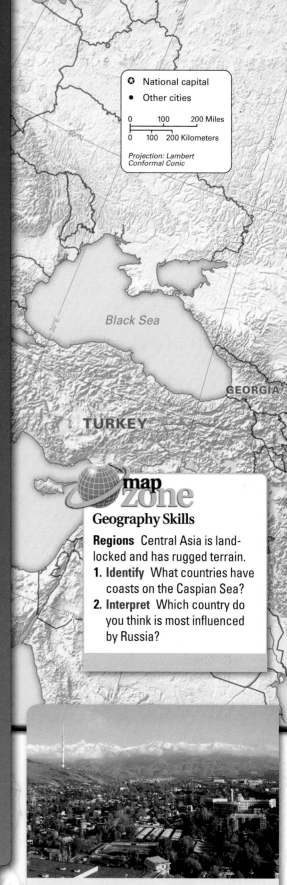

CHAPTER 6

Central Asia

Essential Question How have foreign invasion and influence affected the societies and cultures of Central Asia?

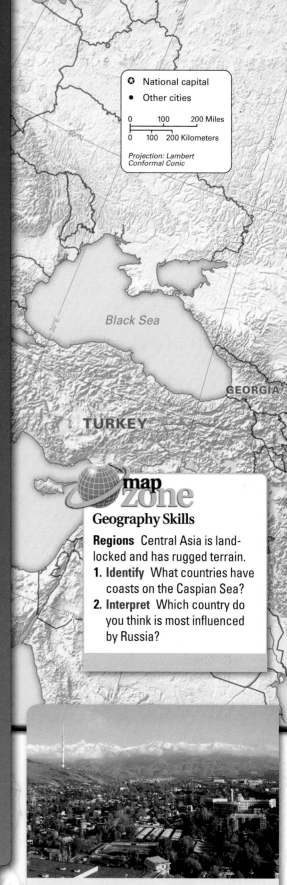

What You Will Learn...

In this chapter you will learn about the rugged physical geography of Central Asia. This physical geography has affected the region's history. You will also learn about the many influences on Central Asia throughout history. Finally, you will see how these influences have affected the region's culture, governments, and economies today.

FOCUS ON READING AND VIEWING

Using Context Clues As you read, you may come across words in your textbook that you do not know. When this happens, look for context clues that restate the unknown word in other words that you know. **See the lesson, Using Context Clues, on page 167.**

Giving a Travel Presentation You work for a travel agency, and you are going to give a presentation encouraging people to visit Central Asia. Gather information from the chapter to help you prepare your presentation. Later you will view your classmates' presentations and provide feedback to them.

map Zone

Geography Skills

Regions Central Asia is landlocked and has rugged terrain.
1. **Identify** What countries have coasts on the Caspian Sea?
2. **Interpret** Which country do you think is most influenced by Russia?

Geography Much of Central Asia's land is rugged. Here, mountains rise behind the city of Almaty, Kazakhstan.

Central Asia: Political

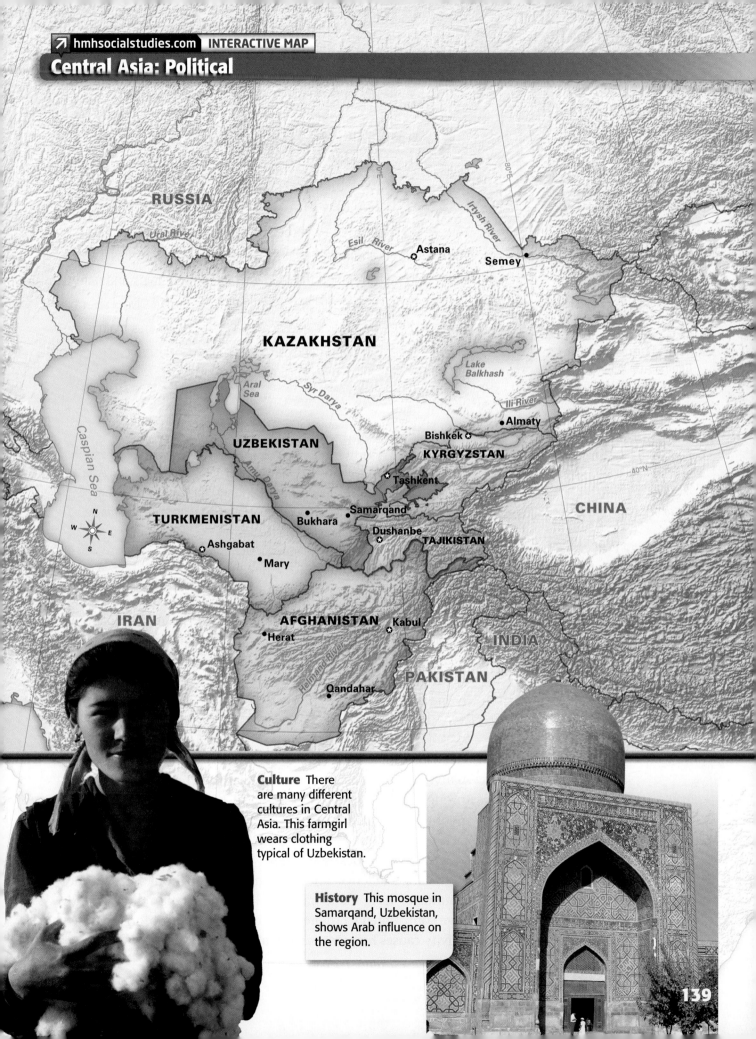

RUSSIA

Ural River

Esil River

Irtysh River

Astana

Semey

KAZAKHSTAN

Aral Sea

Syr Darya

Lake Balkhash

Ili River

UZBEKISTAN

Almaty

Caspian Sea

Bishkek

KYRGYZSTAN

Tashkent

Samarqand

TURKMENISTAN

Amu Darya

Bukhara

Dushanbe

TAJIKISTAN

CHINA

Ashgabat

Mary

N
W E
S

IRAN

AFGHANISTAN

Kabul

Herat

INDIA

PAKISTAN

Helmand River

Qandahar

Culture There are many different cultures in Central Asia. This farmgirl wears clothing typical of Uzbekistan.

History This mosque in Samarqand, Uzbekistan, shows Arab influence on the region.

139

Physical Geography

What You Will Learn...

Main Ideas

1. Key physical features of landlocked Central Asia include rugged mountains.
2. Central Asia has a harsh, dry climate that makes it difficult for vegetation to grow.
3. Key natural resources in Central Asia include water, oil and gas, and minerals.

The Big Idea

Central Asia, a dry, rugged, landlocked region, has oil and other valuable mineral resources.

Key Terms and Places

landlocked, *p. 140*
Pamirs, *p. 140*
Fergana Valley, *p. 141*
Kara-Kum, *p. 142*
Kyzyl Kum, *p. 142*
Aral Sea, *p. 143*

hmhsocialstudies.com
TAKING NOTES

Use the graphic organizer online to take notes on the physical geography of Central Asia.

If **YOU** lived there...

You are flying in a plane low over the mountains of Central Asia. You look down and notice that the area below you looks as if a giant hand has crumpled the land into steep mountains and narrow valleys. Icy glaciers fill some of the valleys. A few silvery rivers flow out of the mountains and across a green plain. This plain is the only green spot you can see in this rugged landscape.

How would this landscape affect people?

BUILDING BACKGROUND The physical geography of Central Asia affects the lives of the people who live there. This region has been shaped throughout its history by its isolated location, high mountains, dry plains, and limited resources.

Physical Features

As the name suggests, Central Asia lies in the middle of Asia. All of the countries in this region are landlocked. **Landlocked** means completely surrounded by land with no direct access to the ocean. This isolated location is just one challenge presented by the physical features of the region.

Mountains

Much of Central Asia has a rugged landscape. In the south, many high mountain ranges, such as the Hindu Kush, stretch through Afghanistan. Tajikistan and Kyrgyzstan are also very mountainous. Large glaciers are common in high mountains such as the **Pamirs**.

Like its landlocked location, Central Asia's rugged terrain presents a challenge for the region. Throughout history, the mountains have made travel and communication difficult and have contributed to the region's isolation. In addition, tectonic activity causes frequent earthquakes there.

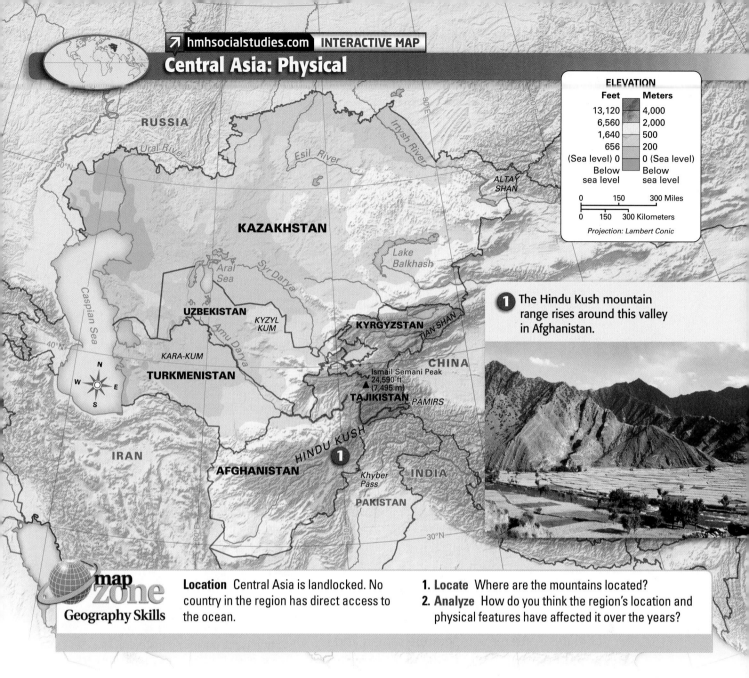

Central Asia: Physical

ELEVATION

Feet	Meters
13,120	4,000
6,560	2,000
1,640	500
656	200
(Sea level) 0	0 (Sea level)
Below sea level	Below sea level

0   150   300 Miles
0   150   300 Kilometers
Projection: Lambert Conic

RUSSIA

Ural River

Esil River

Irtysh River

ALTAY SHAN

KAZAKHSTAN

Lake Balkhash

Aral Sea

Syr Darya

Caspian Sea

UZBEKISTAN

KYZYL KUM

KYRGYZSTAN

TIAN SHAN

CHINA

KARA-KUM

Amu Darya

TURKMENISTAN

Ismail Semani Peak
24,590 ft
▲ (7,495 m)

TAJIKISTAN   PAMIRS

HINDU KUSH

IRAN

AFGHANISTAN

Khyber Pass

INDIA

PAKISTAN

1 The Hindu Kush mountain range rises around this valley in Afghanistan.

map zone
Geography Skills

Location Central Asia is landlocked. No country in the region has direct access to the ocean.

1. **Locate** Where are the mountains located?
2. **Analyze** How do you think the region's location and physical features have affected it over the years?

Plains and Plateaus

From the mountains in the east, the land gradually slopes toward the west. There, near the Caspian Sea, the land is as low as 95 feet (29 m) below sea level. The central part of the region, between the mountains and the Caspian Sea, is covered with plains and low plateaus.

The plains region is the site of the fertile **Fergana Valley**. This large valley has been a major center of farming in the region for thousands of years.

Rivers and Lakes

The Fergana Valley is fertile because of two rivers that flow through it—the Syr Darya (sir duhr-YAH) and the Amu Darya (uh-MOO duhr-YAH). These rivers flow from eastern mountains into the Aral Sea, which is really a large lake. Another important lake, Lake Balkhash, has freshwater at one end and salty water at the other end.

READING CHECK **Generalizing** What challenges do the mountains present to this region?

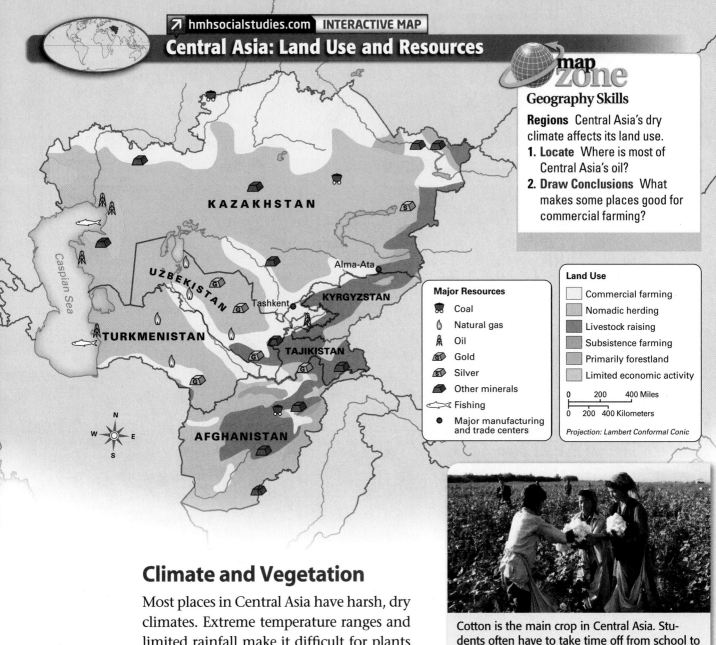

map zone
Geography Skills

Regions Central Asia's dry climate affects its land use.
1. **Locate** Where is most of Central Asia's oil?
2. **Draw Conclusions** What makes some places good for commercial farming?

KAZAKHSTAN

Caspian Sea

UZBEKISTAN

Alma-Ata

Tashkent

KYRGYZSTAN

TURKMENISTAN

TAJIKISTAN

AFGHANISTAN

N W E S

Major Resources
- Coal
- Natural gas
- Oil
- Gold
- Silver
- Other minerals
- Fishing
- ● Major manufacturing and trade centers

Land Use
- Commercial farming
- Nomadic herding
- Livestock raising
- Subsistence farming
- Primarily forestland
- Limited economic activity

0   200   400 Miles
0 200 400 Kilometers

Projection: Lambert Conformal Conic

Climate and Vegetation

Most places in Central Asia have harsh, dry climates. Extreme temperature ranges and limited rainfall make it difficult for plants to grow there.

One area with harsh climates in the region is the mountain area in the east. The high peaks in this area are too cold, dry, and windy for vegetation.

West of the mountains and east of the Caspian Sea is another harsh region. Two deserts—the **Kara-Kum** (kahr-uh-KOOM) in Turkmenistan and the **Kyzyl Kum** (ki-ZIL KOOM) in Uzbekistan and Kazakhstan—have extremely high temperatures in the summer. Rainfall is limited, though both deserts contain several settlements. Rivers crossing this dry region make settlements

Cotton is the main crop in Central Asia. Students often have to take time off from school to help harvest the cotton.

possible, because they provide water for irrigation. Irrigation is a way of supplying water to an area of land.

The only part of Central Asia with a milder climate is the far north. There, temperature ranges are not so extreme and rainfall is heavy enough for grasses and trees to grow.

READING CHECK **Generalizing** Why is it hard for plants to grow in much of Central Asia?

Natural Resources

In this dry region, water is one of the most valuable resources. Although water is scarce, or limited, the countries of Central Asia do have oil and other resources.

Water

The main water sources in southern Central Asia are the Syr Darya and Amu Darya rivers. Since water is so scarce there, different ideas over how to use the water from these rivers have led to conflict between Uzbekistan and Turkmenistan.

Today farmers use river water mostly to irrigate cotton fields. Cotton grows well in Central Asia's sunny climate, but it requires a lot of water. Irrigation has taken so much water from the rivers that almost no water actually reaches the **Aral Sea** today. The effect of this irrigation has been devastating to the Aral Sea. It has lost more than 75 percent of its water since 1960. Large areas of seafloor are now exposed.

In addition to water for irrigation, Central Asia's rivers supply power. Some countries have built large dams on the rivers to generate hydroelectricity.

Oil and Other Resources

The resources that present the best economic opportunities for Central Asia are oil and gas. Uzbekistan, Kazakhstan, and Turkmenistan all have huge reserves of oil and natural gas.

However, these oil and gas reserves cannot benefit the countries of Central Asia unless they can be exported. Since no country in the region has an ocean port, the only way to transport the oil and gas efficiently is through pipelines. But the rugged mountains, along with economic and political turmoil in some surrounding countries, make building and maintaining pipelines difficult.

In addition to oil and gas, some parts of Central Asia are rich in other minerals. They have deposits of gold, silver, copper, zinc, uranium, and lead. Kazakhstan, in particular, has many mines with these minerals. It also has large amounts of coal.

FOCUS ON READING
What context clues give you a restatement of the term *scarce*?

READING CHECK **Categorizing** What are three types of natural resources in Central Asia?

SUMMARY AND PREVIEW In this section you learned about Central Asia's rugged terrain, dry climate, and limited resources. In the next section you will learn about the history and culture of Central Asia.

Section 1 Assessment
hmhsocialstudies.com
ONLINE QUIZ

Reviewing Ideas, Terms, and Places

1. **a. Identify** What fertile area has been a center of farming in Central Asia for many years?
   b. Make Inferences How does Central Asia's terrain affect life there?
2. **a. Describe** Where do people find water in the deserts?
   b. Make Generalizations What is the climate like in most of Central Asia?
3. **a. Recall** What mineral resources does Central Asia have?
   b. Explain How have human activities affected the **Aral Sea**?
   c. Elaborate What kinds of situations would make it easier for countries of Central Asia to export oil and gas?

Critical Thinking

4. **Finding Main Ideas** Look at your notes on this section. Then, using a chart like the one here, write a main idea statement about each topic.

	Main Idea
Physical Features	
Climate and Vegetation	
Natural Resources	

FOCUS ON VIEWING

5. **Describing Physical Geography** Note information about physical features, climates, and resources of this region. Highlight information to include in your presentation.

History and Culture

What You Will Learn...

Main Ideas

1. Throughout history, many different groups have conquered Central Asia.
2. Many different ethnic groups and their traditions influence culture in Central Asia.

The Big Idea

The countries of Central Asia share similar histories and traditions, but particular ethnic groups give each country a unique culture.

Key Terms and Places

Samarqand, *p. 144*
nomads, *p. 146*
yurt, *p. 146*

hmhsocialstudies.com
TAKING NOTES

Use the graphic organizer online to take notes on the history and culture of Central Asia. Be sure to pay attention to the different peoples that influenced the region.

If **YOU** lived there...

Your family has always farmed a small plot of land. Most days you go to school and work in the fields. One day you get news that invaders have taken over your country. They don't look like you and they speak a different language, but now they are in charge.

How do you think your life will change under the new rulers?

BUILDING BACKGROUND You may have noticed that the names of the countries in this region all end with *stan*. In the language of the region, *stan* means "land of." So, for example, Kazakhstan means "land of the Kazakhs." However, throughout history many different groups have ruled these lands.

History

Central Asia has been somewhat of a crossroads for traders and invaders for hundreds of years. As these different peoples have passed through Central Asia, they have each left their own unique and lasting influences on the region.

Trade

At one time, the best trade route between Europe and India ran through Afghanistan. The best route between Europe and China ran through the rest of Central Asia. Beginning in about 100 BC, merchants traveled along the China route to trade European gold and wool for Chinese spices and silk. As a result, this route came to be called the Silk Road. Cities along the road, such as **Samarqand** and Bukhara, grew rich from the trade.

By 1500 the situation in Central Asia had changed, however. When Europeans discovered they could sail to East Asia through the Indian Ocean, trade through Central Asia declined. The region became more isolated and poor.

Invasions

Because of its location on the Silk Road, many groups of people were interested in Central Asia. Group after group swarmed into the region. Among the first people to establish a lasting influence in the region were Turkic-speaking nomads who came from northern Asia in AD 500.

In the 700s Arab armies took over much of the region. They brought a new religion—Islam—to Central Asia. Many of the beautiful mosques in Central Asian cities date from the time of the Arabs.

Arabs, followed by other invaders, ruled Central Asia until the 1200s. Then, Mongol armies conquered Central Asia, destroying many cities with their violent attacks. Eventually, their empire crumbled. With the fall of the Mongols, various tribes of peoples, such as the Uzbeks, Kazakhs, and Turkmens moved into parts of the region.

Russian and Soviet Rule

In the mid-1800s the Russians became the next major group to conquer Central Asia. Although the Russians built railroads and expanded cotton and oil production, people began to resent their rule.

After the Russian Revolution in 1917, the new Soviet government wanted to weaken resistance to its rule. The new Soviet leaders did this by dividing the land into republics. The Soviets encouraged ethnic Russians to move to these areas and made other people settle on government-owned farms. The Soviets also built huge irrigation projects to improve cotton production.

The Soviet Union collapsed in 1991. As the Soviet government and economy fell apart, it could no longer control its huge territory. The Central Asian republics finally became independent countries.

READING CHECK **Generalizing** What groups of people influenced Central Asia?

Influences on Central Asia

The Arabs, Mongols, and Soviets all had a major influence on Central Asia.

Arab Influence

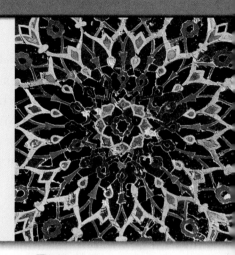

- The Arabs ruled Central Asia in the 700s and 800s.
- They introduced Islam and built beautiful mosques.
- They influenced styles of art and architecture in the region.

Mongol Influence

- The Mongols ruled from 1220 to the mid-1300s.
- They destroyed cities and irrigation systems.
- Eventually, they supported literature and the arts at Samarqand.

Soviet Influence

- The Soviet Union controlled Central Asia from 1917 to 1991.
- The Soviets separated ethnic groups and banned religious practices.
- They began growing cotton and constructed many useful but stark buildings.

Culture

The people who came through Central Asia influenced culture in the region. They brought new languages, religions, and ways of life that mixed with traditional ways of life in Central Asia.

Traditional Lives

For centuries, Central Asians have made a living by raising horses, cattle, sheep, and goats. Many herders live as **nomads**, people who move often from place to place. The nomads move their herds from mountain pastures in the summer to lowland pastures in the winter. Today most people in Central Asia live in more permanent settlements, but many others still live as nomads. The nomadic lifestyle is especially common in Kyrgyzstan.

Unique homes, called yurts, make moving with the herds possible. A **yurt** is a movable round house made of wool felt mats hung over a wood frame. Today the yurt is a symbol of the region's nomadic heritage. Even people who live in cities may put up yurts for special events such as weddings and funerals.

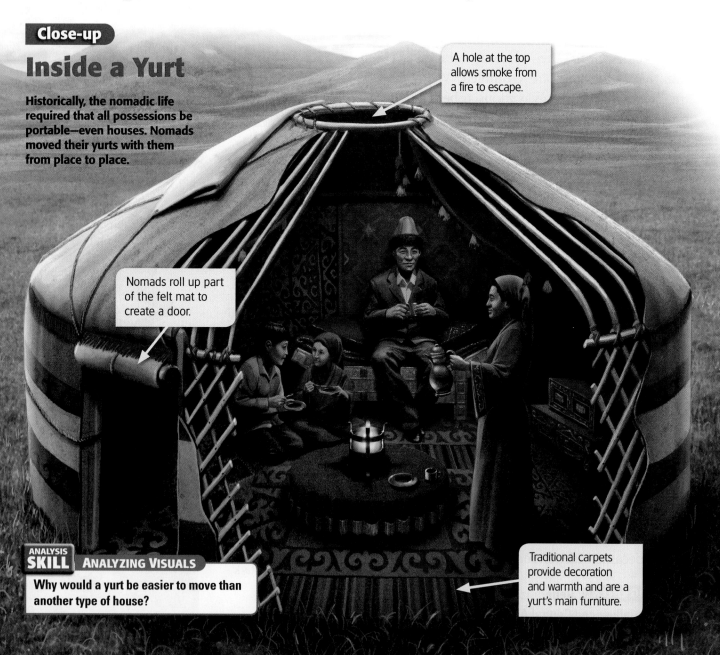

Close-up

Inside a Yurt

Historically, the nomadic life required that all possessions be portable—even houses. Nomads moved their yurts with them from place to place.

A hole at the top allows smoke from a fire to escape.

Nomads roll up part of the felt mat to create a door.

Traditional carpets provide decoration and warmth and are a yurt's main furniture.

ANALYSIS SKILL **ANALYZING VISUALS**

Why would a yurt be easier to move than another type of house?

Languages of Central Asia

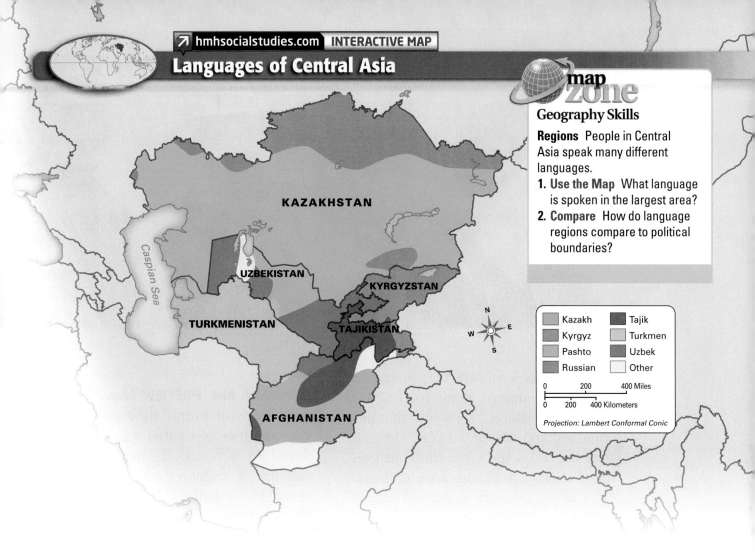

map zone

Geography Skills

Regions People in Central Asia speak many different languages.
1. **Use the Map** What language is spoken in the largest area?
2. **Compare** How do language regions compare to political boundaries?

Legend:
- Kazakh
- Kyrgyz
- Pashto
- Russian
- Tajik
- Turkmen
- Uzbek
- Other

0 — 200 — 400 Miles
0 — 200 — 400 Kilometers

Projection: Lambert Conformal Conic

People, Languages, and Religion

Most people in Central Asia today belong to one of several ethnic groups that are part of a larger ethnic group called Turkic. Some of these ethnic groups are Kazakh (kuh-ZAHK), Kyrgyz (KIR-giz), Turkmen, and Uzbek (OOZ-bek). Another group, ethnic Russians, came to Central Asia when Russia conquered the region. They still live in every Central Asian country.

Each ethnic group speaks its own language. Look at the map above to see where a particular language is the primary language. In most countries in the region, more than one language is spoken.

When the Russians conquered Central Asia, they **established** their own language as the official language for business and government. It is still an official language in some Central Asian countries. The Russians also introduced the Cyrillic alphabet, the alphabet used to write the Russian language. Most countries in Central Asia now use the Latin alphabet, however, which is the one used to write English. Afghanistan also has its own alphabet. It is used for writing Pashto, one of that country's official languages.

Just as people in the region are of many ethnic groups and speak different languages, they also practice different religions. Traders and conquerors brought their religious beliefs and practices to the region. Islam, brought by the Arabs, is the main religion in Central Asia. Some people there also practice Christianity. Most of the region's Christians belong to the Russian Orthodox Church.

FOCUS ON READING

What context clues give a restatement of *Cyrillic alphabet*?

ACADEMIC VOCABULARY

establish to set up or create

Ethnic Groups of Central Asia

Traditional clothing, such as the hats men wear, distinguishes members of different ethnic groups in Central Asia.

ANALYZING VISUALS
Why do you think men wear different hats?

Uzbek

Kyrgyz

Turkmen

During the Soviet era, the government closed or destroyed more than 35,000 religious buildings, such as mosques, churches, and Islamic schools. However, since the end of the Soviet Union in 1991, many religious buildings have reopened. They are in use once again and are also beautiful symbols of the region's past.

READING CHECK Summarizing How did Russian and Soviet rule influence culture in Central Asia?

SUMMARY AND PREVIEW Many different groups of people have influenced the countries of Central Asia over the years. As a result, the region has a mixture of languages and religions. In the next section you will learn about the governments and economies of the countries of Central Asia today. You will also study some of the challenges these countries face.

Section 2 Assessment

hmhsocialstudies.com
ONLINE QUIZ

Reviewing Ideas, Terms, and Places

1. **a. Identify** What people brought Islam to Central Asia?
   b. Analyze What impact did the Silk Road have on Central Asia?
   c. Elaborate How might Central Asia's history have been different without the influence of the Silk Road?
2. **a. Define** What is a **yurt**?
   b. Analyze What are some of the benefits of nomadic life, and what are some of the challenges of this lifestyle?
   c. Elaborate How might the mix of ethnic groups, languages, and religions in Central Asian countries affect life there today?

Critical Thinking

3. **Sequencing** Review your notes on the history of Central Asia. Then organize your information using a time line like the one below. You may add more dates if you need to.

100 BC — 1991

FOCUS ON VIEWING

4. **Taking Notes on History and Culture** What information about the history and culture of the region might encourage travelers to visit Central Asia? What sites might they be interested in visiting? Jot down a few notes.

Central Asia Today

If YOU lived there...

Your country, Kyrgyzstan, has just had an election. You listen to the radio with your brother, anxiously awaiting the results of the election. When the radio announcer says that the same president has won again, your brother is very angry. He says the election was unfair, and he is going to protest outside the president's palace. He expects there to be a big crowd.

Will you join your brother? Why or why not?

BUILDING BACKGROUND Political protests have been fairly common in some Central Asian countries in recent years. Political instability is just one of the challenges facing Central Asia today as the region learns to deal with independence.

Central Asia Today

A history of invasions and foreign rule has made an impact on Central Asia. Because of years of fighting and changes in the region, today many countries of Central Asia face similar issues in building stable governments and strong economies.

Afghanistan

The situation in Afghanistan today is in many ways a result of a long war with the Soviet Union in the 1980s. The Soviets left in 1989. However, turmoil continued under an alliance of Afghan groups. In the mid-1990s a radical Muslim group known as the **Taliban** arose. The group's leaders took over most of the country, including the capital, **Kabul**.

The Taliban used a strict interpretation of Islamic teachings to rule Afghanistan. For example, the Taliban severely limited the role of women in society. They forced women to wear veils and to stop working outside the home. They also banned all music and dancing. Although most Muslims sharply disagreed with the Taliban's policies, the group remained in power for several years.

What You Will Learn...

Main Ideas

1. The countries of Central Asia are working to develop their economies and to improve political stability in the region.
2. The countries of Central Asia face issues and challenges related to the environment, the economy, and politics.

The Big Idea

Central Asian countries are mostly poor, but they are working to create stable governments and sound economies.

Key Terms and Places

Taliban, *p. 149*
Kabul, *p. 149*
dryland farming, *p. 151*
arable, *p. 151*

hmhsocialstudies.com
TAKING NOTES

Use the graphic organizer online to take notes on governments, economies, and challenges in Central Asia today.

Reforms in Afghanistan

Some reforms have taken place in Afghanistan since the end of Taliban rule. However, the country still faces many challenges.

ANALYZING VISUALS What opportunities might education create for this girl?

Since the End of Taliban Rule . . .

- Afghanistan has a new constitution and an elected president.
- Many people are registered to vote.
- Afghanistan's rules are written and accessible to citizens for the first time.
- New clinics and trained doctors provide more people with access to health care.
- Women can work outside the home.
- Girls can attend school.

Eventually, the Taliban came into conflict with the United States. Investigation of the September 11, 2001, terrorist attacks on New York City and Washington, D.C., led to terrorist leader Osama bin Laden and his al Qaeda network, based in Afghanistan. U.S. and British forces attacked Taliban and al Qaeda targets and toppled Afghanistan's Taliban government.

Since the fall of the Taliban, Afghanistan's government has changed in many ways. The country has a new constitution. Also, all men and women age 18 and older can vote for the president and for the members of a national assembly. Some members of the assembly are appointed by the president, and the constitution requires that half of these appointees be women.

FOCUS ON READING

What is a restatement of *factions*?

Many Afghans hope their government will be stable. However, political factions, or opposing groups, disagree with some of the recent changes. These groups threaten violence, which may make Afghanistan's new government less stable.

Kazakhstan

Kazakhstan was the first part of Central Asia to be conquered by Russia. As a result, Russian influence remains strong in that country today. About one-third of Kazakhstan's people are ethnic Russians. Kazakh and Russian are both official languages. Many ethnic Kazakhs grow up speaking Russian at home and have to learn Kazakh in school.

Kazakhstan's economy was once tied to the former Soviet Union's. It was based on manufacturing. When the Soviet Union collapsed, the economy suffered. However, due to its valuable oil reserves and quick adaptation to the free market, Kazakhstan's economy is now growing steadily. The country is the richest in Central Asia.

Kazakhstan also has one of the more stable governments in Central Asia. The country is a democratic republic with an elected president and parliament. In 1998 Kazakhstan moved its capital from Almaty to Astana, which is closer to Russia.

Kyrgyzstan

The word *kyrgyz* means "forty clans." Throughout history, clan membership has been an important part of Kyrgyzstan's social, political, and economic life. Many people still follow nomadic traditions.

Many other people in Kyrgyzstan are farmers. Fertile soils there allow a mix of irrigated crops and **dryland farming**, or farming that relies on rainfall instead of irrigation. Farming is the most important industry in Kyrgyzstan. However, it does not provide much income for the country.

Although the standard of living in Kyrgyzstan is low, the economy shows signs of strengthening. Tourism might also help Kyrgyzstan's economy. The country has a Muslim pilgrimage site as well as the beautiful Lake Issyk-Kul.

Kyrgyzstan's government is changing. The country has been fairly stable for some years. However, protests in 2005 over what some people thought were unfair elections could signal that times are changing.

Tajikistan

Like other countries in Central Asia, Tajikistan is struggling to overcome its problems. In the mid-1990s the country's Communist government fought against a group of reformers. Some reformers demanded democracy. Others called for a government that ruled by Islamic law. The groups came together and signed a peace agreement in 1997. As a result, Tajikistan is now a republic with an elected president.

Years of civil war damaged Tajikistan's economy. Both industrial and agricultural production declined. Even with the decline in agricultural production, Tajikistan still relies on cotton farming for much of its income. However, only 7 percent of the country's land is **arable**, or suitable for growing crops. Lack of arable land makes progress there difficult.

Turkmenistan

Turkmenistan's president holds all power in the country. He was voted president for life by the country's parliament. He has used his power to name a month of the year after himself, and his face appears on almost everything in Turkmenistan.

The Turkmen government supports Islam and has ordered schools to teach Islamic principles. However, it also views Islam with caution. It does not want Islam to become a political movement.

Turkmenistan's economy is based on oil, gas, and cotton. Although the country is a desert, about half of it is planted with cotton fields. Farming is possible because Turkmenistan has the longest irrigation channel in the world.

FOCUS ON CULTURE

Turkmen Carpets

Decorative carpets are an essential part of a nomad's home. They are also perhaps the most famous artistic craft of Turkmenistan. Carpet factories operate in cities all through Turkmenistan, but some women still weave carpets by hand. These weavers memorize hundreds of intricate designs so they can make rugs that look the same. Each of several different Turkmen tribes has its own rug design.

Analyzing Why are carpets good for a nomadic way of life?

Uzbekistan

Uzbekistan has the largest population of the Central Asian countries. It also has the largest cities in the region. Two cities—Bukhara and Samarqand—are famous for their mosques and monuments.

As in Turkmenistan, Uzbekistan's elected president holds all the political power. The United States has criticized the government for not allowing political freedom or respecting human rights.

The government also closely controls the economy. Uzbekistan's economy, based on oil, gold, and cotton, is fairly stable even though it is growing only very slowly.

READING CHECK **Drawing Inferences** How does physical geography affect the economies of Kyrgyzstan and Tajikistan?

Issues and Challenges

As you have read, the countries of Central Asia face similar issues and challenges. Their greatest challenges are in the areas of environment, economy, and politics.

Environment

One of the most serious environmental problems is the shrinking of the Aral Sea. Winds sweep the dry seafloor and blow dust, salt, and pesticides hundreds of miles. Also, towns that once relied on fishing are now dozens of miles from the shore.

Another problem is the damage caused by Soviet military practices. The Soviets tested nuclear bombs in Central Asia. Now people there suffer poor health because of radiation left over from the tests.

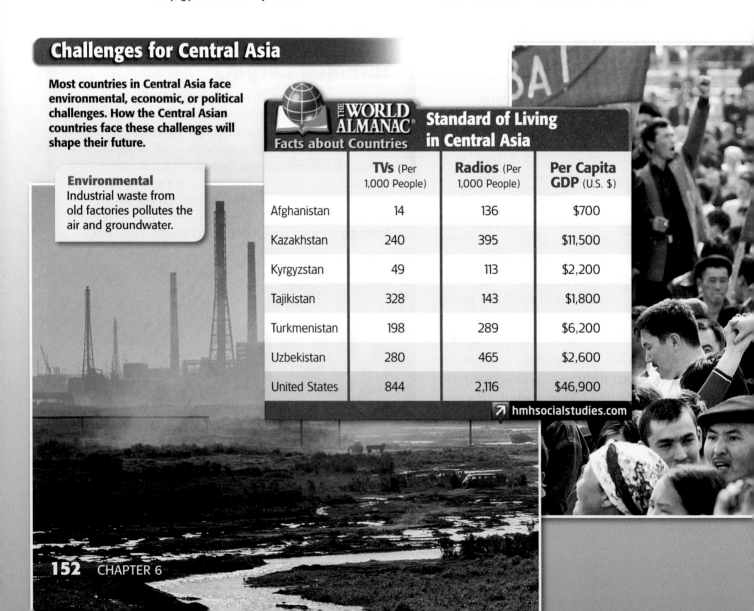

Challenges for Central Asia

Most countries in Central Asia face environmental, economic, or political challenges. How the Central Asian countries face these challenges will shape their future.

Environmental
Industrial waste from old factories pollutes the air and groundwater.

THE WORLD ALMANAC Facts about Countries
Standard of Living in Central Asia

	TVs (Per 1,000 People)	Radios (Per 1,000 People)	Per Capita GDP (U.S. $)
Afghanistan	14	136	$700
Kazakhstan	240	395	$11,500
Kyrgyzstan	49	113	$2,200
Tajikistan	328	143	$1,800
Turkmenistan	198	289	$6,200
Uzbekistan	280	465	$2,600
United States	844	2,116	$46,900

↗ hmhsocialstudies.com

Another environmental problem has been caused by the overuse of chemicals to increase crop production. These chemicals have ended up ruining some farmlands. Instead of increasing crop production, the chemicals have hurt the economy.

Economy

Many of Central Asia's economic problems are due to reliance on one crop—cotton. Suitable farmland is limited, so employment in the cotton industry is limited. Also, the focus on cotton has not encouraged countries to develop manufacturing.

Some countries have oil and gas reserves that may someday make them rich. For now, though, outdated equipment, lack of funds, and poor transportation systems slow development in Central Asia.

Politics

The other main challenge in Central Asia today is lack of political stability. In some countries, such as Kyrgyzstan, people do not agree on the best kind of government. People who are dissatisfied with their government sometimes turn to violence. These countries today are often faced with terrorist threats from different political groups within their own countries.

READING CHECK **Summarizing** What environmental challenges does Central Asia face?

SUMMARY Central Asia is recovering from a history of foreign rule. The region is struggling to develop sound economies and stable governments.

Political Protesters show their opposition to the government in Kyrgyzstan.

ANALYSIS SKILL **ANALYZING VISUALS**

What do you think could be done to improve the environment in Central Asia?

Section 3 Assessment

hmhsocialstudies.com
ONLINE QUIZ

Reviewing Ideas, Terms, and Places

1. **a. Describe** How did the **Taliban** affect Afghanistan?
   b. Contrast What are some major differences between Afghanistan and Kazakhstan?
   c. Elaborate What is one way a country might create more **arable** land?
2. **a. Identify** What three types of challenges does Central Asia face today?
   b. Make Generalizations Why does much of Central Asia face political instability?

Critical Thinking

3. **Categorizing** Using your notes and a chart like the one here, categorize your information on each Central Asian country. You will have to add more lines as needed.

	Government	Economy
Afghanistan		
Kazakhstan		

FOCUS ON VIEWING

4. **Describing Central Asia Today** Write notes about each country in Central Asia. Which countries might you suggest travelers visit? What details might encourage them?

CENTRAL ASIA **153**

The Aral Sea

In 1960 the Aral Sea was the world's fourth-largest lake. However, human activities over the years have caused the Aral Sea to shrink drastically. The lake's former seafloor is now a desert of sand and salt. Also, towns that once benefited from their lakeside location are now left without access to the water. Area governments have built dams to control the flow of water to restore parts of the lake, but so far their efforts have had little success.

Cause
Farmers have taken water from the Amu Darya and the Syr Darya to irrigate cotton fields. Now, less water flows into the sea than evaporates from it.

Effect
Stranded boats are a reminder of the fishing industry once based near the Aral Sea. The fishing industry is dying with the sea.

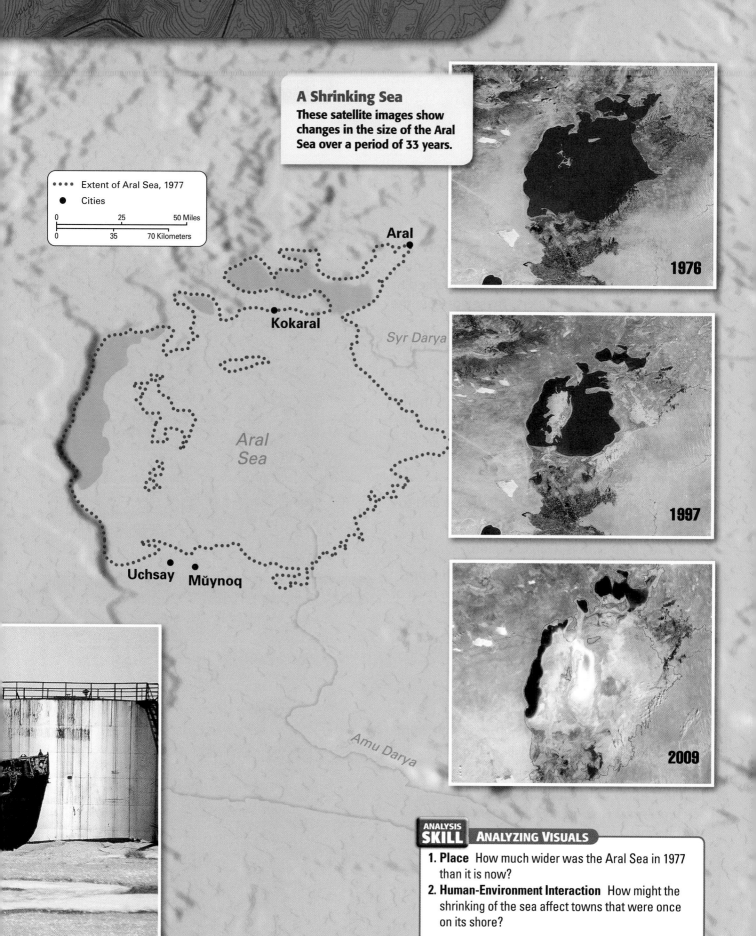

A Shrinking Sea

These satellite images show changes in the size of the Aral Sea over a period of 33 years.

···· Extent of Aral Sea, 1977
● Cities

0   25   50 Miles
0   35   70 Kilometers

Aral

Kokaral

Syr Darya

Aral Sea

Uchsay   **Mŭynoq**

Amu Darya

1976

1997

2009

ANALYSIS SKILL   ANALYZING VISUALS

1. **Place** How much wider was the Aral Sea in 1977 than it is now?
2. **Human-Environment Interaction** How might the shrinking of the sea affect towns that were once on its shore?

Using Scale

Learn

Mapmakers use scales to represent distances between points on a map. On each map legend in this book, you will notice some lines marked to measure miles and kilometers. These lines are the map's scale.

To find the distance between two points on a map, place a piece of paper so that the edge connects the two points. Mark the location of each point on the paper with a line or dot. Then compare the distance between the two dots with the map's scale.

Practice

Use the maps here to practice using scale and to answer the following questions.

❶ Which map shows a larger region?

❷ About how many miles does one inch represent on the map of Kyrgyzstan? on the map of Bishkek?

❸ How far is it from Dubovy Park to Victory Square in Bishkek?

Apply

Use the map of Southwest Asia in the unit opener to answer the following questions.

1. How many miles does one inch represent? How many kilometers does one inch represent?

2. How long is the Caspian Sea from north to south?

3. How far is Turkmenistan from the Persian Gulf?

Bishkek

Kyrgyzstan

Geography's Impact
video series
Review the video to answer the closing question:
What challenges do the people of Afghanistan face today?

Visual Summary

Use the visual summary below to help you review the main ideas of the chapter.

QUICK FACTS

Central Asia is a dry, rugged region. However, people use irrigation to grow cotton, the region's main crop.

Some people follow traditional ways of life. For example, nomads move their yurts from place to place.

Central Asia faces environmental, economic, and political challenges. One challenge is the Aral Sea's shrinking.

Reviewing Vocabulary, Terms, and Places

Unscramble each group of letters below to spell a term that matches the given definition.

1. **mnodsa**—people who move often from place to place

2. **yrddnal mrignaf**—farming that relies on rainfall, not irrigation

3. **tryu**—a moveable round house of wool felt mats hung over a wood frame

4. **ssblhieat**—to set up or create

5. **fgrenaa vlyela**—fertile region that has been a center of farming for thousands of years

6. **tlbania**—a radical Muslim group

7. **dknadclleo**—completely surrounded by land with no direct access to the ocean

8. **kluba**—the capital of Afghanistan

9. **aabler**—suitable for growing crops

10. **aalr sae**—body of water that is shrinking because of use of water for irrigation

Comprehension and Critical Thinking

SECTION 1 *(Pages 140–143)*

11. **a. Describe** How are farmers able to grow crops in Central Asia's dry landscapes?

    b. Analyze What factors make it difficult for the countries of Central Asia to export their oil and gas resources?

    c. Evaluate Do you think Central Asia's location or its mountains do more to keep the region isolated? Explain your answer.

SECTION 2 *(Pages 144–148)*

12. **a. Describe** How did life in Central Asia change under Russian and Soviet rule?

    b. Analyze In what ways do the people of Central Asia show their pride in their past and their culture?

    c. Evaluate Why do you think many former nomads now live in cities? Why do you think other people still choose to live as nomads?

13. a. Identify What are some reforms that have taken place in Afghanistan since the fall of the Taliban?

b. Analyze How does having a limited amount of arable land affect Tajikistan's economy?

c. Elaborate How do you think political and environmental challenges in Central Asia affect the region's economy?

Map Activity

14. Central Asia On a separate sheet of paper, match the letters on the map with their correct labels.

Aral Sea	Pamirs
Caspian Sea	Astana, Kazakhstan
Afghanistan	Tashkent, Uzbekistan

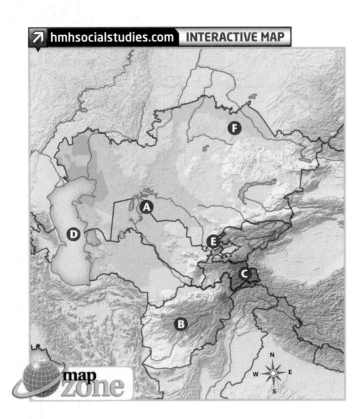

hmhsocialstudies.com **INTERACTIVE MAP**

Social Studies Skills

Using Scale *Use the physical map of Central Asia in Section 1 to answer the following questions.*

15. How many miles does one inch represent?

16. How far is it from the shore of the Caspian Sea to Ismail Samani Peak?

17. How many kilometers long is the Amu Darya?

Using the Internet

18. Activity: Writing Home For thousands of years, nomads have traveled the lands of Central Asia. They move their herds to several different pasture areas as the seasons change. Through the online book, join a caravan of nomads. Find out what it is like to pack up your house, clothes, and all you own as you move from place to place. Then create a postcard to share your adventures with friends and family back home in the United States.

hmhsocialstudies.com

FOCUS ON READING AND VIEWING

19. Using Context Clues Look through your book for examples of restatement. Note one or two examples of restatement for each section of the chapter.

20. Giving a Travel Presentation Review your notes and select one country in Central Asia your audience might want to visit. Look for pictures of at least five locations in that country: buildings, monuments, or other interesting places. As you plan your presentation, create a brief introduction, a brief description of each location and its picture, and a conclusion. Hold up each picture and point out important features as you make your presentation.

As you watch your classmates' presentations, listen carefully. Make note of their eye contact with the audience, use of gestures to add interest, use of interesting pictures, and persuasiveness.

Standardized Test Prep

DIRECTIONS: Read questions 1 through 7 and write the letter of the best response. Then read question 8 and write your own well-constructed response.

1 **What is the main crop grown in Central Asia?**

A wheat

B olives

C cotton

D corn

2 **Which of the following descriptions *best* describes the landscape of Central Asia?**

A dry and rugged

B dry and flat

C humid and landlocked

D humid and cold

3 **How did the Arabs influence Central Asia in the 700s and 800s?**

A separated ethnic groups

B destroyed cities and irrigation systems

C built railroads and expanded oil production

D introduced Islam

4 **Which of the following statements about the nomadic lifestyle is false?**

A Nomads move their herds depending on the season.

B Nomads decorate their yurts with carpets.

C It is a symbol of the region's heritage.

D Nomads often move from one dwelling to another.

5 **What country did the Taliban rule?**

A Kazakhstan

B Afghanistan

C Kyrgyzstan

D Uzbekistan

Farmland in Central Asia

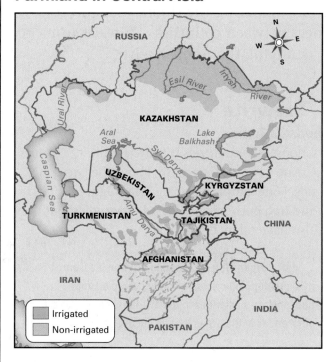

6 **Based on the map above, what country has the most non-irrigated farmland?**

A Kazakhstan

B Tajikistan

C Turkmenistan

D Uzbekistan

7 **Based on the map above and your knowledge of the physical geography of Central Asia, what is the main reason there is little farmland in eastern Kyrgyzstan and Tajikistan?**

A There are too many rivers.

B Most people live as nomads there.

C The area is too mountainous.

D The area is a desert.

8 **Extended Response** Using the map and your knowledge of Central Asia, write a brief essay explaining how irrigation has affected the region.

Compare and Contrast

How are two countries alike? How are they different? Comparing the similarities and contrasting the differences between countries can teach us more than we can learn by studying them separately.

Assignment

Write a paper comparing and contrasting two countries from this unit. Consider physical geography, government, and/or culture.

1. Prewrite

Choose a Topic

- Choose two countries to write about.
- Create a big idea, or thesis, about the two counries. For example, your big idea might be "Iran and Iraq both have oil-based economies, but they also have many differences."

> **TIP** **Organizing Information** A Venn diagram (two overlapping circles) can help you plan your paper. Write similarities in the overlapping area and differences in the areas that do not overlap.

Gather and Organize Information

- Identify at least three similarities or differences between the countries.
- Decide whether to write about each country one at a time or to discuss each point of similarity or difference one at a time.

2. Write

Use a Writer's Framework

> **A Writer's Framework**
>
> **Introduction**
> - Start with a fact or question relating to both countries.
> - Identify your big idea.
>
> **Body**
> - Write at least one paragraph for each country or each point of similarity or difference. Include facts and details to help explain each point.
> - Use block style or point-by-point style.
>
> **Conclusion**
> - Summarize the process in your final paragraph.

3. Evaluate And Revise

Review and Improve Your Paper

- Re-read your draft, then ask yourself the questions below to see if you have followed the framework.
- Make any changes needed to improve your comparison and conrast paper.

Evaluation Questions for a Compare and Contrast Paper

1. Do you begin with an interesting fact or question that relates to both countries?
2. Does your first paragraph clearly state your big idea and provide background information?
3. Do you discuss at least three similarities and differences between the countries?
4. Do you include facts and details to explain each similarity or difference?
5. Is your paper clearly organized by country or by similarities and differences?

4. Proofread And Publish

Give Your Explanation the Finishing Touch

- Make sure you have capitalized the names of countries and cities.
- Check for punctuation around transitional words and phrases like and, but, or similarly.
- Share your compare-and-contrast paper by reading it aloud in class or in small groups.

5. Practice And Apply

Use the steps outlined in this workshop to write a compare-and-contrast paper. Compare and contrast your paper to those of your classmates.

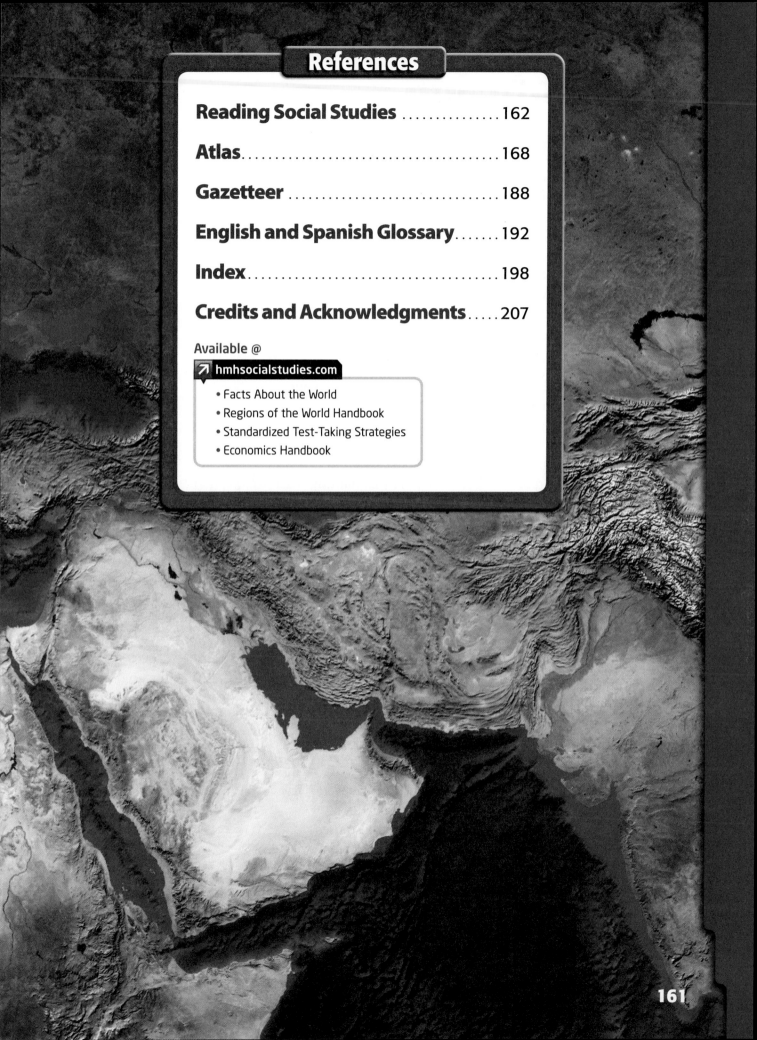

References

Available @

⬈ **hmhsocialstudies.com**

- Facts About the World
- Regions of the World Handbook
- Standardized Test-Taking Strategies
- Economics Handbook

Paraphrasing

FOCUS ON READING

When you paraphrase, you explain someone else's idea in your own words. When you put an idea in your own words, you will understand it better and remember it longer. To paraphrase a passage, first read it carefully. Make sure you understand the main ideas. Then, using your own words, restate what the writer is saying. Keep the ideas in the same order and focus on using your own, familiar vocabulary. Your sentences may be shorter and simpler, but they should match the ideas in the text. Below is an example of a paraphrased passage.

Original Text	**Paraphrase**
Priests, people who performed or led religious ceremonies, had great status in Sumer. People relied on them to help gain the gods' favor. Priests interpreted the wishes of the gods and made offerings to them. These offerings were made in temples, special buildings where priests performed their religious ceremonies.	Priests hold the religious services, so people respect them. People want the priests to help them get on the gods' good side. Priests do this by explaining what the gods want and by making offerings. They make offerings in a special building where they lead services.

From Section 2, The Rise of Sumer

To paraphrase:
- Understand the ideas.
- Use your own words.
- Keep the same order.
- Make it sound like you.
- Keep it about the same length.

YOU TRY IT!

Read the following passage, and then write a paraphrase using the steps described above.

Irrigation increased the amount of food farmers were able to grow. In fact, farmers could produce a food surplus, or more than they needed. Farmers also used irrigation to water grazing areas for cattle and sheep. As a result, Mesopotamians ate a variety of foods. Fish, meat, wheat, barley, and dates were plentiful.

From Section 1, Geography of the Fertile Crescent

Understanding Implied Main Ideas

FOCUS ON READING

Do you ever "read between the lines" when people say things? You understand what people mean even when they don't come right out and say it. You can do the same thing with writing. Writers don't always state the main idea directly, but you can find clues to the main idea in the details. To understand an implied main idea, first read the text carefully and think about the topic. Next, look at the facts and details and ask yourself what the paragraph is saying. Then create a statement that sums up the main idea. Notice the way this process works with the paragraph below.

As a young man Jesus lived in the town of Nazareth and probably studied with Joseph to become a carpenter. Like many young Jewish men of the time, Jesus also studied the laws and teachings of Judaism. By the time he was about 30, Jesus had begun to travel and teach.

From Section 2, Origins of Christianity

1. What is the topic?
Jesus as a young man

2. What are the facts and details?
• lived in Nazareth
• studied to be a carpenter
• learned about Judaism

3. What is the main idea?
Jesus lived the typical life of a young Jewish man.

YOU TRY IT!

Read the following sentences. Notice the main idea is not stated. Using the three steps described above, develop a statement that expresses the main idea of the paragraph.

Justinian was stopped from leaving by his wife, Theodora. She convinced Justinian to stay in the city. Smart and powerful, Theodora helped her husband rule effectively. With her advice, he found a way to end the riots. Justinian's soldiers killed all the rioters—some 30,000 people—and saved the emperor's throne.

From Section 3, The Byzantine Empire

Sequencing

READING SOCIAL STUDIES

FOCUS ON READING

When you read about how countries and cultures developed, it is necessary to understand the sequence, or order, of events. Writers sometimes signal the sequence by using words or phrases such as *first, before, then, later, soon, next,* or *finally*. Sometimes writers use dates instead to indicate the order of events. Developing a sequence chain is a way to help you mark and understand the order of events. Clue words indicating sequence are underlined in the example.

> As the Muslim community in Medina grew stronger, other Arab tribes began to accept Islam. Conflict with the Meccans, however, increased. In 630, after several years of fighting, the people of Mecca gave in. They accepted Islam as their religion.
>
> Before long, most people in Arabia had accepted Muhammad as their spiritual and political leader and become Muslims. Muhammad died in 632, but the religion he taught would soon spread far beyond the Arabian Peninsula.
>
> *From Section 1, Origins of Islam*

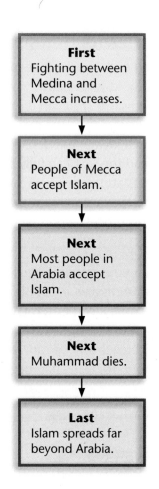

First
Fighting between Medina and Mecca increases.

Next
People of Mecca accept Islam.

Next
Most people in Arabia accept Islam.

Next
Muhammad dies.

Last
Islam spreads far beyond Arabia.

YOU TRY IT!

Read the following passage. Create a graphic organizer like the one above to list the events in sequence. Use as many boxes as you need to create a full sequence chain.

> In 711 a combined Arab and Berber army invaded Spain and quickly conquered it. Next, the army moved into what is now France, but it was stopped by a Christian army near the city of Tours. Despite this defeat, Muslims called Moors ruled parts of Spain for the next 700 years.
>
> *From Section 3, Muslim Empires*

Setting a Purpose

FOCUS ON READING

When you start on a trip, you have a purpose or a destination in mind. When you read, you should also have a purpose in mind before you start. This purpose keeps you focused and moving toward your goal. To decide on a purpose, look over the headings, pictures, and study tips before you read. Then ask yourself a question that can guide your reading. See how a heading suggested a purpose for the passage below.

Israeli Teens for Peace

Peace between Israeli Jews and Palestinian Arabs has not been easy in the past. Moreover, some believe peace in the region might be impossible ever to accomplish. But don't tell that to a group of more than 2,000 Jewish and Arab teenagers who are making a difference in Israel. These teens belong to an organization called Seeds of Peace. To learn more about each other's culture and thus understand each other better, these teens meet regularly.

From Section 3, Israel

Notice Headings, Pictures or Tips
Here's a heading about teenagers and a picture.

↓

Set a Purpose
I wonder who these teenagers are and what they're doing for peace. I'll read to find out.

↓

Ask Questions
What's so important about these teenagers?

YOU TRY IT!

Read the following introduction to the section on Israel. Ask yourself questions that can set a purpose for your reading. Following the steps given above, develop a purpose for reading about Israel. State this purpose in one to two sentences.

Do you know that Israel is often referred to as the Holy Land? Some people call Israel the Holy Land because it is home to sacred sites for three of the world's major religions—Judaism, Christianity, and Islam. Throughout the region's history, these three groups have fought over their right to the land.

From Section 3, Israel

Re-Reading

FOCUS ON READING

When you read about other countries, you will come across some information that is completely new to you. Sometimes it can seem difficult to keep all the people, places, dates, and events straight. Re-reading can help you absorb new information and understand the main facts of a passage. Follow these three steps in re-reading. First, read the whole passage. Look over the passage and identify the main details you need to focus on. Then re-read the passage slowly. As you read, make sure you understand the details by restating the details silently. If necessary, go back and re-read until you have the details firmly in your mind. Here's how this process works with the following passage.

> The Persian Empire was later conquered by several Muslim empires. Muslims converted the Persians to Islam, but most people retained their Persian culture. They built beautiful mosques with colorful tiles and large domes.
>
> *From Section 4, Iran*

1. Read the passage.

2. Identify the main details to focus on.
Persian Empire, Muslims, culture

3. Re-read and restate the details silently.
The Persian Empire was first. Then it was conquered by Muslims. Persian and Muslim cultures blended. Mosques show the region's culture.

YOU TRY IT!

Read the following sentences. Then, following the three steps above, write down the main details to focus on. After you re-read the paragraph, write down the information restated in your own words to show that you understood what you read.

> The Tigris and Euphrates rivers flow across a low, flat plain in Iraq. They join together before they reach the Persian Gulf. The Tigris and Euphrates are what are known as exotic rivers, or rivers that begin in humid regions and then flow through dry areas. The rivers create a narrow fertile area, which in ancient times was called Mesopotamia, or the "land between rivers."
>
> *From Section 1, Physical Geography*

Using Context Clues

FOCUS ON READING

One way to figure out the meaning of an unfamiliar word or term is by finding clues in its context, the words or sentences surrounding it. A common context clue is a restatement. Restatements simply define the new word using ordinary words you already know. Notice how the following passage uses a restatement to define nomads.

For centuries, Central Asians have made a living by raising horses, cattle, sheep, and goats. Many herders live as <u>nomads</u>, people who move often from place to place. The nomads move their herds from mountain pastures in the summer to lowland pastures in the winter.

From Section 2, History and Culture

Restatement: people who move often from place to place

YOU TRY IT!

Read the following sentences and identify the restatement for each underlined term.

Many other people in Kyrgyzstan are farmers. Fertile soils there allow a mix of irrigated crops and <u>dryland farming</u>, or farming that relies on rainfall instead of irrigation.

Even with the decline in agricultural production, Tajikistan still relies on cotton farming for much of its income. However, only 5 to 6 percent of the country's land is <u>arable</u>, or suitable for growing crops.

From Section 3, Central Asia Today

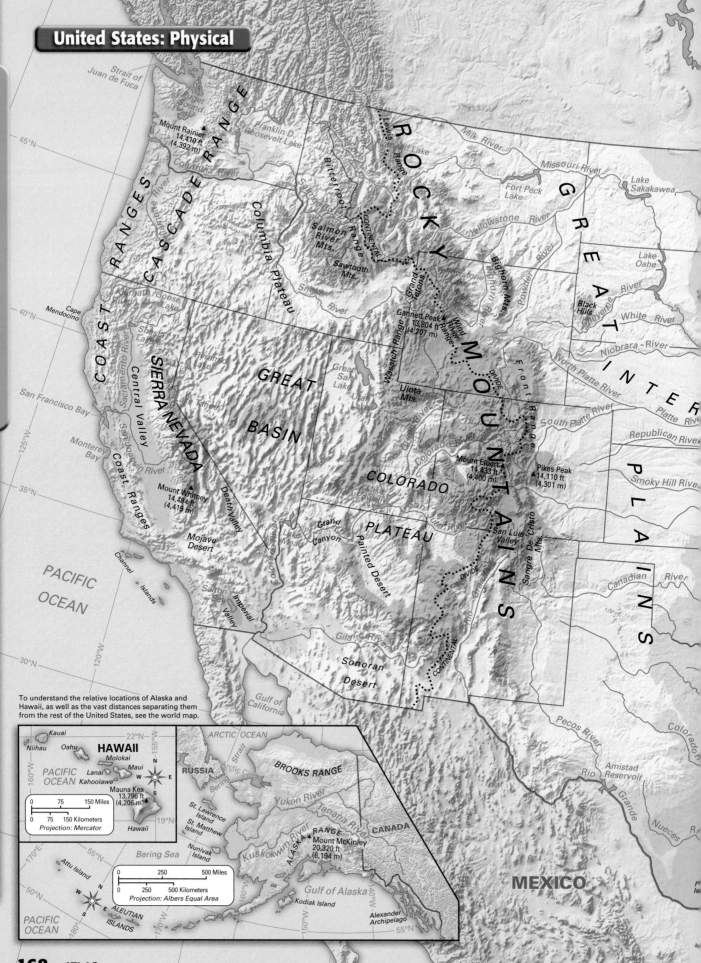

ATLAS

Strait of Juan de Fuca

Puget Sound

Mount Rainier
14,410 ft
(4,392 m)

Franklin D. Roosevelt Lake

Milk River

Missouri River

Lake Sakakawea

45°N

COLUMBIA River

Columbia River

Willamette River

Bitterroot Range

Lewis Range

CONTINENTAL

Lake

Fort Peck Lake

Yellowstone River

ROCKY

GREAT

Columbia Plateau

Salmon River Mts.

Sawtooth Mts.

Klamath

Goose Lake

Snake River

Grand Tetons

Gannett Peak
13,804 ft
(4,207 m)

Wind River Range

Yellowstone River

Bighorn Mts.

Powder River

Lake Oahe

40°N

Cape Mendocino

Shasta Lake

Pyramid Lake

Great Salt Lake

Wasatch Range

Uinta Mts.

DIVIDE

Front Range

Black Hills

Cheyenne River

White River

Niobrara River

INTER

125°W

San Francisco Bay

Sacramento River

Central Valley

San Joaquin River

SIERRA NEVADA

Lake Tahoe

GREAT

BASIN

Utah Lake

Green River

Colorado River

North Platte River

South Platte River

Platte River

Republican River

PLAINS

Monterey Bay

Coast Ranges

Mount Whitney
14,494 ft
(4,419 m)

Death Valley

Lake Mead

Grand Canyon

Great Salt Lake

COLORADO

PLATEAU

Mount Elbert
14,433 ft
(4,400 m)

San Luis Valley

Pikes Peak
14,110 ft
(4,301 m)

Smoky Hill River

35°N

MOUNTAINS

Sangre De Cristo Mts.

Channel Islands

PACIFIC

OCEAN

Mojave Desert

Salton Sea

Imperial Valley

Painted Desert

DIVIDE

Rio Grande

Canadian River

120°W

30°N

Gila River

Sonoran Desert

Gulf of California

CONTINENTAL

Pecos River

MEXICO

Colorado

To understand the relative locations of Alaska and Hawaii, as well as the vast distances separating them from the rest of the United States, see the world map.

Amistad Reservoir

Rio Grande

Nueces River

Kauai

Niihau

Oahu

HAWAII

Molokai

Maui

Lanai

Kahoolawe

PACIFIC OCEAN

22°N

155°W

ARCTIC OCEAN

Arctic Strait

RUSSIA

Arctic Circle

Bering Strait

BROOKS RANGE

CANADA

160°W

Mauna Kea
13,796 ft
(4,206 m)

Hawaii

19°N

0   75   150 Miles

0   75   150 Kilometers

Projection: Mercator

St. Lawrence Island

St. Matthew Island

Yukon River

Tanana River

ALASKA

RANGE

Mount McKinley
20,320 ft
(6,194 m)

170°E

55°N

Bering Sea

Nunivak Island

Kuskokwim River

250   500 Miles

0   250   500 Kilometers

Projection: Albers Equal Area

Kodiak Island

Gulf of Alaska

Alexander Archipelago

55°N

50°N

180°

Attu Island

ALEUTIAN ISLANDS

PACIFIC OCEAN

CANADA

Isle Royale

Mesabi Range

Lake Superior

St. Lawrence River

St. Lawrence Seaway

Longfellow Mts.

Penobscot River

St. John River

Minnesota River

Wisconsin River

Mississippi River

Lake Michigan

Lake Huron

Lake Champlain

Adirondack Mts.

Green Mts.

White Mts.

Connecticut River

Cape Cod

Missouri River

Des Moines River

Illinois River

Wabash River

Scioto River

ALLEGHENY PLATEAU

Catskill Mts.

Susquehanna River

Delaware River

Long Island Sound

Long Island

40°N

Lake Ontario

Lake Erie

P L A I N S

Ohio River

Kanawha River

Monongahela R.

Potomac River

APPALACHIAN MOUNTAINS

Delaware Bay

James River

Chesapeake Bay

ATLANTIC OCEAN

Minnesota River

Arkansas R.

Lake of the Ozarks

OZARK PLATEAU

Keystone Lake

White River

Arkansas River

Lake Barkley

Kentucky Lake

Cumberland River

Cumberland Plateau

Great Smoky Mts.

BLUE RIDGE MOUNTAINS

PIEDMONT

Roanoke River

Pamlico Sound

Cape Hatteras

35°N

70°W

Ouachita Mts.

Tennessee River

Coosa River

Oconee River

Savannah River

Toledo Bend Reservoir

Saline River

Red River

Pearl River

Mississippi River

Tombigbee River

Alabama R.

Chattahoochee River

Altamaha River

Sea Islands

Trinity River

COASTAL PLAIN

Chandeleur Islands

Mississippi Delta

Okefenokee Swamp

FLORIDA PENINSULA

Cape Canaveral

GULF

Gulf of Mexico

N W E S

Lake Okeechobee

BAHAMAS

25°N

The Everglades

Cape Sable

Florida Keys

Straits of Florida

ELEVATION

Feet		Meters
13,120		4,000
6,560		2,000
1,640		500
656		200
(Sea level) 0		0 (Sea level)
Below sea level		Below sea level

0   100   200 Miles

0   100   200 Kilometers

Projection: Albers Equal Area

95°W   90°W   85°W   80°W   75°W

ATLAS

Strait of
Juan de Fuca

Seattle
Olympia ★ ● Tacoma
● Spokane

WASHINGTON

Puget
Sound

Franklin D.
Roosevelt Lake

Pend
Oreille

Portland ●
Columbia River

Flathead
Lake

Great Falls ●

Helena ★ **MONTANA**

Fort Peck
Lake

Missouri River

★ Salem

Billings ●

Yellowstone River

NORTH DAKOT

Lake
Sakakawea

● Bismarck

● Eugene

OREGON

IDAHO

Boise ★
● Sun Valley

Snake
River

Pocatello ●

Yellowstone
Lake

WYOMING

Cheyenne ★

Lake
Oahe

SOUTH DAKOTA

Pierre ★

Rapid City ●

NEBRASKA

Platte Ri

Cape
Mendocino

Goose
Lake

Shasta
Lake

Sacramento River

Pyramid
Lake

Reno ●
★ Carson City
Lake Tahoe

NEVADA

Great
Salt
Lake

Ogden ●
★ Salt Lake City
● Provo

Utah
Lake

UTAH

Green River

Boulder ●
Vail ●
Aspen ●
Salt Lake City

★ Denver
Colorado
Springs ●

COLORADO

Pueblo ●

Arkansas River

KANS

Berkeley ●
Oakland ●
San Francisco ●
★ Sacramento
San Jose ●
San Joaquin River
San Francisco Bay

Monterey
Bay

● Fresno

CALIFORNIA

Las
Vegas ●

Colorado River

Lake
Mead

Lake
Powell

Flagstaff ●

ARIZONA

Taos ●
Santa Fe ★
● Albuquerque

NEW MEXICO

Canadian River

Oklahoma ●

OKLAHO

● Amarillo

Lav

**PACIFIC
OCEAN**

Santa Barbara ●
Ventura ●
Long
Beach ●
Channel
Islands

Los
Angeles ●
Riverside ●
Palm Springs ●
Anaheim ●
Santa Ana ●
San Diego ●

Salton
Sea

Phoenix ★

Gila River

Casa Grande ●

● Tucson

Las Cruces ●

El Paso ●

Rio Grande

● Lubbock

Brazos River

● Abilene

Midland ●
Odessa ●

Colorado Rive

Fort W

TEXAS

Aust

Pecos River

San Antonio ●

Amistad
Reservoir

Corpus Chr

● Laredo

MEXICO

To understand the relative locations of Alaska and
Hawaii, as well as the vast distances separating them
from the rest of the United States, see the world map.

Gulf of
California

Kauai
Niihau Oahu
Honolulu ★ Molokai
PACIFIC Lanai Maui
OCEAN Kahoolawe
Hilo ●
Hawaii

HAWAII

22°N
155°W

ARCTIC OCEAN

Arctic Circle

RUSSIA

Bering Strait

St. Lawrence
Island
St. Matthew
Island

● Nome

Yukon River

Fairbanks ●

CANADA

0   75   150 Miles
0   75   150 Kilometers
Projection: Mercator

19°N

Nunivak
Island

ALASKA

Anchorage ●
● Valdez

● Skagway

Attu Island

**PACIFIC
OCEAN**

170°E

55°N

**ALEUTIAN
ISLANDS**

Bering Sea

0   250   500 Miles
0   250   500 Kilometers
Projection: Albers Equal Area

160°W

Gulf of Alaska

Kodiak Island

Juneau ★

Alexander
Archipelago

55°N

CANADA

MINNESOTA

Grand Forks
Fargo
Duluth
Superior
Marquette
Sault Ste. Marie

Red River
Minnesota River
Lake Superior

WISCONSIN
Minneapolis
St. Paul
Green Bay
Madison
Milwaukee

MICHIGAN
Grand Rapids
Saginaw
Lansing
Detroit
Ann Arbor

Lake Michigan
Lake Huron

Sioux Falls
Sioux City

IOWA
Cedar Rapids
Davenport
Des Moines
Rockford
Chicago
Gary
South Bend
Fort Wayne
Peoria
Springfield

Mississippi River
Missouri River
Illinois River

Cleveland
Toledo
Youngstown
Akron

INDIANA
Indianapolis

OHIO
Columbus
Dayton
Cincinnati

ILLINOIS
St. Louis
East St. Louis

Omaha
Lincoln

MISSOURI
Kansas City
Kansas City
Jefferson City

Topeka
Wichita

Lake of the Ozarks
Keystone Lake

Springfield

KENTUCKY
Louisville
Evansville
Frankfort
Lexington

Ohio River

Tulsa
Fayetteville

ARKANSAS
Little Rock
Pine Bluff

Eufaula Lake
Lake Texoma

Memphis

Kentucky Lake
Lake Barkley
Kentucky River

TENNESSEE
Nashville
Knoxville
Chattanooga

MISSISSIPPI
Vicksburg
Jackson
Meridian

ALABAMA
Huntsville
Birmingham
Montgomery

Dallas
Waco

LOUISIANA
Shreveport
Baton Rouge
Biloxi
New Orleans

Beaumont
Houston
Galveston

Red River
Toledo Bend Reservoir

Chandeleur Islands

Mobile
Pensacola

Gulf of Mexico

GEORGIA
Atlanta
Macon
Columbus
Savannah

Chattahoochee River
Savannah River
Sea Islands

Charleston

SOUTH CAROLINA
Columbia
Greenville

NORTH CAROLINA
Winston-Salem
Greensboro
Durham
Raleigh
Asheville
Charlotte

Cape Hatteras

Tallahassee
Gainesville
Jacksonville

FLORIDA
Orlando
Tampa
St. Petersburg
Fort Myers
Fort Lauderdale
Miami

Cape Canaveral
Lake Okeechobee
Cape Sable
Florida Keys
Straits of Florida

BAHAMAS

NEW YORK
Rochester
Syracuse
Buffalo
Albany

Lake Ontario
Lake Erie

MAINE
Augusta
Portland

St. Lawrence River
Lake Champlain
Burlington
Montpelier
VT
NH
Concord
Manchester
Boston
Worcester
Providence
Springfield
MA
Hartford
CT **RI**
New Haven
Bridgeport
Yonkers
Newark
Jersey City
New York City
Long Island
Long Island Sound
Cape Cod

Hudson R.
Connecticut R.

PENNSYLVANIA
Allentown
Trenton
Harrisburg
Pittsburgh
Philadelphia
Camden
NJ
Atlantic City
DE
Dover
Baltimore
MD
Annapolis
Washington D.C.

Susquehanna River
Delaware Bay
Chesapeake Bay

WEST VIRGINIA
Charleston

VIRGINIA
Richmond
Newport News
Norfolk
Virginia Beach

ATLANTIC OCEAN

40°N
35°N
30°N
25°N
70°W
75°W
80°W
85°W
90°W
95°W

N E S W

Legend
- National capital
- State capitals
- Other cities

0 100 200 Miles
0 100 200 Kilometers

Projection: Albers Equal Area

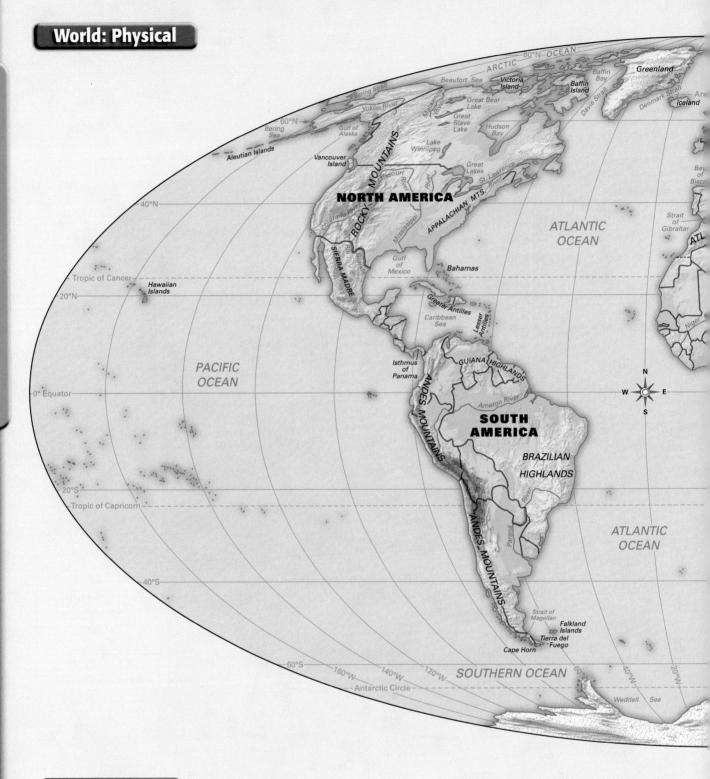

ARCTIC 80°N OCEAN
Beaufort Sea
Victoria Island
Baffin Bay
Greenland
Bering Strait
Great Bear Lake
Baffin Island
Davis Strait
Denmark Strait
Iceland
Yukon River
Mackenzie River
Great Slave Lake
Hudson Bay
60°N
Bering Sea
Gulf of Alaska
Lake Winnipeg
Great Lakes
St. Lawrence River
Bay of Biscay
Aleutian Islands
Vancouver Island
ROCKY MOUNTAINS
Missouri River
NORTH AMERICA
40°N
APPALACHIAN MTS.
ATLANTIC OCEAN
Strait of Gibraltar
ATL
Colorado River
Mississippi
Rio Grande
SIERRA MADRE
Gulf of Mexico
Bahamas
Tropic of Cancer
Hawaiian Islands
20°N
Greater Antilles
Caribbean Sea
Lesser Antilles
Niger
PACIFIC OCEAN
Isthmus of Panama
GUIANA HIGHLANDS
0° Equator
ANDES MOUNTAINS
Amazon River
SOUTH AMERICA
N
W E
S
BRAZILIAN HIGHLANDS
20°S
Paraná River
Tropic of Capricorn
ATLANTIC OCEAN
40°S
ANDES MOUNTAINS
Strait of Magellan
Falkland Islands
Tierra del Fuego
Cape Horn
60°S
160°W
140°W
120°W
SOUTHERN OCEAN
40°W
20°W
Antarctic Circle
Weddell Sea

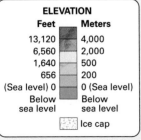

ELEVATION

Feet	Meters
13,120	4,000
6,560	2,000
1,640	500
656	200
(Sea level) 0	0 (Sea level)
Below sea level	Below sea level

Ice cap

0   500   1,000   1,500   2,000 Miles
0   1,000   2,000 Kilometers

Projection: Mollweide

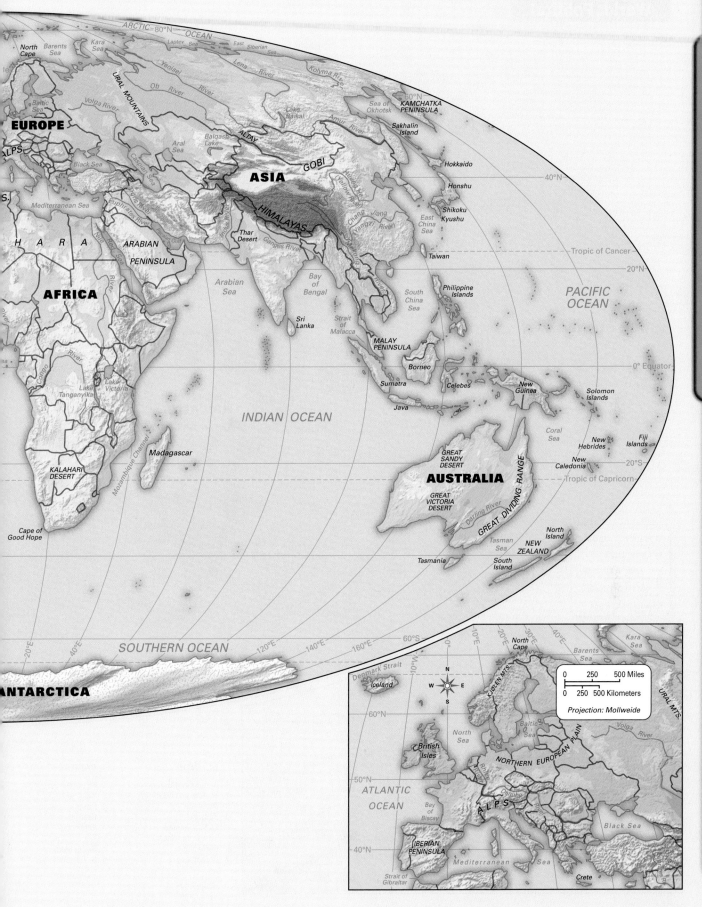

EUROPE

ALPS

U.S.

Mediterranean Sea

S A H A R A

AFRICA

Congo River

Lake Tanganyika

Lake Victoria

KALAHARI DESERT

Cape of Good Hope

River

North Cape

Barents Sea

Kara Sea

Baltic Sea

Black Sea

URAL MOUNTAINS

Volga River

Ob River

Yenisei River

Lena River

ARCTIC 80°N OCEAN

Laptev Sea

East Siberian Sea

Kolyma River

Aral Sea

Caspian Sea

Balqash Lake

ALTAY

ASIA

GOBI

HIMALAYAS

Tien Shan

Thar Desert

Euphrates River

Tigris River

ARABIAN PENINSULA

Arabian Sea

Sri Lanka

Indus River

Ganges River

Bay of Bengal

Chang Jiang (Yangzi) River

Huang He

Yellow River

Mekong River

Amur River

50°N

Sea of Okhotsk

KAMCHATKA PENINSULA

Sakhalin Island

Hokkaido

Honshu

Shikoku

Kyushu

40°N

Taiwan

East China Sea

South China Sea

Philippine Islands

Tropic of Cancer

20°N

PACIFIC OCEAN

Strait of Malacca

MALAY PENINSULA

Sumatra

Java

Borneo

Celebes

New Guinea

Solomon Islands

0° Equator

INDIAN OCEAN

Madagascar

Mozambique Channel

GREAT SANDY DESERT

AUSTRALIA

GREAT VICTORIA DESERT

Darling River

GREAT DIVIDING RANGE

Coral Sea

New Hebrides

New Caledonia

Fiji Islands

20°S

Tropic of Capricorn

Tasman Sea

Tasmania

South Island

North Island

NEW ZEALAND

60°S

20°E

40°E

120°E

140°E

160°E

SOUTHERN OCEAN

ANTARCTICA

Denmark Strait

Iceland

ATLANTIC OCEAN

British Isles

60°N

50°N

Bay of Biscay

40°N

IBERIAN PENINSULA

Strait of Gibraltar

North Cape

10°E

20°E

30°E

40°E

0°

10°W

KJØLEN MTS.

North Sea

Baltic Sea

NORTHERN EUROPEAN PLAIN

Rhine

Danube

ALPS

Mediterranean Sea

Crete

Black Sea

Kara Sea

Barents Sea

Volga River

URAL MTS.

N W E S

| 0 | 250 | 500 Miles |
| 0 | 250 | 500 Kilometers |

Projection: Mollweide

World: Political

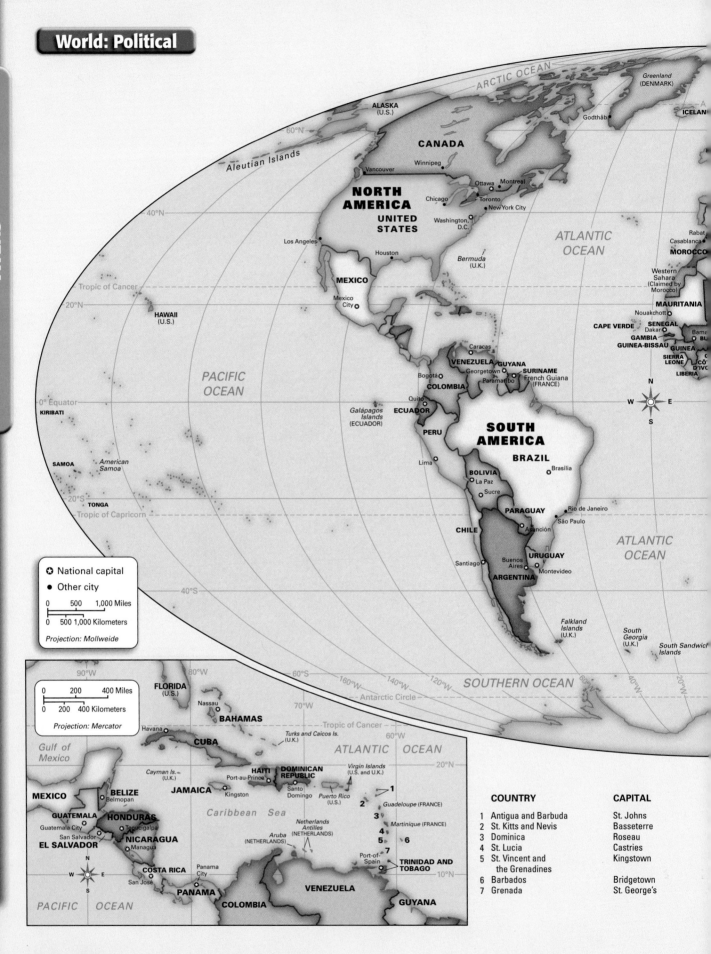

ARCTIC OCEAN

Greenland
(DENMARK)

ALASKA
(U.S.)

ICELAN

CANADA

Godthåb

Aleutian Islands

Vancouver
Winnipeg

Ottawa Montreal

NORTH
AMERICA

Chicago
Toronto

New York City

UNITED
STATES

Washington,
D.C.

ATLANTIC
OCEAN

Rabat
Casablanca

Los Angeles

Houston

Bermuda
(U.K.)

MOROCCO

MEXICO

Tropic of Cancer

Western
Sahara
(Claimed by
Morocco)

Mexico
City

MAURITANIA

HAWAII
(U.S.)

Nouakchott

CAPE VERDE

SENEGAL
Dakar

Bama
BU

Caracas

GAMBIA
GUINEA-BISSAU

GUINEA

VENEZUELA
GUYANA

Georgetown
SURINAME

SIERRA
LEONE

CÔ
D'IVC

PACIFIC
OCEAN

Bogotá

Paramaribo
French Guiana
(FRANCE)

LIBERIA

COLOMBIA

KIRIBATI

0° Equator

Quito

ECUADOR

Galápagos
Islands
(ECUADOR)

PERU

SOUTH
AMERICA

SAMOA

American
Samoa

Lima

BRAZIL

Brasília

BOLIVIA
La Paz

Sucre

Rio de Janeiro

TONGA

Tropic of Capricorn

PARAGUAY

São Paulo

CHILE

Asunción

ATLANTIC
OCEAN

Santiago

Buenos
Aires

URUGUAY

Montevideo

ARGENTINA

☼ National capital
● Other city

0   500   1,000 Miles
0   500 1,000 Kilometers

Projection: Mollweide

40°S

Falkland
Islands
(U.K.)

South
Georgia
(U.K.)

South Sandwich
Islands

60°S

SOUTHERN OCEAN

Antarctic Circle

90°W   80°W

FLORIDA
(U.S.)

0   200   400 Miles
0   200   400 Kilometers

Projection: Mercator

Nassau

BAHAMAS

Tropic of Cancer

Gulf of
Mexico

Havana

CUBA

Turks and Caicos Is.
(U.K.)

ATLANTIC   OCEAN

20°N

Cayman Is.
(U.K.)

HAITI
Port-au-Prince

DOMINICAN
REPUBLIC

Virgin Islands
(U.S. and U.K.)

1

MEXICO

BELIZE
Belmopan

JAMAICA

Kingston

Santo
Domingo

Puerto Rico
(U.S.)

2

Guadeloupe (FRANCE)

GUATEMALA

HONDURAS

Caribbean Sea

3

Guatemala City

Tegucigalpa

Netherlands
Antilles
(NETHERLANDS)

Martinique (FRANCE)

San Salvador

NICARAGUA

4

EL SALVADOR

Managua

Aruba
(NETHERLANDS)

5

6

7

COSTA RICA

Panama
City

Port-of-
Spain

TRINIDAD AND
TOBAGO

San José

PANAMA

PACIFIC   OCEAN

VENEZUELA

COLOMBIA

GUYANA

10°N

	COUNTRY	CAPITAL
1	Antigua and Barbuda	St. Johns
2	St. Kitts and Nevis	Basseterre
3	Dominica	Roseau
4	St. Lucia	Castries
5	St. Vincent and the Grenadines	Kingstown
6	Barbados	Bridgetown
7	Grenada	St. George's

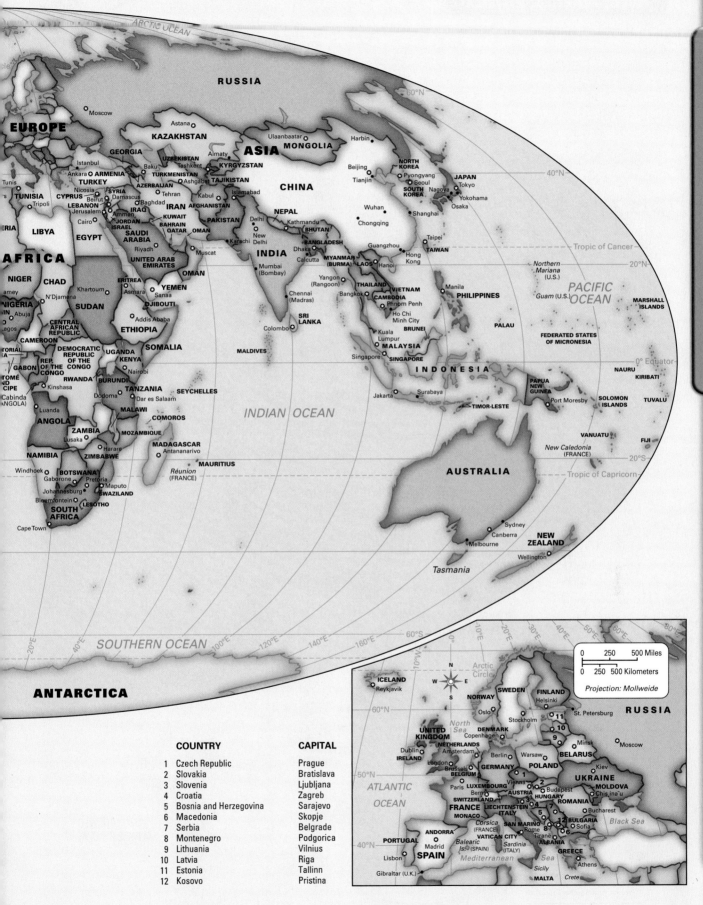

COUNTRY	CAPITAL
1 Czech Republic	Prague
2 Slovakia	Bratislava
3 Slovenia	Ljubljana
4 Croatia	Zagreb
5 Bosnia and Herzegovina	Sarajevo
6 Macedonia	Skopje
7 Serbia	Belgrade
8 Montenegro	Podgorica
9 Lithuania	Vilnius
10 Latvia	Riga
11 Estonia	Tallinn
12 Kosovo	Pristina

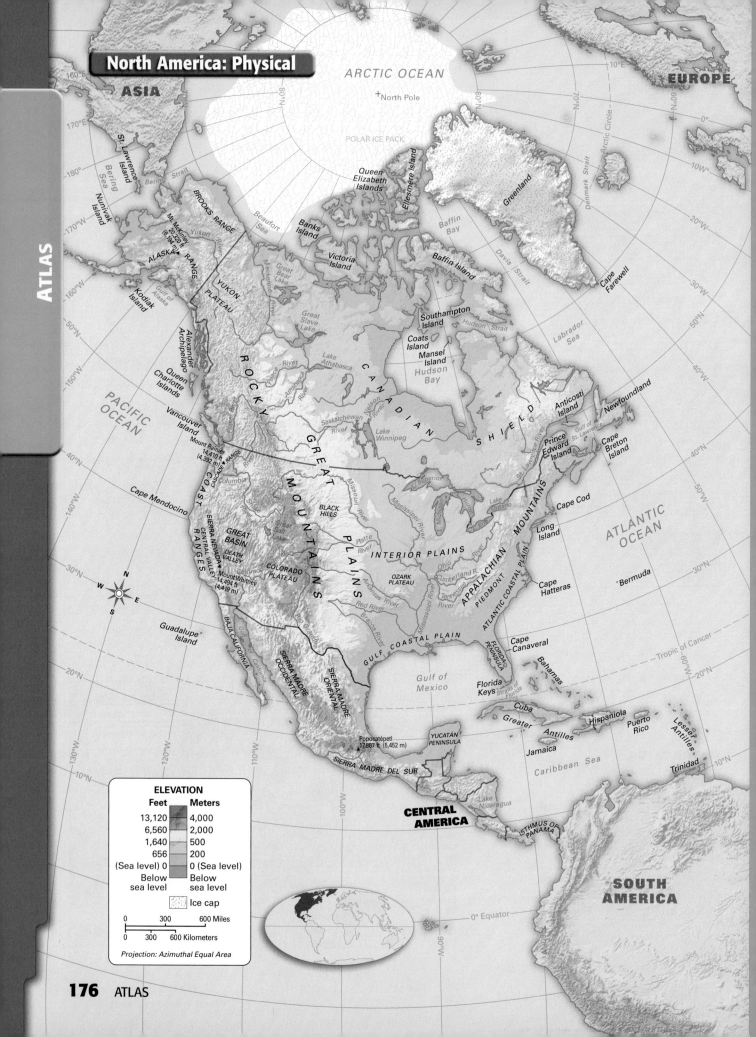

North America: Physical

ARCTIC OCEAN

ASIA

EUROPE

+ North Pole

POLAR ICE PACK

Queen
Elizabeth
Islands

Greenland

Beaufort
Sea

Banks
Island

BROOKS RANGE

Mt. McKinley
20,320 ft
(6,194 m)
ALASKA RANGE

Victoria
Island

Baffin
Bay

Baffin Island

Ellesmere Island

Denmark Strait

St. Lawrence
Island

Bering
Sea

Nunivak
Island

Bering Strait

Yukon River

YUKON PLATEAU

Great
Bear
Lake

Mackenzie River

Southampton
Island

Hudson Strait

Davis Strait

Cape
Farewell

Kodiak
Island

Gulf of
Alaska

Alexander
Archipelago

Queen
Charlotte
Islands

Vancouver
Island

ROCKY

Great
Slave
Lake

Lake
Athabasca

C A N A D I A N

Coats
Island

Mansel
Island

Hudson
Bay

S H I E L D

Labrador
Sea

PACIFIC
OCEAN

Peace River

Athabasca River

Saskatchewan
River

Nelson River

Lake
Winnipeg

Prince
Edward
Island

Anticosti
Island

Newfoundland

Gulf of
St. Lawrence

Cape
Breton
Island

Mount Rainier
14,410 ft
(4,394 m)

Cape Mendocino

COAST RANGE

CASCADE RANGE

Columbia River

M O U N T A I N S

G R E A T

Missouri River

St. Lawrence River

Superior

BLACK
HILLS

Mississippi River

Lake
Ontario

MOUNTAINS

Cape Cod

ATLANTIC
OCEAN

SIERRA NEVADA

CENTRAL VALLEY

GREAT
BASIN

DEATH
VALLEY

Great
Salt
Lake

P L A I N S

Platte River

INTERIOR PLAINS

L. Michigan

Ohio River

APPALACHIAN

Long
Island

Mount Whitney
14,494 ft
(4,419 m)

COLORADO
PLATEAU

Colorado River

OZARK
PLATEAU

Arkansas River

Cumberland R.

Tennessee
River

PIEDMONT

Cape
Hatteras

Bermuda

Guadalupe
Island

BAJA CALIFORNIA

California

SIERRA MADRE
OCCIDENTAL

SIERRA MADRE
ORIENTAL

Rio Grande

Red River

Brazos River

GULF COASTAL PLAIN

ATLANTIC COASTAL PLAIN

FLORIDA
PENINSULA

Cape
Canaveral

Bahamas

Gulf of
Mexico

Florida
Keys

Straits of
Florida

Cuba

Greater

Antilles

Jamaica

Hispaniola

Puerto
Rico

Lesser
Antilles

Popocatépetl
17,887 ft (5,452 m)

YUCATÁN
PENINSULA

Caribbean Sea

Trinidad

SIERRA MADRE DEL SUR

CENTRAL
AMERICA

Lake
Nicaragua

ISTHMUS OF
PANAMA

SOUTH
AMERICA

ELEVATION

Feet		Meters
13,120		4,000
6,560		2,000
1,640		500
656		200
(Sea level) 0		0 (Sea level)
Below sea level		Below sea level
	Ice cap	

0   300   600 Miles

0   300   600 Kilometers

Projection: Azimuthal Equal Area

0° Equator

ARCTIC OCEAN

ASIA

EUROPE

North Pole

St. Lawrence Island

Bering Sea

Nunivak Island

Point Barrow

Beaufort Sea

Banks Island

Queen Elizabeth Islands

Ellesmere Island

Greenland (DENMARK)

ICELAND

Denmark Strait

Arctic Circle

ALASKA (U.S.)

Anchorage

Kodiak Island

Gulf of Alaska

Juneau

Alexander Archipelago

Queen Charlotte Islands

Great Bear Lake

Victoria Island

Baffin Island

Baffin Bay

Davis Strait

Cape Farewell

Labrador Sea

PACIFIC OCEAN

Vancouver Island

Great Slave Lake

Southampton Island

Coats Island

Mansel Island

Hudson Strait

Edmonton

Calgary

CANADA

Lake Winnipeg

Hudson Bay

Anticosti Island

Newfoundland

Vancouver

Seattle

Portland

Winnipeg

Lake Superior

Lake Michigan

Lake Huron

Lake Ontario

Lake Erie

Prince Edward Island

Cape Breton Island

St. Pierre and Miquelon (FRANCE)

Gulf of St. Lawrence

Québec

Montréal

Ottawa

Toronto

Minneapolis

Milwaukee

Chicago

Detroit

Cleveland

Columbus

Boston

Cape Cod

New York City

Philadelphia

Baltimore

Washington, D.C.

ATLANTIC OCEAN

San Francisco

San Jose

Great Salt Lake

Salt Lake City

Denver

Kansas City

Indianapolis

St. Louis

UNITED STATES

Norfolk

Los Angeles

San Diego

Tijuana

Phoenix

Memphis

Atlanta

Birmingham

Bermuda (U.K.)

Dallas

Jacksonville

Austin

San Antonio

Houston

New Orleans

Monterrey

Gulf of Mexico

Florida Keys

Miami

BAHAMAS

Nassau

Turks and Caicos Islands (U.K.)

DOMINICAN REPUBLIC

Puerto Rico (U.S.)

San Juan

ST. KITTS & NEVIS

ANTIGUA & BARBUDA

Guadeloupe (FRANCE)

DOMINICA

Tropic of Cancer

MEXICO

Gulf of California

Guadalajara

Mexico City

Puebla

Mérida

Cayman Is. (U.K.)

Havana

CUBA

Straits of Florida

Kingston

JAMAICA

HAITI

Port-au-Prince

Santo Domingo

Virgin Is. (U.S., U.K.)

Martinique (FRANCE)

ST. LUCIA

BARBADOS

ST. VINCENT AND THE GRENADINES

Netherlands Antilles (NETHERLANDS)

GRENADA

Belmopan

BELIZE

GUATEMALA

Guatemala City

Caribbean Sea

Aruba (NETHERLANDS)

TRINIDAD AND TOBAGO

HONDURAS

Tegucigalpa

San Salvador

EL SALVADOR

NICARAGUA

Managua

Panama Canal

San José

Panama City

COSTA RICA

PANAMA

SOUTH AMERICA

✪ National capital

● Other city

0   300   600 Miles

0   300   600 Kilometers

Projection: Azimuthal Equal-Area

CENTRAL
AMERICA

Caribbean Sea

Panama
Canal

Margarita
Island

Tobago

Trinidad

Orinoco River
Delta

Lake
Maracaibo

LLANOS

Orinoco River

Meta
River

Angel Falls

GUIANA

HIGHLANDS

Devil's Island

Cape Orange

Gulf
of
Panama

Malpelo
Island

Mount Tolima
18,425 ft
(5,616 m)

Orinoco River

Río
Negro

Amazon

River

Amazon
River Delta

Caqueta
River

Japurá
River

A M A Z O N

Galápagos
Islands

0° Equator

Mount Chimborazo
20,561 ft
(6,267 m)

Amazo
River

B A S I N

Tapajós River

Xingu

River

Tocantins

River

0° Equator

Gulf of Guayaquil

Marañón River

Juruá

River

River

Río

River

Parnaíb

River

Purus

Madeira

River

ANDES

Mount Huascarán
22,205 ft
(6,768 m)

BRAZILIAN

Beni River

Mamoré

MATO GROSSO

PLATEAU

Araguaia

São
Francisco

HIGHLANDS

PACIFIC
OCEAN

Ancohuma Peak
20,958 ft
(6,388 m)

River

River

ATLANTIC
OCEAN

Lake
Poopó

Pilcomayo

River

ATACAMA DESERT

Lake
Titicaca

C H A C O

BRAZILIAN

River

River

Paraguay

PLATEAU

Tropic of Capricorn

San Ambrosio
Island

ANDES

Salado

River

Paraná

Tropic of Capricorn

San Félix Island

San Félix Island

Salado
River

Mount Aconcagua
22,834 ft
(6,960 m)

Uruguay River

Juan Fernández
Islands

PAMPAS

Río de la Plata

ATLANTIC
OCEAN

Colorado
River

Gulf of San Matias

ELEVATION

Feet	Meters
13,120	4,000
6,560	2,000
1,640	500
656	200
(Sea level) 0	0 (Sea level)
Below sea level	Below sea level

Chiloé
Island

Chonos
Archipelago

PATAGONIA

Gulf of
San Jorge

Cape Tres Puntas

0   250   500 Miles

0   250   500 Kilometers

Projection: Azimuthal Equal Area

Bahía
Grande

Strait of
Magellan

Falkland
Islands

South
Georgia
Islands

Tierra del
Fuego

Cape Horn

ATLAS

South America: Political

CENTRAL AMERICA

Caribbean Sea

Barranquilla
Cartagena
Caracas

VENEZUELA

Medellín
Bogotá
COLOMBIA
Cali

Georgetown
Paramaribo
GUYANA
Cayenne
SURINAME French Guiana (FRANCE)

Lake Maracaibo

Malpelo Island (COLOMBIA)

Quito
ECUADOR
Guayaquil

Galápagos Islands (ECUADOR)

0° Equator

PERU

Trujillo

Callao Lima

PACIFIC OCEAN

Arequipa

Lake Titicaca
La Paz
Lake Poopó
BOLIVIA
Sucre

Belém

BRAZIL

Brasília

Recife

Salvador

Belo Horizonte

Campinas
São Paulo
Rio de Janeiro
Curitiba

ATLANTIC OCEAN

PARAGUAY
Asunción

San Félix Island (CHILE) *San Ambrosio Island (CHILE)*

Tropic of Capricorn

CHILE

Juan Fernández Islands (CHILE)

Córdoba
Rosario
URUGUAY

Valparaíso
Santiago
Buenos Aires
Montevideo

Pôrto Alegre

ARGENTINA

⬡ National capital
● Other city

0   250   500 Miles
0   250   500 Kilometers

Projection: Azimuthal Equal-Area

Strait of Magellan
Falkland Islands (U.K.)

Tierra del Fuego

South Georgia Island (U.K.)

Europe: Physical

ELEVATION

Feet	Meters
13,120	4,000
6,560	2,000
1,640	500
656	200
(Sea level) 0	0 (Sea level)
Below sea level	Below sea level

Ice cap

300 Miles
0   150   300 Kilometers
0   150

Projection: Azimuthal Equal Area

ASIA

SOUTHWEST ASIA

AFRICA

URAL MOUNTAINS

Pechora River

Dvina River

Kama River

Volga River

Ural River

NORTHERN EUROPEAN PLAIN

Caspian Sea

Mt. Elbrus (5,642 m)
18,510 ft

CAUCASUS MTS.

Don River

Sea of Azov

CRIMEAN PENINSULA

Black Sea

Dnipro

Rybinsk Reservoir

Oka River

Lake Onega

Lake Ladoga

White Sea

KOLA PENINSULA

North Cape

Barents Sea

ARCTIC OCEAN

BALTIC PLAINS

Gulf of Finland

Gulf of Bothnia

Dvina R.

Dnister River

Dnestr River

CARPATHIAN

TRANSYLVANIAN ALPS

BALKAN PENINSULA

Sea of Marmara

Rhodes

Crete

Aegean Sea

DINARIC ALPS

Danube

Adriatic Sea

APENNINES

Tiber River

Tyrrhenian Sea

Sicily

Malta

Corsica

Sardinia

Balearic Islands

Mediterranean Sea

Vistula River

Oder River

Elbe River

Baltic Sea

Kattegat

Skagerrak

Lake Vättern

Lake Vänern

KJØLEN MOUNTAINS

Norwegian Sea

Arctic Circle

Iceland

Faeroe Islands

Shetland Islands

Orkney Islands

Hebrides

British Isles

Irish Sea

PENNINES

North Sea

Danube River

Rhine River

A L P S

Lake Geneva

Mont Blanc
15,781 ft (4,810 m)

Rhône River

Po River

PYRENEES

Ebro River

IBERIAN PENINSULA

Douro River

Tagus River

Guadiana River

Guadalquivir River

Strait of Gibraltar

Cape Finisterre

Bay of Biscay

Garonne River

Loire River

Seine River

Thames River

English Channel

ATLANTIC OCEAN

N E W S

70°E
60°E
50°E
40°E
30°E
20°E
10°E
0°
10°W
20°W
30°W
40°W
20°E
30°E

80°N
70°N
60°N
50°N
40°N

Europe: Political

Legend:
- ✪ National capital
- • Other city

Scale:
0 — 150 — 300 Miles
0 — 150 — 300 Kilometers

Projection: Azimuthal Equal-Area

ASIA

URAL MOUNTAINS

RUSSIA

Nizhny Novgorod
Moscow

Barents Sea

White Sea

North Cape

ARCTIC OCEAN

Arctic Circle

ICELAND
Reykjavik

Faeroe Islands (DENMARK)

Shetland Islands

FINLAND
Helsinki

Gulf of Bothnia

St. Petersburg

Gulf of Finland
Tallinn

ESTONIA

LATVIA
Riga

LITHUANIA
Vilnius

Minsk

BELARUS

UKRAINE
Kiev

MOLDOVA
Chisinau

ROMANIA
Bucharest

Black Sea

SOUTHWEST ASIA

Rhodes
Crete
Aegean Sea
GREECE
Athens

BULGARIA
Sofia

Skopje
MACEDONIA
Tirana
ALBANIA

Pristina
KOSOVO
MONTENEGRO
Podgorica
SERBIA
Belgrade

SWEDEN
Stockholm
Göteborg

Baltic Sea

RUSSIA

Warsaw
Krakow

POLAND

SLOVAKIA
Bratislava
Budapest
HUNGARY

CZECH REPUBLIC
Prague

Berlin
Dresden

NORWAY
Oslo
Bergen

DENMARK
Copenhagen

North Sea

Hamburg

GERMANY
Cologne
Bonn

Amsterdam
THE NETHERLANDS

Brussels
BELGIUM
LUXEMBOURG
Luxembourg

Munich
Vienna
AUSTRIA
LIECHTENSTEIN
Vaduz
SLOVENIA
Ljubljana
Zagreb
CROATIA
BOSNIA AND HERZEGOVINA
Sarajevo

SWITZERLAND
Lake Geneva
Bern

SAN MARINO
San Marino

ITALY
Rome
VATICAN CITY
Naples

MONACO
Monaco

Corsica (FRANCE)

Milan
Lyon

FRANCE
Paris

UNITED KINGDOM
SCOTLAND
Edinburgh
Belfast
NORTHERN IRELAND
Dublin
IRELAND
Liverpool
ENGLAND
London
WALES

British Isles

English Channel
Channel Islands (U.K.)

Marseille

Sardinia (ITALY)

Sicily
Naples

MALTA
Valletta

Mediterranean Sea

PYRENEES
Andorra la Vella
ANDORRA
Barcelona

Balearic Islands (SPAIN)

Bay of Biscay

SPAIN
Madrid
Valencia
Seville
Gibraltar (U.K.)
Strait of Gibraltar

PORTUGAL
Lisbon

AFRICA

ATLANTIC OCEAN

70°N
60°N
50°N
40°N

30°W
20°W
10°W
0°
10°E
20°E
30°E
40°E

70°N
60°N

Asia: Physical

ELEVATION

Feet	Meters
13,120	4,000
6,560	2,000
1,640	500
656	200
0 (Sea level)	0 (Sea level)
Below sea level	Below sea level

Ice cap

0 250 500 750 Miles
0 250 500 750 Kilometers

Projection: Two-Point Equidistant

EUROPE
AFRICA
AUSTRALIA

PACIFIC OCEAN
INDIAN OCEAN

North Pole
Arctic Circle

Wrangel Island
New Siberian Islands
Aleutian Islands
KAMCHATKA PENINSULA
Bering Sea
Sea of Okhotsk
Sakhalin Island
Kuril Islands
Hokkaido
Honshu
Shikoku
Kyushu
Sea of Japan (East Sea)
Korea Strait
Okinawa
Ryukyu Islands
East China Sea
Taiwan
Luzon Strait
Luzon
Philippines
Mindanao
Celebes Sea
Celebes
Molucca S.
Banda Sea
Maoke Mountains
New Guinea
Arafura Sea

Franz Josef Land
Novaya Zemlya
North Land
TAYMYR PENINSULA
Kara Sea
Barents Sea
Laptev Sea
KOLYMA MTS.
CHERSKIY RANGE
VERKHOYANSKIY RANGE
STANOVOY MOUNTAINS
CENTRAL RANGE
Lena River
Aldan River
Amur River
Vilyuy River
YABLONOVY RANGE
Stanovoy Range
GREATER KHINGAN RANGE
MONGOLIAN PLATEAU
GOBI
NORTH CHINA PLAIN
QIN LING
BOHAI HILLS
Yellow Sea
Huang He (Yellow River)
Chang Jiang (Yangzi River)
Xi Jiang
Gulf of Tonkin
Hainan
South China Sea
INDOCHINA PENINSULA
Mekong River
Chao Phraya River
Gulf of Thailand
MALAY PENINSULA
Sumatra
Borneo
Java
Java Sea
Bangka
Mentawai Islands
Andaman Islands
Nicobar Islands
Andaman Sea

CENTRAL SIBERIAN PLATEAU
SIBERIA
Lower Tunguska River
Angara River
Yenisey River
SAYAN MOUNTAINS
ALTAY MOUNTAINS
TIAN SHAN
TARIM BASIN
TAKLIMAKAN DESERT
KUNLUN MOUNTAINS
PLATEAU OF TIBET
Mount Everest 29,035 ft (8,850 m)
HIMALAYAS
INDO-GANGETIC PLAIN
Ganges River
Brahmaputra River
Irrawaddy River
Bay of Bengal
DECCAN PLATEAU
EASTERN GHATS
WESTERN GHATS
Godavari River
Sri Lanka
Maldives
Lakshadweep Islands

WEST SIBERIAN PLAIN
Ob River
Irtysh River
Ishim River
KAZAKH UPLANDS
Balqash Lake
Syr Darya
TURAN LOWLAND
KYZYL KUM
KARA KUM
Amu Darya
Aral Sea
USTYURT PLATEAU
HINDU KUSH
THAR DESERT
Sutlej River
Indus River
URAL MOUNTAINS
Ural River
Caspian Sea
GREAT SALT DESERT
ZAGROS MTS.
Persian Gulf
Gulf of Oman
Arabian Sea
Socotra Island
Gulf of Aden

CAUCASUS MTS.
Mount Ararat 16,945 ft (5,165 m)
ANATOLIAN PLATEAU
Black Sea
Bosporus
Tigris River
Euphrates River
SYRIAN DESERT
AN-NAFUD
RUB' AL-KHALI
SINAI PENINSULA
Red Sea
Cyprus
Mediterranean Sea

Asia: Political

National capitals ⭐
Other cities •

| 0 | 250 | 500 | 750 Miles |
| 0 | 250 | 500 | 750 Kilometers |

Projection: Two-Point Equidistant

EUROPE

RUSSIA

Moscow

Yakutsk

URAL MOUNTAINS

Yekaterinburg
Chelyabinsk
Omsk
Novosibirsk
Irkutsk

Lake Baykal

MONGOLIA

Ulaanbaatar

Astana

KAZAKHSTAN

Aral Sea
Lake Balkhash

Almaty
Bishkek
KYRGYZSTAN
Tashkent
UZBEKISTAN
TAJIKISTAN
Dushanbe
TURKMENISTAN
Ashgabat

Caspian Sea

GEORGIA
Tbilisi
ARMENIA
Yerevan
Baku
AZERBAIJAN

Black Sea

Istanbul
Ankara
TURKEY
Izmir

CYPRUS
Nicosia
LEBANON
Beirut
Tel Aviv
ISRAEL
Jerusalem
Amman
JORDAN
SYRIA
Damascus

Mediterranean Sea

IRAQ
Mosul
Baghdad
Basra
KUWAIT
Kuwait City

Tehran
IRAN
Shiraz

Persian Gulf
BAHRAIN
Manama
QATAR
Doha
Abu Dhabi
UNITED ARAB EMIRATES
Masqat (Muscat)
OMAN

SAUDI ARABIA
Riyadh
Mecca
Jidda

Red Sea

YEMEN
Sanaa

Gulf of Aden

Socotra (YEMEN)

AFRICA

Arabian Sea

AFGHANISTAN
Kabul

PAKISTAN
Islamabad
Lahore
Karachi

Ahmadabad
New Delhi
Delhi
Jaipur
Mumbai (Bombay)

INDIA

Bangalore

Lakshadweep Islands (INDIA)

MALDIVES
Male

NEPAL
Kathmandu

BHUTAN
Thimphu

BANGLADESH
Dhaka

Kolkata (Calcutta)

Chennai (Madras)

Bay of Bengal

SRI LANKA
Colombo

INDIAN OCEAN

Andaman Islands (INDIA)

Nicobar Islands (INDIA)

MYANMAR (BURMA)
Mandalay
Yangon (Rangoon)

CHINA

Chengdu
Chongqing
Wuhan
Nanjing
Beijing
Fushun
Harbin

Qingdao
Shanghai
Yellow Sea

Guangzhou
Hong Kong
Macao
Hainan (CHINA)

East China Sea

Tropic of Cancer

LAOS
Vientiane
THAILAND
Bangkok
CAMBODIA
Phnom Penh
Gulf of Thailand
VIETNAM
Hanoi
Ho Chi Minh City

South China Sea

TAIWAN
Taipei

PHILIPPINES
Manila

Luzon Strait

MALAYSIA
Kuala Lumpur
SINGAPORE
Singapore

BRUNEI
Bandar Seri Begawan

Medan

Andaman Sea

INDONESIA

Java Sea
Ujung Pandang
Jakarta
Bandung
Surabaya

Celebes Sea

TIMOR-LESTE
Dili

Arafura Sea

New Guinea

AUSTRALIA

PACIFIC OCEAN

Equator

JAPAN
Tokyo
Yokohama
Sapporo
Sendai
Osaka
Kyoto
Hiroshima
Nagasaki

NORTH KOREA
Pyongyang
SOUTH KOREA
Seoul
Pusan

Vladivostok

Kuril Islands (RUSSIA)

Sakhalin Island

Sea of Okhotsk

Ryukyu Islands (JAPAN)

Dalian

RUSSIA

Bering Sea

Aleutian Islands

North Pole

Arctic Circle

Barents Sea
Kara Sea
Laptev Sea

Bering Strait

ATLAS

EUROPE

SOUTHWEST ASIA

Azores

Strait of Gibraltar

Madeira Islands

ATLAS MOUNTAINS

Mediterranean Sea

Gulf of Sidra

Suez Canal

QATTARA DEPRESSION

Canary Islands

Cape Blanc

EL DJOUF

S A H A R A

AHAGGAR MOUNTAINS

AIR MTS.

TIBESTI MOUNTAINS

LIBYAN DESERT

Nile River

Lake Nasser

NUBIAN DESERT

Red Sea

Persian Gulf

Tropic of Cancer

Cape Verde Islands

Cape Verde

S A H E L

S U D A N

Niger River

Senegal R.

Lake Chad

CHAD BASIN

Gulf of Aden

White Nile

Blue Nile

Lake Tana

FOUTA DJALLON

Black Volta R.

White Volta R.

Benue River

Lake Volta

SUDAN BASIN

ETHIOPIAN HIGHLANDS

HORN OF AFRICA

SOMALI PENINSULA

Cape Palmas

Gulf of Guinea

ADAMAWA MTS.

Ubangi River

Congo River

Lake Albert

Lake Edward

Lake Turkana

Mount Kenya 17,058 ft ▲ (5,199 m)

Cape Lopez

CONGO BASIN

Kasai River

Lake Kivu

Lake Victoria

RIFT VALLEY

Mount Kilimanjaro 19,340 ft (5,895 m)

0° Equator

INDIAN OCEAN

Ascension

Cuanza River

MITUMBA MOUNTAINS

Lake Tanganyika

SERENGETI PLAIN

MASAI STEPPE

Zanzibar

WESTERN RIFT VALLEY

EASTERN

Lake Rukwa

Seychelles

ATLANTIC OCEAN

Lake Mweru

Lake Malawi (Nyasa)

Cape Delgado

Comoro Islands

Zambezi River

Mozambique Channel

Madagascar

Lake Kariba

Victoria Falls

Okavango Delta

Limpopo River

Mauritius

Réunion

NAMIB DESERT

KALAHARI BASIN

KALAHARI DESERT

Tropic of Capricorn

Orange River

Vaal River

GREAT KARROO

DRAKENSBERG MOUNTAINS

Cape of Good Hope

ELEVATION

Feet		Meters
13,120		4,000
6,560		2,000
1,640		500
656		200
(Sea level) 0		0 (Sea level)
Below sea level		Below sea level

0 250 500 Miles

0 250 500 Kilometers

Projection: Azimuthal Equal-Area

N W E S

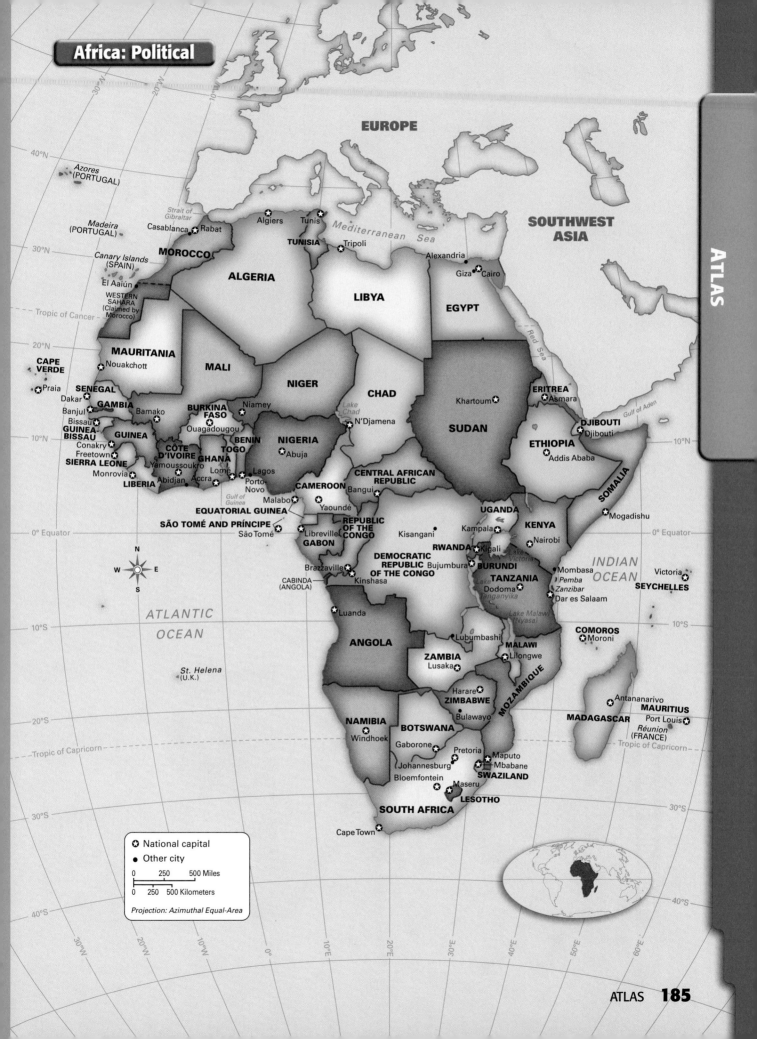

EUROPE

SOUTHWEST
ASIA

ATLAS

40°N

Azores
(PORTUGAL)

Madeira
(PORTUGAL)

Strait of
Gibraltar

Algiers   Tunis

Mediterranean   Sea

Casablanca   ✪ Rabat

30°N

MOROCCO

TUNISIA   ✪ Tripoli

Alexandria

Canary Islands
(SPAIN)

El Aaiún

ALGERIA

LIBYA

Giza ● Cairo

EGYPT

WESTERN
SAHARA
(Claimed by
Morocco)

Tropic of Cancer

20°N

MAURITANIA

MALI

Red Sea

CAPE
VERDE

✪ Nouakchott

NIGER

CHAD

Khartoum ✪

ERITREA
Asmara

● Praia

SENEGAL

Niamey

SUDAN

DJIBOUTI
Djibouti

Gulf of Aden

10°N

Dakar

GAMBIA

BURKINA
FASO

N'Djamena

ETHIOPIA

10°N

Bamako

Banjul

Bissau

Ouagadougou

BENIN
TOGO

NIGERIA

Addis Ababa

GUINEA-
BISSAU

GUINEA

CÔTE
D'IVOIRE
GHANA

Abuja

CENTRAL AFRICAN
REPUBLIC

SOMALIA

Conakry

Freetown

Yamoussoukro

Lomé ● Lagos

SIERRA LEONE

Abidjan

Porto-
Novo

Accra

CAMEROON

Bangui

Mogadishu

Monrovia

LIBERIA

Gulf of
Guinea

Malabo

UGANDA

KENYA

0° Equator

EQUATORIAL GUINEA

Yaoundé

Kisangani ●

Kampala

Nairobi

0° Equator

SÃO TOMÉ AND PRÍNCIPE

São Tomé

REPUBLIC
OF THE
CONGO

RWANDA
Kigali

INDIAN
OCEAN

Victoria

Libreville

GABON

DEMOCRATIC
REPUBLIC
OF THE CONGO

Bujumbura

BURUNDI

Lake
Victoria

SEYCHELLES

Brazzaville

Mombasa

CABINDA
(ANGOLA)

Kinshasa

TANZANIA

Dodoma

Pemba
Zanzibar

10°S

ATLANTIC

OCEAN

● Luanda

Lake
Tanganyika

Dar es Salaam

10°S

COMOROS
Moroni

St. Helena
(U.K.)

ANGOLA

Lubumbashi ●

Lake Malawi
(Nyasa)

MALAWI
Lilongwe

ZAMBIA

Lusaka

Harare

Antananarivo

MAURITIUS

20°S

ZIMBABWE

MOZAMBIQUE

Port Louis

NAMIBIA

Bulawayo

MADAGASCAR

Réunion
(FRANCE)

Tropic of Capricorn

BOTSWANA

Tropic of Capricorn

Windhoek

Gaborone

Pretoria

Maputo

Johannesburg

Mbabane

Bloemfontein

SWAZILAND

SOUTH AFRICA

Maseru

LESOTHO

30°S

Cape Town

30°S

✪ National capital

● Other city

0   250   500 Miles

0   250   500 Kilometers

Projection: Azimuthal Equal-Area

40°S

40°S

30°W   20°W   10°W   0°   10°E   20°E   30°E   40°E   50°E   60°E

NORTH AMERICA

The Pacific: Political

ASIA

NORTH PACIFIC OCEAN

SOUTH PACIFIC OCEAN

Tropic of Cancer

30°N

15°N

0° Equator

15°S

Tropic of Capricorn

30°S

45°S

International Date Line

Hawaiian Islands

Hawaii (U.S.)

Midway (U.S.)

Johnston Island (U.S.)

Kingman Reef (U.S.)

Palmyra Island (U.S.)

Washington Island (U.S.)

Fanning Island (U.S.)

Jarvis I. (U.S.)

Howland I. (U.S.)

Baker I. (U.S.)

McKean I.

Gardner

Phoenix Islands

Starbuck Island

KIRIBATI

P O L Y N E S I A

Marquesas Islands (FRANCE)

Tuamotu Archipelago (FRANCE)

French Polynesia

Society Islands (FRANCE)

Tahiti (FRANCE)

Papeete

Tubuai Islands (FRANCE)

Rapa Island (FRANCE)

Easter Island (CHILE)

Pitcairn (U.K.)

Pitcairn Island

Ducie Island

Manihiki Island

Cook Islands (NEW ZEALAND)

Rarotonga Island

Tokelau (N.Z.)

American Samoa

Pago Pago

Niue (N.Z.)

SAMOA

Apia

TONGA

Nuku'alofa

Wallis & Futuna (FR.)

TUVALU

Funafuti

FIJI

Suva

M E L A N E S I A

Kermadec Islands (N.Z.)

Chatham Islands (N.Z.)

Auckland

Wellington

Christchurch

North Island

South Island

NEW ZEALAND

Bounty Islands (N.Z.)

Auckland Islands (NEW ZEALAND)

MARSHALL ISLANDS

Eniwetok I.

Kwajalein Island

Majuro

Tarawa

Gilbert Islands

Wake Island (U.S.)

M I C R O N E S I A

Palikir

NAURU

Truk Is.

FEDERATED STATES OF MICRONESIA

SOLOMON ISLANDS

Honiara

Guadalcanal I.

VANUATU

Port-Vila

Espiritu Santo I.

Malekula I.

Loyalty Islands (FRANCE)

New Caledonia (FRANCE)

Noumea

Norfolk Island (AUSTRALIA)

Bismarck Archipelago

PAPUA NEW GUINEA

Port Moresby

New Guinea

PALAU

Koror

Northern Marianas (U.S.)

Guam (U.S.)

Agana

Bonin Islands (JAPAN)

Volcano Islands (JAPAN)

Coral Sea

Arafura Sea

Timor Sea

Tasman Sea

AUSTRALIA

Darwin

Brisbane

Sydney

Canberra

Melbourne

Adelaide

Perth

Hobart

INDIAN OCEAN

Philippine Sea

South China Sea

Christmas Island (AUSTRALIA)

Legend:
- National capital
- Other city

1,000 Miles
1,000 Kilometers
500

Projection: Azimuthal Equal-Area

N E S W

120°W

135°W

150°W

165°W

180°

165°E

150°E

135°E

120°E

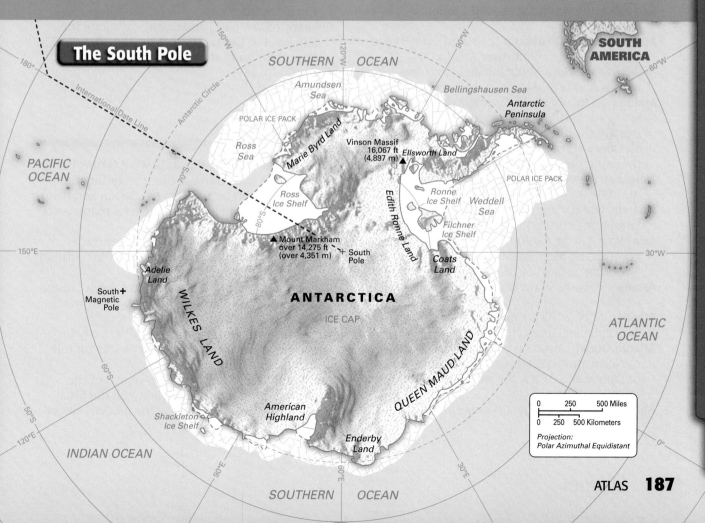

The North Pole

0   200   400 Miles
0   200   400 Kilometers

Projection:
Polar Azimuthal Equidistant

Kara
Sea

Barents
Sea

EUROPE

Norwegian
Sea

60°E

Laptev
Sea

90°E

ARCTIC
OCEAN

0°

Arctic Circle

Greenland
Sea

120°E

80°N

+ North
Pole

30°E

ASIA

150°E

International Date Line

POLAR ICE PACK

Greenland
(DENMARK)

ATLANTIC
OCEAN

30°W

150°W

North
Magnetic
Pole +

Baffin
Bay

60°N

60°W

180°

Beaufort
Sea

90°W

50°N

Bering Sea

NORTH
AMERICA

The South Pole

180°

International Date Line

SOUTHERN   OCEAN

150°W

Antarctic Circle

120°W

Amundsen
Sea

90°W

Bellingshausen Sea

SOUTH
AMERICA

60°W

Antarctic
Peninsula

PACIFIC
OCEAN

POLAR ICE PACK

Ross
Sea

70°S

Marie Byrd Land

Vinson Massif
16,067 ft
(4,897 m) ▲

Ellsworth Land

POLAR ICE PACK

Ross
Ice Shelf

80°S

Edith Ronne Land

Ronne
Ice Shelf

Weddell
Sea

150°E

▲ Mount Markham
over 14,275 ft
(over 4,351 m)

+ South
Pole

Filchner
Ice Shelf

30°W

Coats
Land

South +
Magnetic
Pole

Adelie
Land

WILKES LAND

ANTARCTICA

ICE CAP

QUEEN MAUD LAND

ATLANTIC
OCEAN

60°S

120°E

Shackleton
Ice Shelf

American
Highland

Enderby
Land

0°

50°S

INDIAN OCEAN

90°E

30°E

0   250   500 Miles
0   250   500 Kilometers

Projection:
Polar Azimuthal Equidistant

SOUTHERN   OCEAN

Gazetteer

A

Afghanistan a landlocked country in Central Asia (p. 139)

Africa the second-largest continent; surrounded by the Atlantic Ocean, Indian Ocean, and Mediterranean Sea (p. 184)

Akkad a city in Mesopotamia, now in modern Iraq; it was the center of the Akkadian empire (p. 19)

Almaty (ahl-mah-TUH) (43°N, 77°E) the former capital of Kazakhstan (p. 139)

Amman (32°N, 36°E) the capital of Jordan (p. 91)

Amu Darya (uh-MOH duhr-YAH) a river in Central Asia that flows along Afghanistan's border with Tajikistan, Uzbekistan and Turkmenistan to the Aral Sea (p. 141)

Anatolia (a-nuh-TOH-lee-uh) a mountainous region in Southwest Asia forming most of Turkey; also referred to as Asia Minor (p. 182)

Ankara (40°N, 33°E) the capital and second-largest city of Turkey (p. 98)

An Nafud (ahn nah-FOOD) a large desert in northern Saudi Arabia; known for its giant sand dunes (p. 117)

Antarctica the continent around the South Pole (p. 187)

Arabia or Arabian Peninsula the world's largest peninsula; located in Southwest Asia (p. 117)

Arabian Sea an arm of the Indian Ocean that surrounds Arabia (p. 81)

Aral Sea an inland sea in Central Asia fed by the Syr Darya and Amu Darya rivers; it has been steadily shrinking (p. 155)

Arctic Ocean the ocean north of the Arctic Circle; the world's fourth-largest ocean (p. 187)

Ashgabat (38°N, 58°E) the capital of Turkmenistan (p. 139)

Asia the world's largest continent; located between Europe and the Pacific Ocean (p. 182)

Asia Minor a large peninsula in Southwest Asia, between the Black Sea and the Mediterranean Sea, forming most of Turkey (p. 13)

Astana (51°N, 72°E) the capital of Kazakhstan (p. 139)

Athens (38°N, 24°E) an ancient city and the modern capital of Greece (p. 53)

Atlantic Ocean the ocean between the continents of North and South America and the continents of Europe and Africa; the world's second-largest ocean (p. 172)

Atlas Mountains a mountain range in northwestern Africa (p. 184)

Australia the only country occupying an entire continent (also called Australia); located between the Indian Ocean and the Pacific Ocean (p. 186)

B

Babylon an ancient city in Mesopotamia on the Euphrates River; it was the capital of the Babylonian Empire (p. 30)

Baghdad (33°N, 44°E) the capital of Iraq (p. 115)

Bahrain a small country on the Persian Gulf (p. 115)

Beirut (34°N, 36°E) the capital of Lebanon (p. 91)

Bethlehem (BETH-li-hem) (32°N, 35°E) a town in Judea; traditionally regarded as the birthplace of Jesus (p. 49)

Bishkek (43°N, 75°E) the capital of Kyrgyzstan (p. 139)

Blue Mosque (41°N, 29°E) a mosque in Istanbul built in the 1600s; it is known for its beautiful blue-colored interior tiles (p. 84)

Bosporus (bahs-puh-ruhs) a narrow strait in Turkey that connects the Mediterranean Sea with the Black Sea (p. 93)

Bukhara (40°N, 64°E) an ancient city along the Silk Road in Central Asia; it has long been an important trade and cultural center in the region (p. 139)

C

Canaan (KAY-nuhn) a region in what is now Israel near the Mediterranean coast; according to the Bible, Abraham settled in Canaan and his Hebrew descendants lived there for many years (p. 47)

Carthage (KAHR-thij) (37°N, 10°E) a key trade center built by the Phoenicians on the northern coast of Africa (p. 33)

Caspian Sea an inland sea located between Europe and Asia; it is the largest inland body of water in the world (p. 141)

Córdoba (KAWR-doh-bah) (38°N, 5°W) a city in southern Spain; it was a center of Muslim rule in Spain (p. 64)

Constantinople (41°N, 29°E) the capital of the Byzantine Empire, located between the Black Sea and Mediterranean Sea; the modern city of Istanbul (p. 57)

Damascus (34°N, 36°E) the capital of Syria (p. 91)

Dardanelles (dahrd-uhn-ELZ) a strait between the Aegean Sea and the Sea of Marmara; part of a waterway that connects the Black Sea and the Mediterranean Sea (p. 92)

Dead Sea the saltiest lake and lowest point on Earth; located on the border between Israel and Jordan and fed by the Jordan River (p. 93)

Doha (26°N, 51°E) the capital of Qatar (p. 115)

Dushanbe (39°N, 69°E) the capital of Tajikistan (p. 139)

E

Eastern Hemisphere the half of the globe between the prime meridian and 180° longitude that includes most of Africa and Europe as well as Asia, Australia, and the Indian Ocean (p. H7)

Egypt an ancient kingdom in North Africa along the Nile River; now a modern country (p. 30)

Elburz Mountains a mountain range in northern Iran south of the Caspian Sea (p. 117)

equator the imaginary line of latitude that circles the globe halfway between the North and South poles (p. H6)

Esfahan (es-fah-HAHN) (33°N, 52°E) ancient capital of the Safavid Empire; now a city in central Iran (p. 80)

Euphrates River (yoo-FRAY-teez) a major river in Southwest Asia; with the Tigris River it defined the "land between the rivers" known as Mesopotamia (p. 13)

Europe the continent between the Ural Mountains and the Atlantic Ocean (p. 180)

F, G, H

Fergana Valley a fertile plains region of Uzbekistan in Central Asia (p. 141)

Fertile Crescent a large arc of fertile lands between the Persian Gulf and the Mediterranean Sea; the world's earliest civilizations began in the region (p. 13)

Gaul an ancient region in Western Europe that included parts of modern France and Belgium (p. 54)

Gaza (32°N, 34°E) a city in southwestern Israel on the Mediterranean Sea (p. 103)

Hagia Sophia (HAH-juh soh-FEE-uh) a famous Byzantine church in Constantinople built for Emperor Justinian I in the AD 500s (p. 59)

Himalayas a mountain range that separates the Indian Subcontinent from the rest of Asia; it is the highest mountain range on Earth (p. 81)

Hindu Kush a mountain system that stretches from northern Pakistan into northeastern Afghanistan (p. 141)

India a large country in South Asia (p. 183)

Indian Ocean the world's third-largest ocean; located east of Africa, south of Asia, and west of Australia (p. 182)

Indonesia the largest country in Southeast Asia; it includes thousands of tropical islands (p. 183)

Iran a country in the Persian Gulf region; it includes the ancient region of Persia (p. 115)

Iraq a country in the Persian Gulf region; it includes the ancient region of Mesopotamia (p. 115)

Israel a country between the Mediterranean Sea and Jordan; it was the homeland of the ancient Hebrews (p. 91)

Istanbul (41°N, 29°E) the largest city in Turkey; formerly known as Constantinople and was the capital of the Byzantine Empire and Ottoman Empire (p. 90)

Italy a country on the Mediterranean Sea in Southern Europe (p. 33)

Jerusalem (32°N, 35°E) the capital of Israel; it contains holy sites of Judaism, Christianity, and Islam (p. 103)

Jordan a country east of Israel and the Jordan River (p. 91)

Jordan River a river between Israel and Jordan that empties into the Dead Sea (p. 93)

Judah (JOO-duh) one of the two kingdoms created when Israel was divided; the Hebrews in Judah came to be called Jews (p. 42)

GAZETTEER

K

Kabul (35°N, 69°E) the capital of Afghanistan (p. 139)

Kara-Kum (kahr-uh-koom) a desert in Central Asia east of the Caspian Sea (p. 141)

Kazakhstan a country in Central Asia; it was part of the Soviet Union until 1991 (p. 142)

Kopet-Dag a group of mountains in northern Iran bordering Turkmenistan (p. 117)

Kyrgyzstan a country in Central Asia; it was part of the Soviet Union until 1991 (p. 139)

Kyzyl Kum (ki-ZIL KOOM) a vast desert region in Uzbekistan and Kazakhstan (p. 141)

Kuwait a small country on the Persian Gulf (p. 115)

L, M

Lebanon a country on the Mediterranean Sea north of Israel (p. 91)

Lydia an ancient region in western Anatolia (p. 33)

Manama (26°N, 51°E) capital of Bahrain (p. 115)

Mecca (21°N, 40°E) an ancient city in Arabia and the birthplace of Muhammad (p. 65)

Medina (muh-DEE-nuh) (24°N, 40°E) a city in western Saudi Arabia north of Mecca; people there were among the first to accept Islam (p. 65)

Mediterranean Sea a large sea surrounded by Europe, Africa, and Asia; it played a vital role in the development of ancient civilizations (p. 13)

Memphis (30°N, 31°E) an ancient Egyptian capital city at the southern tip of the Nile Delta; built around 3100 BC, it was the political and cultural center of Egypt for centuries (p. 16)

Mesopotamia (mes-uh-puh-TAY-mee-uh) the region in Southwest Asia between the Tigris and Euphrates rivers; it was the site of some of the world's earliest civilizations (p. 13)

Middle East the region around the eastern Mediterranean, northeastern Africa, and Southwest Asia that links the continents of Europe, Asia, and Africa (p. 11)

Muscat (24°N, 59°E) the capital of Oman (p. 115)

N

Nazareth (33°N, 35°E) an ancient town between the Sea of Galilee and the Mediterranean Sea in modern Israel; said to be the boyhood home of Jesus (p. 49)

Negev (NE-gev) an arid region of southern Israel (p. 93)

Nineveh (NI-nuh-vuh) (37°N, 43°E) an ancient capital of Assyria, located on the Tigris River (p. 30)

North America a continent including Canada, the United States, Mexico, Central America, and the Caribbean islands (p. 176)

Northern Hemisphere the northern half of the globe, between the equator and the North Pole (p. H7)

North Pole (90°N) the northern point of Earth's axis (p. 187)

O, P

Oman a country on the Arabian Peninsula (p. 115)

Pacific Ocean the world's largest ocean; located between Asia and the Americas (p. 186)

Palestine a region between the Jordan River and the Mediterranean Sea in modern Israel (p. 103)

Pamirs a highland region in Central Asia, mainly in Tajikistan (p. 141)

Persian Gulf a body of water located between the Arabian Peninsula and the Zagros Mountains in Iran; the Tigris and Euphrates rivers empty into the Persian Gulf, which has enormous oil deposits along its shores (p. 13)

Phoenicia (fi-NI-shuh) an ancient region on the shores of the Mediterranean Sea in the Fertile Crescent; modern Lebanon includes most of the area (p. 33)

Pontic Mountains a group of mountains in northern Turkey bordering the Black Sea (p. 93)

prime meridian an imaginary line that runs through Greenwich, England, at 0° longitude (p. H6)

Q, R

Qatar (KUH-tahr) a country on the Arabian Peninsula (p. 115)

Red Sea a sea between the Arabian Peninsula and Africa (p. 117)

Riyadh (25°N, 47°E) the capital of Saudi Arabia (p. 115)

Rome (42°N, 13°E) the capital of Italy; in ancient times it was the capital of the Roman Empire (p. 42)

Rub´ al-Khali (ROOB ahl-KAH-lee) a huge sandy desert on the Arabian Peninsula; its name means "empty quarter" (p. 117)

GAZETTEER

Russia a huge country that extends from Eastern Europe to the Pacific Ocean; it is the largest country in the world (p. 183)

Samarqand (40°N, 67°E) an ancient city on the Silk Road in modern Uzbekistan (p. 139)

Saudi Arabia a large country on the Arabian Peninsula; it has the world's largest known oil deposits and contains Mecca, the most sacred site in Islam (p. 115)

Sea of Marmara (MAHR-muh-ruh) a small sea in Turkey; with the Bosporus and the Dardanelles, it forms a waterway that separates Europe and Asia and connects the Mediterranean Sea and Black Sea (p. 93)

Silk Road an ancient trade route from China through Central Asia to the Mediterranean Sea (p. 144)

South America a continent in the Western and Southern hemispheres (p. 178)

Southern Hemisphere the southern half of the globe, between the equator and the South Pole (p. H7)

South Pole (90°S) the southern point of Earth's axis (p. 187)

Soviet Union a former country that included Russia and the former Soviet Republics; it broke up in 1991 (p. 145)

Sumer (SOO-muhr) the region in southern Mesopotamia where the world's first civilization developed (p. 19)

Syr Darya (sir duhr-YAH) the longest river in Central Asia; it flows through the Fergana Valley and Kazakhstan, Tajikistan, and Uzbekistan on its way to the Aral Sea (p. 141)

Syria a country on the eastern Mediterranean Sea (p. 91)

Syrian Desert a desert in Southwest Asia covering much of the Arabian Peninsula between the Mediterranean coast and the Euphrates River (p. 30)

Tajikistan a country in Central Asia; it was part of the Soviet Union until 1991 (p. 141)

Taj Mahal (27°N, 78°E) a tomb in the Indian city of Agra built by the Mughal emperor Shah Jahan for his wife; it is considered one of the world's most beautiful buildings (p. 81)

Tachkent (41°N, 69°E) the capital of Uzbekistan; in ancient times it was an important trading city along the Silk Road in Central Asia (p. 139)

Taurus Mountains a mountain range in southern Turkey along the Mediterranean Sea (p. 93)

Tehran (36°N, 51°E) the capital of Iran (p. 115)

Tigris River (ty-gruhs) a major river in Southwest Asia; with the Euphrates River it defined the "land between the rivers" known as Mesopotamia (p. 13)

Tropic of Cancer the parallel 23.5° north of the equator; parallel on the globe at which the sun's most direct rays strike Earth during the June solstice (p. 172)

Tropic of Capricorn the parallel at 23.5° south of the equator; parallel on the globe at which the sun's most direct rays strike Earth during the December solstice (p. 172)

Turkey a country on the eastern Mediterranean, it includes the regions of Anatolia and Asia Minor (p. 91)

Turkmenistan a country in Central Asia; it was part of the Soviet Union until 1991 (p. 139)

United Arab Emirates a country on the Arabian Peninsula (p. 115)

Ur a city in ancient Sumer on the Euphrates River near the Persian Gulf; it was one of the largest cities of ancient Mesopotamia (p. 19)

Uzbekistan a country in Central Asia; it was part of the Soviet Union until 1991 (p. 139)

W, Y, Z

West Bank a disputed territory in eastern Israel (p. 103)

Western Hemisphere the half of the globe between 180° and the prime meridian that includes North and South America and the Pacific and Atlantic oceans (p. H7)

Yemen a country on the Arabian Peninsula bordering the Red Sea and the Gulf of Aden (p. 115)

Zagros Mountains a mountain range in Iran; it forms the western boundary of the Plateau of Iran (p. 117)

GAZETTEER

English and Spanish Glossary

MARK	AS IN	RESPELLING	EXAMPLE
a	alphabet	a	*AL-fuh-bet
ā	Asia	ay	AY-zhuh
ä	cart, top	ah	KAHRT, TAHP
e	let, ten	e	LET, TEN
ē	even, leaf	ee	EE-vuhn, LEEF
i	it, tip, British	i	IT, TIP, BRIT-ish
ī	site, buy, Ohio	y	SYT, BY, oh-HY-oh
	iris	eye	EYE-ris
k	card	k	KAHRD
kw	quest	kw	KWEST
ō	over, rainbow	oh	OH-vuhr, RAYN-boh
u̇	book, wood	ooh	BOOHK, WOOHD
ȯ	all, orchid	aw	AWL, AWR-kid
ȯi	foil, coin	oy	FOYL, KOYN
au̇	out	ow	OWT
ə	cup, butter	uh	KUHP, BUHT-uhr
ü	rule, food	oo	ROOL, FOOD
yü	few	yoo	FYOO
zh	vision	zh	VIZH-uhn

*A syllable printed in small capital letters receives heavier emphasis than the other syllable(s) in a word.

Phonetic Respelling and Pronunciation Guide

Many of the key terms in this textbook have been respelled to help you pronounce them. The letter combinations used in the respelling throughout the narrative are explained in this phonetic respelling and pronunciation guide. The guide is adapted from *Merriam-Webster's Collegiate Dictionary, Eleventh Edition; Merriam-Webster's Geographical Dictionary;* and *Merriam-Webster's Biographical Dictionary.*

A

alphabet a set of letters that can be combined to form words (p. 33)
   alfabeto conjunto de letras que pueden combinarse para formar palabras (pág. 33)
arable land that is suitable for growing crops (p. 151)
   cultivable tierra buena para el cultivo (pág. 151)
architecture the science of building (p. 26)
   arquitectura ciencia de la construcción (pág. 26)

B

Bedouins Arabic-speaking nomads that live mostly in the deserts of Southwest Asia (p. 108)
   beduinos nómadas que hablan árabe y viven principalmente en los desiertos del suroeste de Asia (pág. 108)
Bible the holy book of Christianity (p. 48)
   Biblia libro sagrado del cristianismo (pág. 48)
Byzantine Empire (bi-zuhn-teen) the society that developed in the eastern Roman Empire after the west fell (p. 58)
   Imperio bizantino sociedad que surgió en el Imperio romano de oriente tras la caída del Imperio romano de occidente (pág. 58)

caliph (KAY-luhf) a title that Muslims use for the highest leader of Islam (p. 76)
califa título que los musulmanes le dan al líder supremo del Islam (pág. 76)

calligraphy decorative writing (p. 85)
caligrafía escritura decorativa (pág. 85)

canal a human-made waterway (p. 14)
canal vía de agua hecha por el ser humano (pág. 14)

chariot a wheeled, horse-drawn cart used in battle (p. 30)
carro de guerra carro tirado por caballos usado en las batallas (pág. 30)

Christianity a major world religion based on the teachings of Jesus (p. 48)
cristianismo una de las principales religiones del mundo, basada en las enseñanzas de Jesús (pág. 48)

city-state a political unit consisting of a city and its surrounding countryside (p. 18)
ciudad estado unidad política formada por una ciudad y los campos que la rodean (pág. 18)

cuneiform (kyoo-NEE-uh-fohrm) the world's first system of writing; it developed in Sumer (p. 23)
cuneiforme primer sistema de escritura del mundo; desarrollado en Sumeria (pág. 23)

Diaspora the scattering of the Jewish population outside of Israel (p. 100)
Diáspora dispersión de la población judía fuera de Israel (pág. 100)

disciples (di-SY-puhls) followers (p. 49)
discípulos seguidores (pág. 49)

division of labor an arrangement in which each worker specializes in a particular task or job (p. 14)
división del trabajo organización mediante la que cada trabajador se especializa en un trabajo o tarea en particular (pág. 14)

dryland farming farming that relies on rainfall instead of irrigation (p. 151)
cultivo de secano cultivo que depende de la lluvia en vez de la irrigación (pág. 151)

embargo a limit on trade (p. 127)
embargo límite impuesto al comercio (pág. 127)

empire land with different territories and peoples under a single rule (p. 19)
imperio zona que reúne varios territorios y pueblos bajo un mismo gobierno (pág. 19)

epics long poems that tell the stories of heroes (p. 24)
poemas épicos poemas largos que narran relatos de héroes (pág. 24)

Exodus the journey in which Moses led his people out of Egypt (p. 41)
Éxodo viaje en el que Moisés guió a su pueblo para salir de Egipto (pág. 41)

F

Fertile Crescent an area of rich farmland in Southwest Asia where the first civilizations began (p. 13)
Creciente Fértil zona de ricas tierras de cultivo situada en el suroeste de Asia, en donde comenzaron las primeras civilizaciones (pág. 13)

ENGLISH AND SPANISH GLOSSARY

ENGLISH AND SPANISH GLOSSARY

Five Pillars of Islam five acts of worship required of all Muslims (p. 72)
los cinco pilares del Islam cinco prácticas religiosas que los musulmanes tienen que observar (pág. 72)

fossil water water underground that is not being replaced by rainfall (p. 119)
aguas fósiles agua subterránea que no es reemplazada por el agua de lluvia (pág. 119)

Hammurabi's Code a set of 282 laws governing daily life in Babylon; the earliest known collection of written laws (p. 29)
Código de Hammurabi conjunto de 282 leyes que regían la vida cotidiana en Babilonia; la primera colección de leyes escritas conocida (pág. 29)

irrigation a way of supplying water to an area of land (p. 14)
irrigación método para suministrar agua a un terreno (pág. 14)

Islam a religion based on the messages that Muhammad is believed to have received from God (p. 68)
Islam religión basada en los mensajes que se cree que Mahoma recibió de Dios (pág. 68)

Janissary an Ottoman slave soldier (p. 78)
jenízaro soldado esclavo otomano (pág. 78)

jihad (ji-HAHD) to make an effort, or to struggle; has also been interpreted to mean holy war (p. 71)
yihad esforzarse o luchar; se ha interpretado también con el significado de guerra santa (pág. 71)

Judaism (JOO-dee-i-zuhm) the religion of the Hebrews (practiced by Jews today); it is the world's oldest monotheistic religion (p. 40)
judaísmo religión de los hebreos (practicada por los judíos hoy en día); es la religión monoteísta más antigua del mundo (pág. 40)

kibbutz (kih-BOOTS) in Israel, a large farm where people share everything in common (p. 102)
kibbutz en Israel, granja grande donde las personas comparten todo (pág. 102)

kosher a term used to refer to Jewish dietary laws; it means "acceptable" in Hebrew (p. 102)
kosher término utilizado para referirse a las leyes alimenticias judías; en hebreo significa aceptable (pág. 102)

landlocked completely surrounded by land with no direct access to the ocean (p. 140)
sin salida al mar que está rodeado completamente por tierra, sin acceso directo al océano (pág. 140)

M

Messiah in Judaism, a new leader that would appear among the Jews and restore the greatness of ancient Israel (p. 48)
Mesías en el judaísmo, nuevo líder que aparecería entre los judíos y restablecería la grandeza del antiguo Israel (pág. 48)

minaret a narrow tower from which Muslims are called to prayer (p. 85)
minarete torre fina desde la que se llama a la oración a los musulmanes (pág. 85)

monotheism the belief only one God (p. 43)
monoteísmo creencia en un solo Dios (p. 43)

mosaic a picture made with pieces of colored stone or glass (p. 59)
mosaico dibujo hecho con trozos de piedra o cristal de colores (pág. 59)

mosque (MAHSK) a building for Muslim prayer (p. 69)
mezquita casa de oración musulmana (pág. 69)

Muslim a follower of Islam (p. 68)
musulmán seguidor del Islam (pág. 68)

N

nomads people who move often from place to place (p. 146)
nómadas personas que se trasladan frecuentemente de un lugar a otro (pág. 146)

O

oasis a wet, fertile area in a desert that forms where underground water bubbles to the surface (p. 118)
oasis lugar húmedo y fértil en el desierto que se forma donde el agua subterránea sale a la superficie (pág. 118)

OPEC an international organization whose members work to influence the price of oil on world markets by controlling the supply (p. 121)
OPEP organización internacional cuyos miembros trabajan para influenciar el precio del petróleo en los mercados mundiales controlando la oferta (pág. 121)

P

phosphate a mineral salt containing the element phosphorus (p. 95)
fosfato sal mineral que contiene el elemento fósforo (pág. 95)

pictograph a picture symbol (p. 24)
pictograma símbolo con imágenes (pág. 24)

polytheism the worship of many gods (p. 20)
politeísmo culto a varios dioses (pág. 20)

priest a person who performs religious ceremonies (p. 21)
sacerdote persona que lleva a cabo ceremonias religiosas (pág. 21)

Q

Qur'an (kuh-RAN) the holy book of Islam (p. 68)
Corán libro sagrado del Islam (pág. 68)

R

rabbi a Jewish religious leader and teacher (p. 45)
rabino líder y maestro religioso judío (pág. 45)

Resurrection (re-suh-REK-shuhn) in Christianity, Jesus's rise from the dead (p. 49)
Resurrección en el cristianismo, la vuelta a la vida de Jesús (pág. 49)

ENGLISH AND SPANISH GLOSSARY

revolution a drastic change in a country's government and way of life (p. 131)
revolución cambio drástico en el gobierno y la forma de vida de un país (pág. 131)

S

saint a person known and admired for his or her holiness (p. 52)
santo persona conocida y admirada por su santidad (pág. 52)

scribe a writer (p. 24)
escriba escritor (pág. 24)

secular the separation of religion and government; non-religious (p. 99)
secular separación entre la religión y el gobierno; no religioso (pág. 99)

shah a Persian title that means "king" (p. 131)
sha título persa que significa "rey" (pág. 131)

Shia Muslims who believe that true interpretation of Islamic teaching can only come from certain religious and political leaders called imams; they make up one of the two main branches of Islam (p. 120)
chiítas musulmanes que creen que la interpretación correcta de las enseñanzas islámicas solo puede provenir de ciertos líderes religiosos y políticos llamados imanes; forman una de las dos ramas principales del Islam (pág. 120)

silt a mixture of rich soil and tiny rocks that can make land ideal for farming (p. 13)
cieno mezcla de tierra fértil y piedrecitas que pueden crear un terreno ideal para el cultivo (pág. 13)

social hierarchy the division of society by rank or class (p. 21)
jerarquía social división de la sociedad en clases o niveles sociales (pág. 21)

Sufism (soo-fi-zuhm) a movement in Islam that taught people they can find God's love by having a personal relationship with God (p. 83)
sufismo movimiento perteneciente al Islam que enseñaba a las personas que pueden hallar el amor de Dios si establecen una relación personal con Él (pág. 83)

Sunnah (SOOH-nuh) a collection of writings about the way Muhammad lived that provides a model for Muslims to follow (p. 71)
Sunna conjunto de escritos sobre la vida de Mahoma que proporciona un modelo de comportamiento para los musulmanes (pág. 71)

Sunni Muslims who believe in the ability of the majority of the community to interpret Islamic teachings; they make up one of the two main branches of Islam (p. 120)
sunitas musulmanes que creen en la capacidad de la mayor parte de la comunidad de interpretar las enseñanzas islámicas; forman una de las dos ramas principales del Islam (pág. 120)

surplus more of something than is needed (p. 14)
excedente más cantidad de algo de lo que se necesita (pág. 14)

T

Taliban a radical Muslim group that rose to power in Afghanistan in the mid-1990s (p. 149)
talibanes grupo radical musulmán que llegó al poder en Afganistán a mediados de la década de 1990 (pág. 149)

theocracy a government ruled by religious leaders (p. 132)
teocracia gobierno dirigido por líderes religiosos (pág. 132)

tolerance acceptance (p. 78)
   tolerancia aceptación (pág. 78)
Torah the most sacred text of Judaism (p. 44)
   Torá el texto más sagrado del judaísmo (pág. 44)

wadi a dry streambed (p. 119)
   uadi cauce seco de un río o arroyo (pág. 119)

yurt a movable round house made of wool felt mats hung over a wood frame (p. 146)
   yurt tienda redonda y portátil de fieltro de lana que se coloca sobre una armazón de madera (pág. 146)

ziggurat a pyramid-shaped temple in Sumer (p. 26)
   zigurat templo sumerio en forma de pirámide (pág. 26)
Zionism a nationalist movement that began in the late 1800s and called for Jews to reestablish a Jewish state in their original homeland (p. 101)
   sionismo movimiento nacionalista que comenzó a finales del siglo XIX y que alentaba a los judíos a reestablecer un estado judío en su tierra natal (pág. 101)

ENGLISH AND SPANISH GLOSSARY

Index

INDEX

INDEX

Credits and Acknowledgments

HISTORY Unless otherwise indicated below, all video reference screens are © 2010 A&E Television Networks, LLC. All rights reserved.

For permission to reproduce copyrighted material, grateful acknowledgment is made to the following sources:

David Higham Associates Limited:
From *Travels in Asia and Africa 1325–1354* by Ibn Battuta, translated by H.A.R. Gibb. Copyright 1929 by Broadway House, London.

The Jewish Publication Society:
Exodus 20:12–14 from *Tanakh: A New Translation of the Holy Scriptures According to the Traditional Hebrew Text*. Copyright © 1985 by The Jewish Publication Society.

Naomi Shihab Nye: "Red Brocade" from *19 Varieties of Gazelle: Poems of the Middle East* by Naomi Shihab Nye. Copyright © 1994, 1995, 2002 by Naomi Shihab Nye.

Penguin Books, Ltd.: From "The Blood Clots" from *The Koran,* translated with notes by N. J. Dawood. Copyright © 1956, 1959, 1966, 1968, 1974, 1990 by N. J. Dawood.

Sources Cited:

Quote from *Seeds of Peace* Web site, accessed August 23, 2005, at http://www.seedsofpeace.org/site/PageServer?pagename=BakerEvent.

From "Adoration of Inanna of Ur" from *The Ancient Near East, Volume II* by James D. Pritchard. Published by Princeton University Press, Princeton, NJ, 1976.

Sources used by The World Almanac® for charts and graphs:

Geographical Extremes: Southwest and Central Asia: *The World Almanac and Book of Facts, 2005; The World Factbook, 2005;* World Oil Reserves: Energy Information Administration of the U.S. Department of Energy; Southwest and Central Asia: *The World Factbook, 2005;* U.S. Bureau of the Census, International Database; United Nations Statistical Yearbook; Largest Oil Reserves by Country: Energy Information Administration of the U.S. Department of Energy; Origin of Israel's Jewish Population: Central Bureau of Statistics, Israel; Saudi Arabia's Oil Production: Energy Information Administration of the U.S. Department of Energy; Saudi Arabia's Exports: OPEC, International Monetary Fund; Standard of Living in Central Asia: *The World Factbook, 2005;* United Nations Statistical Yearbook

Illustrations and Photo Credits

www.seedsofpeace.org; 107, Alison Wright/CORBIS; 108, Siegfried Tauqueur/eStock Photo; 109 (tr), Anthony Ham/Lonely Planet Images; 109 (tl), Ayman Trawi, *Beirut's Memory*; 111 (r), Ayman Trawi, *Beirut's Memory*; 111 (c), The Image Bank/Getty Images; 111 (l), Hanan Isachar/CORBIS.

Chapter 5: 114, Nader/Sygma/CORBIS; 115 (tr), 2010 A&E Television Networks, LLC. All rights reserved; 115 (bl), CORBIS; 115 (br), K.M. Westermann/CORBIS; 117 (b), Nik Wheeler/CORBIS; 117 (cr), CORBIS; 118, Chris Mellor/Lonely Planet Images; 119, Worldsat; 121, The Granger Collection, New York; 122 (br), Frank Perkins/Index Stock Imagery/PictureQuest/Jupiter Images; 122 (bl), Ludovic Maisant/CORBIS; 123, Abbie Enock; Travel Ink/CORBIS;

125 (t), Tom Hanley/Alamy; 128 (tr), U.S. Air Force Photo by Staff Sgt. Vanessa Valentine; 128 (cl), Andrew Parsons/AP/Wide World Photos; 128 (cr), Ivan Sekretarev/AP/Wide World Photos; 131 (b), Michael Yamashita/IPN/Aurora & Quantas Productions; 132 (br), Bob Daemmrich/Stock Boston; 132 (bl), Kaveh Kazemi/CORBIS; 133, Scanpix/Tor Richardsen/Reuters/CORBIS; 135 (r), Michael Yamashita/IPN/Aurora & Quantas Productions; 135 (c), Andrew Parsons/AP/Wide World Photos; 135 (l), Chris Mellor/Lonely Planet Images.

Chapter 6: 138, Martin Moos/Lonely Planet Images; 139 (br), SuperStock; 139 (bl), Robert Harding Picture Library/SuperStock; 141, Francoise de Mulder/CORBIS; 142, Robert Harding Picture Library Ltd./Alamy;

145 (br), Christine Osborne/Lonely Planet Images; 145 (tr), Gerard Degeorge/CORBIS; 148 (tr), Nevada Wier/CORBIS; 148 (tc), Michele Molinari/DanitaDelimont.com; 148 (tl), Martin Moos/Lonely Planet Images; 150, Reuters/CORBIS; 151, Martin Moos/Lonely Planet Images; 152, David Samuel Robbins/CORBIS; 152-153, David Mdzinarishvili/CORBIS; 154 (b), Howell Paul/CORBIS; 154 (cl), Reuters; 155 (c), Worldsat; 155 (t), Worldsat; 155 (b), Jesse Allen/USGS LPDAAC; 157 (r), Howell Paul/CORBIS; 157 (l), Robert Harding Picture Library Ltd./Alamy.

Backmatter: 196 (bl), Scanpix/Tor Richardsen/Reuters/Corbis; 196 (tl), The Granger Collection, New York.

Staff Credits

The people who contributed to *Holt McDougal: Southwest and Central Asia* are listed below. They represent editorial, design, production, emedia, and permissions.

Melanie Baccus, Angela Beckmann, Julie Beckman-Key, Genick Blaise, Ed Blake, Jennifer Campbell, Henry Clark, Grant Davidson, Nina Degollado, Rose Degollado, Christine Devall, Michelle Dike, Lydia Doty, Chase Edmond, Susan Franques, Stephanie Friedman, Bob Fullilove, Matthew Gierhart, Bill Gillis, Ann Gorbett, Janet Harrington, Betsy Harris, Wendy Hodge, Tim Hovde, Cathy Jenevein, Carrie Jones, Kadonna Knape, David Knowles, Aylin Koker, Laura Lasley, Sarah Lee, Sean McCormick, Joe Melomo, Richard Metzger, Andrew Miles, Joeleen Ornt, Debra O'Shields, Jarred Prejean, Paul Provence, Shelly Ramos, Curtis Riker, Michelle Rimsa, Michael Rinella, Jennifer Rockwood, Carole Rollins, Beth Sample, Annette Saunders, Jenny Schaeffer, Kay Selke, Chris Smith, Jeremy Strykul, Jeannie Taylor, Terri Taylor, Joni Wackwitz, Mary Wages, Diana Holman Walker, Nadyne Wood, Robin Zaback